New Media, Development and Globalization

For my three girls – Jo, Bella and Rosa – without whom this book might have been finished years ago but life wouldn't have been so much fun.

And for Eileen Cadman (1950–2013): author, editor, intellectual, feminist, gardener, astrologer, etc. . . .

New Media, Development and Globalization

Making Connections in the Global South

Don Slater

polity

The right of Don Slater to be identified as Author of this Work has been
asserted in accordance with the UK Copyright, Designs and Patents Act 1988.

First published in 2013 by Polity Press

Polity Press
65 Bridge Street
Cambridge CB2 1UR, UK

Polity Press
350 Main Street
Malden, MA 02148, USA

ISBN-13: 978-0-7456-3832-4
ISBN-13: 978-0-7456-3833-1 (pb)

A catalogue record for this book is available from the British Library.

Typeset in 10 on 12 pt Sabon
by Toppan Best-set Premedia Limited
Printed and bound in Great Britain by TJ International Ltd, Padstow, Cornwall

The publisher has used its best endeavours to ensure that the URLs for
external websites referred to in this book are correct and active at the time of
going to press. However, the publisher has no responsibility for the websites
and can make no guarantee that a site will remain live or that the content is
or will remain appropriate.

Every effort has been made to trace all copyright holders, but if any have been
inadvertently overlooked the publisher will be pleased to include any necessary
credits in any subsequent reprint or edition.

For further information on Polity, visit our website: www.politybooks.com

Contents

Acknowledgements

This book draws on many partnerships and conversations, formal and informal, because of its roots in numerous collaborative research projects and because of its over-long gestation.

Firstly, being so project-based, there are funders and co-workers to whom I am indebted. More specific acknowledgements are made in context, but overall the research projects on which I've drawn are as follows:

- US/UK (1996–7): Sexpics trading on IRC (self-funded).
- Trinidad (1998–2000): Daniel Miller (UCL) and Don Slater (LSE). Travel funded by the University of London; the rest by credit card debt.
- Sri Lanka (2002): *Monitoring and Evaluation of Kothmale Community Radio and Internet Centre.* Lead researchers: Don Slater (LSE), Jo Tacchi (QUT), Peter Lewis (LSE). Funded by the Department for International Development; research conducted under the auspices of UNESCO. Particular thanks are due to Wijayananda Jayaweera (UNESCO) and the main researchers, Lasanthi Daskon and Tanya Notley.
- *ictPR* (ICTs for Poverty Reduction) (2002–4): Lead researchers: Don Slater (LSE), Jo Tacchi (QUT); project co-ordinator, Ian Pringle.

Funded and implemented by UNESCO. Particular thanks are again due to Mr Jayaweera for his exceptional leadership of this seriously brave programme, to the research co-ordinator Savithri Subramanian, and to the enormously enterprising and hardworking researchers on that programme. The latter are listed and acknowledged in the table of ictPR projects in Chapter 6.

- *Information Society* (comparative ethnographies of ICTs and poverty reduction) (2003–5): Lead researchers: Don Slater (Ghana), Jo Tacchi (India), Daniel Miller (Jamaica), Andrew Skuse (South Africa). Funded by the Department for International Development. The present book draws exclusively on the Ghana ethnography, which I conducted in partnership with Dr Janet Kwami. My then doctoral students, Dr Jenna Burrell and Dr Matti Kohonen, were conducting their fieldwork in Accra at same time and I benefited enormously – in conversation, ideas, contacts and medical care – from this rare experience of actually being in the field with students.
- Asturias, Spain (2007): *Cultural Maps and Cultural Development: A Study of Youth Culture, Technology and Cultural Policy.* Lead researchers: Don Slater (LSE) and Tomas Ariztia-Larrain (LSE). Funded by CCON and administered through EnterpriseLSE.
- OLPC, Uruguay (2009–present): As referenced in Chapters 1 and 6, I have benefited greatly from supervising the fieldwork and doctoral research of Daiana Beitler from about 2009 onwards; I also benefited greatly from related visits to Montevideo to put together a large research programme there which, though ultimately unsuccessful, was a very important learning experience for me.

Secondly, there are many friends and colleagues with whom I have discussed aspects of this work over the years; to avoid getting too effusive I'll name just a few who have had the most direct formative influence on this book: Daniel Miller, Jo Tacchi, Nick Couldry and Jo Entwistle.

Thirdly, I have been blessed with some fabulous Ph.D. students who have played a huge role in my intellectual development (whatever my role in theirs) during the writing of this book; amongst those who have had the most direct impact are several who are explicitly cited in the text as collaborators as well as interlocutors: I am massively indebted to Tomas Ariztia-Larrain, Daiana Beitler, Jenna Burrell and Lena Simanyi for key aspects of this book; but I would also like to specifically acknowledge Oriana Bernasconi and Sandy Ross for particularly challenging and important conversations that have really helped me figure things out. I would also like to acknowledge several years' worth of my MSc Culture and Society students on whom I piloted many of these arguments and stories, and whose critical responses have been more formative than they might have realized.

Finally, I want to acknowledge the role of three of my oldest friends, none of them academics – Mike Hughes, Andy Moye and the late Eileen Cadman – in forming and challenging the ways I make sense of life in conversations that now go back over thirty years.

1

Introduction:
Frames and Dialogues

Over the past few decades, the three terms in my title – new media, development and globalization – have fused into a holy trinity through which people increasingly organize and act upon their beliefs about the future. Individually, each term invokes cosmologies that structure our conceptual and practical universes around fundamental aspects of life: communication and mediation (new media); social change over historical time (development); and connectedness at different spatial scales (globalization). They are also so tightly interwoven that each term appears as both manifestation and cause of the other two: new media (or ICTs or digital culture or cognate terms) are understood as inherently globalizing and as constituting the inevitable informational future for social development; development is normatively, even commonsensically, narrated as a transition to unimpeded and technically enabled global information flows and associated forms of organization and sociality ('networks'); and globalization designates an informational reconstitution of space and connection that is often taken for granted as describing our collective socio-economic future.

Together they make a compelling and seemingly irrefutable case about the way the world is going within which 'everyone' must position themselves, as if people everywhere were adapting to an altered natural habitat: individuals, households, communities, nations, the globe, have been set, as their fundamental tasks, the need to comprehend these changes, to imagine the new agencies and qualities that will emerge from them and, on the basis of these knowledges and desires, to forge strategies for surviving or advancing or 'developing'. These interlinked processes are confronted as dangers and threats, as challenges, as opportunities, even as final solutions to the problems previously posed by unequal development or capitalism or pre-modern techno-cultures. In all of these cases, however, these interlinked terms have come to be understood in a thoroughly realist mode whereby they provide the analytical frameworks in and through which people are to organize social thought and action. More concretely, as academics who are researching and teaching this stuff, we are channelled into operating within containers labelled 'new media', 'development' and 'globalization', and their interweaving, in our production and circulation of new knowledges.

The aim of this book is to reposition these three terms and their conjoint narrative as just one kind of story about the future, told by certain kinds of people, and therefore as performatively part of the construction of whatever future will actually eventuate: the aim is simply to achieve an anthropological distance from these terms so that they can always be traced to someone's cosmology somewhere, and so that all contributions – northern or southern – to debates about communication, change and connectedness might be treated as equally or symmetrically cosmological. Stated more academically, I am concerned to demote all three from acting as analytical frames or metalanguages that contain (and constrain) research and political action, and to recognize them instead as part of the fields we study and act within, to render them as topics rather than resources. In this sense, I am not primarily concerned with critiquing these concepts, or debunking them as fictions or hype, or presenting new findings that confirm or refute or revise them, or adding new concepts that would help practitioners do (or contest) media, development or globalization 'better', though some of all that will inevitably be involved.

More specifically, and more urgently, the aim is to anthropologize these terms, recognizing them as elements of specifically northern cosmologies: stories 'we' tell about the rest of the world but which then structure and contain 'their' practical and ethical sense of the future and its possibilities. The present discussion is entirely structured by a series of ethnographic fieldwork encounters with new media, development and globalization in several non-northern locations (and a couple of marginal northern ones) – in the Caribbean and Latin America, South Asia and West Africa (detailed below) – in which the three terms of our title were encountered from non-northern standpoints, at the receiving end of beliefs, practices and regulatory controls organized through this trinity, and largely experienced as naturalized and realist terms, as references to objective processes established through impersonal knowledges that all participants regarded as social facts. By looking from the outside – standing in a different place – at northern beliefs about media, development and globalization we can make all three look strange, local, contingent, as part of northern cosmologies of pretty dubious generality. And all three terms are very much northern terms – they are both geographically and historically very specific and they are bound up with histories of northern preoccupations: media and development are inextricably tied to post-war Euro-American history, in the desire – an anxious one throughout post-war reconstruction and the Cold War – to construct a world of liberal democracy that necessarily included undistorted public spheres and private markets. New media and globalization are equally inseparable from a more recent redefinition of the West that envisages renewal through connectedness.

These three terms, naturalized as unchallengeable facts and frameworks, obviously come from somewhere very particular (and indeed originate partly from metropolitan academics like myself), and so another way of putting the problem is the idea that, historically, 'the North provides the theory; the South provides the data'.[1] This phrase captures and condenses a tremendous complexity of power relations, as well as a contemporary division of intellectual labour. Amongst other things it references a colonial history in which southern peoples were simultaneously and inseparably objects of knowledge and of rule, a doubled epistemological and political subordination – a knowledge/power coupling that has arguably continued seamlessly into postcolonial 'development' (Escobar 1995, 2000; Rahnema and Bawtree 1997). It references the extent to which southern experiences are regarded not as *sui generis* histories to be traced and lived but as merely local instances of global developmental logics (progress, modernization, information society) that are defined in the North, modelled on its experiences, hopes and anxieties, but presented as unanswerable and impersonal social facts. And it references an asymmetry of representation and self-representation, of innovation, discovery and creation: the stories we invent and tell ourselves about the way our world is going tend to come from the North (and, if not, they are treated as 'culture' or 'belief' or 'identity'); and in this global division of narration, southern peoples are not narrators (agents) – or, at best, they are unreliable narrators – but are rather facts (objects) which may or may not fit into the story. Indeed, the structuring southern experience of ICTs (information and communication technologies) for/in development has been anxiety or even panic as to whether they fit in to the normative techno-developmental path of becoming an information society (as, for example, in the issue of 'digital divide' or Castells-style 'informational black holes'), whether people or communities or nations will fall into the blank spaces between nodes, and whether their marginality might become irreversible.

The aim of this book, then, is to challenge 'new media', 'development' and 'globalization' as analytical frameworks, with obscured northern origins, into which southern 'facts' (people, lives, histories, plans) must fit themselves, and instead to assert an analytical and political symmetry between people's evolving theorizations and practices of communication, change and connection. Put crudely, the aim of most of the ethnographic storytelling in this book is to consistently portray development 'beneficiaries' in southern places and development agents in northern ones (whether in agencies, academies or government) as in principle identical: they are all treated simply as people trying to make sense of and act upon transformations of communication, change and connection. They clearly do so under extremely and frequently obscenely unequal conditions of knowledge and power (some of which inequalities can be traced precisely through this political division of epistemological standing between northern theories and southern facts); but, in analytical principle, any southern villager and any American professor is identically, and equally fallibly, attempting to theorize social change – as a basis for social action – under conditions of incomplete, contingent and situated knowledges. Let's try starting from there.

The strategy that is pursued here is best described in terms of Latour's (1988a, 1988b, 2005) notion of an 'infra-language' (though in the book I tend to use his simpler injunction to deploy intentionally 'banal and empty' concepts). Unlike the metalanguages of classical and critical social thought, whose universalistic aim is to contain or subsume everyone and everything, infra-languages, in Latour's extension of both ethnomethodology and semiotics, aim simply to provide ways of moving between the different frames of analysis that are at play in the field, including ways of moving between the analyst's frame of analysis and the frames of those they seek to understand. This is done by trying to 'define a completely empty frame that enable[s us] to follow any assemblage of heterogeneous entities' and enables the researcher to identify 'how any entity builds its world' (Latour 1988a), without presuming to specify – in advance and as a matter of theoretical assumption – anything at all about the shape of the entities, actions or worlds to be traced, or, more precisely, to allow the traces to be made by the actor-network to be recorded:

> When [actor-network theory/ANT] says that actors may be human or unhuman, that they are infinitely pliable, heterogeneous, that they are free associationists, know no differences of scale, that there is no

inertia, no order, that they build their own temporality, this does not qualify any real observed actor, but is the necessary condition for the observation and the recording of actors to be possible. Instead of constantly predicting how an actor should behave, and which associations are allowed a priori, A[N]T makes no assumption at all, and in order to remain uncommitted needs to set its instrument by insisting on infinite pliability and absolute freedom. (Latour 1988a)

This is a very promising strategy for dealing with the long-recognized conundrum of social thought that Giddens (1984) described as the 'double hermeneutics' (for use of this concept in development research, see McKemmish, Burstein, Faulkhead et al. 2012; McKemmish, Burstein, Manaszewicz et al. 2012), the recursive relationship between lay and expert concepts, but it is not as easy as Latour makes it sound here. We are dealing with relations between lay and expert knowledges that are not only analytically but also politically, institutionally and processually impossible to separate out. Not only are sociologists limited to producing accounts of accounts (if possibly with more rigour or reflexivity about the rules of the game of knowledge), but their accounts enter into the production of the world they are trying to account for and – as Latour (1988a) himself blithely notes in the same article – they too are actors who may be 'primum inter pares', but who also 'strive for parity or primacy like any other' actor: we academics are always *in* the field; we always influence the field; but we are always also *contestants* within the field. We need only look at the fate of the term 'network' (Barry 2001; Latour 2010; Riles 2000; Strathern 1996, 2004 [1991]) to see the kind of exceptionally fancy footwork required by Latour himself to distinguish an empty infra-linguistic use of the term 'network' from the obsessive and ubiquitous use of the term throughout the fields which he has tried to study using the same term. Others, such as Castells, do not even try to address this politics of lay and expert classification which is so hugely consequential for ordinary lives, academic knowledges and political governance.

Because of this messy relationship to the world, infra-languages are necessarily tactical and provisional, moves in a political game of knowledge rather than devices for nailing down meanings and standpoints. Neologisms rapidly fill up with meaning and start performing in the world; attempts to reclaim or 'queer' older terms soon get defused by entering into routine communication, losing all shock or alienation value. It is hard to stay ahead of this game, even when one properly acknowledges it. The relation between 'our' academic concepts and 'theirs' involves a complex, mobile, reflexive and historicizing dialectic, one that is tactical as much as epistemological, and this comes out very clearly when placed in a development context. Throughout the book we will try out several 'banal and empty' concepts or definitions that aim to place all participants or voices within one frame, or which allow us as scholars to move between frames; but these moves are indeed tactical and provisional and unavoidably inelegant (by virtue of their desire to evade commonsense). In Chapters 2 and 3, for example, we look at what it means to use the words 'media' and 'new media' in academic discourse and in development practice, and this prompts us to retreat to the emptier notions of 'communicative ecology' and 'communicative assemblages'. These neologisms simply seek to enframe all the communicative resources (technologies, institutions, aesthetic forms, practices, interactional rules, material properties, etc.) that people might connect up in order to make and operate means of communicating. The communicative assemblages we observe in the field may include some that look like 'media', or are labelled as 'media' by some or all participants, or are regulated in terms of the idea of 'media', but that is to be observed, not assumed. The banal and empty infra-language of communicative assemblages and ecologies should allow 'media' to be observed and contested as one way in which some actors may organize the field rather than as a universal and unchallengeable category through which we as researchers covertly organize the field and the actors within it (and thereby help development agents and agencies organize the world and its politics in particular and unexamined ways), as well as organizing our own professional worlds through notions like media studies, media sociology and media anthropology. At the same time, however, 'communicative assemblage' should not be reified as an unchallengeable analytical framework; it is itself a move in a game, part of a Gramscian 'war of position'. Were 'communicative assemblage' ever to enter the lexicon of UNESCO development practices, we would of course have to invent a new term to reconstitute the space of symmetrical exchange and dialogue.

Similarly, in Chapter 4, we will try to redefine 'development' (though in this case without adopting a new word) in an empty and generic way that distances it from its place both within modernist thought (development as accounts of the normative path of social change) and within the development industry or bureaucracy (development as technologies for realigning or 'developing' those who have fallen outside or behind that normative path of social change). We might think of development, as above, more simply and banally as a condition of seeking to understand and act upon the future under conditions of uncertain knowledge, a characterization that clearly fits both 'developers' in the North and 'beneficiaries' in the South. Following my definition, everyone *has to be* a development theorist, in the most empty sense that all action is based on fallible hypotheses as to how the world works and changes.

In Chapter 5, globalization is 'demoted' from a framework for dealing with the changing nature of social connectedness to one kind of theory or practice of 'scaling' – of measuring, representing and acting upon connections at different degrees of proximity. Crudely, 'globalization' needs to be understood not as a realist process to which southern actors need to effectively respond (or which they must empirically refute), but rather as what has been described as a genre of 'scaling narrative' (Cameron and Palan 2004b; Gonzalez 2006), involving scaling practices, devices and representations. And again, in unashamedly populist terms, we need to treat seriously and equivalently the ways in which 'beneficiaries' are just as busy theorizing scales, connections and communications as are their 'developers': all social action requires geo-positionings or mappings that place people in the world at different levels of granularity. The question is simply: what maps do we and they produce and act on?

I want to be clear, from the start, that, when encountered in the context of development practice and North–South relations, the problems and strategies I am identifying are explicitly political ones. The problem with 'new media', 'development' and 'globalization' is not a problem of incorrect knowledge or theory but a problem of democracy and power. The move from metalanguages to infra-languages is a move from pretending to an expertise above the level of other people's knowledges and theorizations of their own situation, conditions and practices to an engagement with how people (including oneself and one's development partners) make and understand their worlds, and how they communicatively engage in that process. This is a move from containing, regulating and governing 'their' worlds based on claims to an unchallengeable rationality to an open engagement in dialogue over how the world does, will or should work. The irony of raising these issues in the context of development practice is that development exemplifies both the evils of asymmetries in the framing of social change (as in periods of structural adjustment ruled by economic experts), on the one hand, and, on the other hand, very well-intentioned attempts and procedures for bringing other knowledges into the frame, such as participatory development, the languages of empowerment and capabilities, and even a growing acceptance of new methodologies such as ethnography. Moreover the very centrality of new media, information and networks to narratives of development should give an extra recursive twist to this inclusion of 'the other': shouldn't the world move through the linking of nodes rather than a subsumption under hierarchized categories?

With these questions in mind, the book unsurprisingly ends (Chapter 6) with a discussion of the politics of knowledge and research themselves. The concern is that even the most well-meaning attempts – such as 'participatory research' – to roll back the rule of expertise and the framing of beneficiaries by means of unchallengeable theorizations ('information society', 'network society') involve an insufficiently radical understanding of the epistemological implications of changing the terms of communication. On the one hand, attempts to mobilize and valorize knowledges can simply end up appropriating and co-opting them as local examples of media, development or globalization. On the other hand, attacks on the monolithic and ideological nature of development discourse, such as those by Escobar (1995) and Ferguson (1994, 2006), seem simply to replace a framing by mainstream experts with a framing by critical ones that is no less absolute. The problem is not just about including the excluded or about challenging ideology; it is an almost Habermasian question of discourse ethics: how can knowledges, voices, communications, interactions, meet on a seriously level playing field, defined by the discursive capacity of each participant to identify and call into question (i.e., demand good reasons for) any claim – empirical, ethical, analytical – such that no argument can win simply by making itself the framework that contains, and adjudicates the rationality of, all the others?

In the context of ICTs and development what I particularly appreciate about Latour's strategic response is its pragmatic and profoundly anti-theoretical character. The idea of infra-language foregrounds research as itself a network-constructing activity: we understand our task as researchers as being not to contain or subsume others but to negotiate our relationship to them. This is to understand research as practical politics. The idea of an infra-language, of using banal concepts, is simply a way of making central and unignorable the relationship between my concepts and 'theirs', and therefore to foreground the ways in which that relationship is or isn't transparent, responsive and democratic. It is a move to a neutral or empty space in which conversations can take place and where the baggage that all participants bring with them can be opened up for inspection.

One last introductory point about infra-languages. So far I have been emphasizing *analytical* symmetry, but there is another dimension to asymmetry that runs throughout the book: what might be called 'ethical' asymmetry (see particularly Chapter 4). How do different deployments of our three terms distribute social agency and identify transformations in the nature of both agency and sociality? The conjuncture of new media, development and globalization narratives in the North has been characterized by extreme and often utopian visions of fundamental transformations in the nature of both social agency and sociality, in our sense of what it means to be an actor and how actors are organized within reproducible social forms. These visions characterize not only counter-cultural avant-gardisms such as cyberculture (in which people might become not only networked but post-human), but also mainstream visions of new economy, information society or network society that are seriously entertained within the heartlands of capitalism (Thrift 2005) and international governance (World Summit on the Information Society, WSIS, see below). In all these cases, new media act as a kind of material culture of development through which people imagine, articulate and enact futures. We can characterize this material culture in terms of the idea of 'network ethics': through their engagement with and transaction of these privileged technological objects, people imagine and specify new forms of agency and sociality in terms of the available and emergent possibilities of connecting and associating that they perceive or experience. This should suggest to us another symmetry: rural Ghanaians first encountering a mobile phone will understand and imagine the nature of their agency and social connection through the kinds of communicative assemblages they can operate just as much as – but differently from – geeks in London who experience the expansion of their social networks through the latest iteration of Facebook. In simple terms, we all renegotiate our sense of ourselves and our relationships through the objects we use and transact.

Network ethics as articulated over the past few decades of northern experience of the digital have generally taken the form of universalistic dreams and hopes, often technologically deterministic (e.g., the internet will produce freedom, disintermediation, transcendence of racism and nationalism, etc.), whereby we can imagine fundamental transformations. And yet at the same time, they point to fundamental asymmetries: in development contexts, new media are generally understood not as the material culture of transformation but rather as narrowly instrumental tools for the more efficient achievement of unaltered ends by unaltered agents but under newly modernized conditions. Not the imagination of new selves and sociality through new assemblages but a more efficient way to be who one always was, or to preserve an 'indigenous' culture or identity ('Self' as opposed to 'Net', in Castells' terms), as if we were dealing with anthropological myths of pre-contact authenticity. There is, we might say, an international division of ethics, of agency and transformation, a fundamental ethical asymmetry in how subjectivity and change are imagined and attributed: whereas northerners can excitedly worry about the changing nature of self, work, community and politics, beneficiaries of ICT for Development (ICT4D) are to find work in call centres or data-entry factories that utilize their competitive advantage to better place them within a conventional division of labour and trade, or to use ICTs to meet 'basic needs'. It would be nice, even as a thought experiment, to imagine what development practice might look like if it was based on extending to southern beneficiaries the utopian and radical dreams of transformation for which northerners have used this new material culture, if development were framed in terms of maximal cultural change instead of ICTs as the informational equivalent of digging more wells.

The tensions resulting from this ethical asymmetry, from the unequal distribution of network ethics, are usually easily accessible ethnographically and analytically through material culture studies, as well as sociology of consumption: people don't 'use tools', and tool use as an implicit model for ICT4D is ethically and pragmatically a very bad strategy to adopt. At most this version of object relations only suffices when the 'tools' have become routine, stable and unregarded, and even such moments are at best treated as provisional. People in contact with new machines for communicating are reconfiguring and reimagining who they are, what they can and should do, where they might go or 'develop' in the future, what counts as a relationship, as communication, as information, how people can – or are now expected to – make connections and associations. In the ethical imaginations they articulate in and through the things they transact, the 'beneficiaries' in our ethnographic stories are entirely the same as 'us', and frequently as radical as any northern cybergeek or *Wired*-style entrepreneur. Moreover, they are just as contradictory, diverse and multilingual in the ethics they imagine through these objects: a constant experience in fieldwork is people's ability to articulate simultaneously the official views of ICTs and transformation learned through schools or NGOs and the more radical possibilities imagined through their own social practices. People are always multilingual in their provision of accounts. And it is recognition of this complexity and imaginative capability in people's object relations that needs to be extended from northern digital culture to thinking new media in development and globalization, rather than continuing to try to settle, once and for all, what ICTs 'really are' and how they can best be 'used' by the people we deign to 'help'.

Ethnography

The strategies I've just outlined obviously also account for the consistent methodological commitment to ethnography asserted throughout this book, and to ethnography as, essentially, the most wonderfully banal and empty space available, the research space that most consistently performs the possibility of symmetrical relations between cosmologies. But, then, I'm also clearly biased: probably because I am *not* an anthropologist, I feel I can treat anthropology's endless guilt-ridden worrying over ethnographic representation and power as evidence not that it is dangerous or hopeless but that it is the one research form through which the danger and potential of communicative engagements can be properly explored and acted upon in transformative ways. At the centre of the very idea of ethnography is the commitment not only to hear people's own construction of their worlds, but to build up our own accounts in terms of the logics by which they associate and assemble their worlds, including the part played by their encounters with discourses and practices such as the terms in our title. In this sense, all that I have said about ANT and infra-language above, can be rendered in bog-standard ethnographese. Ethnography, I strongly believe, is fundamentally, even essentially, symmetrical: even though I may return from the field to my domestic certainties, my rooted cosmology – particularly as the feel of the field recedes over time – nonetheless the fundamental structure of ethnography is a dialogical one in which the researcher's classificatory structures come into vulnerable engagement with those at play in the field. Ethnography is a 'fusion of horizons' (Gadamer 1994; Ricoeur 1984) or 'heuristic' (Strathern 1990) in which each side provides leverage on the other. Put more experientially: it really is hard during an ethnography to avoid feeling other than a baffled foreigner whose sense of certainty about his or her own story is undermined in the process of making sense of others'. Clearly, different ethnographers pursue these possibilities to different degrees, and there are limits to the amount of reflexivity that texts (and researcher's brains) can bear and still remain intelligible (and sane); the point is that it is only ethnography that regards these issues as constitutive of its methodology, rather than as technically corrigible problems.

Obviously, ethnography is understood here not as a particular methodological tool, for example one identified with participant observation, but rather as an overarching tradition or 'approach' defined by a commitment to the specificity of lived lives and practices that need to be understood, in the first instance, through their own unique complexity, including participants' self-understandings. By the same token, ethnography is not always understood in this book in terms of more purist anthropology; some of the shorter pieces of fieldwork I rely on here, as well as the very geographical spread of the studies, may be dismissed by some anthropologists as the intellectual tourism that is just typical of a sociologist. My own view (politically and epistemologically) is deeply 'impurist': any ethnography, however quick and dirty, is better than none, is better than leaving the field and the people in it to be defined by standardized and imposed measures; better than allowing the researcher to luxuriate in the certainty of a God's-eye view. My experience of other knowledges in development has consistently confirmed this view.

The projects that I draw on are described in more detail as they arise *in situ* in the text, but it is worth pausing here to give a general idea of the trajectory; the sequence of projects had a huge impact on my arguments, and, of course, vice versa. My own interest in new media had two points of departure: firstly, a long-term engagement with community arts, and particularly with photography, which emphasized the politics of representation and self-representation involved in new media practices (e.g., Slater 1995, 1997b, 1999); and, secondly, a concern with consumption and consumer culture as a history of needs and object relations. It was the latter that led me directly into material culture studies, ANT and ethnography. With this background, my first project on digital culture (only briefly referenced in this book) looked at online trading of pornography. This study was ethnographic in form, based on participant observation in porn-exchange channels, analysis of online traces (websites, hard disk collections and classifications) as well as online and phone interviews with participants. It asked the question I introduced above as a matter of 'network ethics': to what extent did the ethics of transformation proposed by emerging cyberculture (e.g., the possibility of entirely textual/virtual sexual identities that would allow for unconstrained invention) inform participant's practices (Slater 2000a, 2000b, 2002)? A crude conclusion to this project could have been that participants voiced the discourses of cybercultural transformation while actually practising a very constrained and conventional heteronormativity. But this would have been to judge them from the standpoint of cybercultural (and post-structuralist) metanarratives. Participants' own concerns were quite different, and were ethically inventive to an extent that would not have been detectable from this metanarrative perspective and its ostensibly critical project. Participants' aims in trading pornography had less to do with sexual freedoms than with establishing a normative sociality that involved values such as trust, fairness, responsibility and order. And from that perspective – rather than that of sexuality – they were very involved indeed in inventing and articulating agency and sociality through this new material culture (and one of their central tasks was to articulate the very idea of materiality itself in what was then – 1996 – a new digital world). Moreover, participants' constitutive concern with normative sociality could be turned around to face and challenge utopian northern metanarratives (Rival, Slater and Miller 1998), much as I am trying to do in this book on the basis of development experiences.

These themes were pursued into fieldwork in Trinidad with Daniel Miller in 1999–2000 (Miller and Slater 2000, 2003, 2005; Miller, Slater and Suchman 2004). Our initial aim was straightforward: new media research was then dominated by cybercultural metanarratives centred on notions of virtuality and disembedding, on the ways in which digitally networked communication separated sociality from physical bodies and places (Slater 2004). Was any of this relevant or intelligible in a non-northern context? To what extent would projecting these northern concerns onto (any) southern place do analytical violence to the co-configuration of agents and objects that was fundamental to both of us as students of consumption and material culture? What alternative understandings were being generated amongst Trinidadians as to the normative, scalar, identificatory and transformative 'dynamics' or potentials of the internet? This project was ethnographic in a conventional sense, as well as building on Miller's longer-term ethnographic involvement with Trinidad (e.g., Miller 1992, 1994, 1997). Methodologically it included analysis of large numbers of websites and participation in chatrooms, interviews with Trinidadians in London and North America, fieldwork in Trinidad that included interviews with governmental, commercial, religious and educational actors, interviews with a range of 'ordinary users', interviews and a survey in four residential areas representative of Trinidadian socio-economic groupings, and participant observation in several cybercafés.

While the Trinidad research located understandings of digital culture in a North–South context, I had no experience of 'development' until the next project: a monitoring and evaluation study (2002) of Kothmale Community Radio and Internet Project (KCRIP) in Sri Lanka, carried out with Jo Tacchi and Peter Lewis, Tania Notley and Lasanthi Daskon, funded by the UK Department for International Development (DFID) but conducted under the auspices of UNESCO (Slater, Tacchi and Lewis 2002). My own aim in this project was to apply the ethnographic approach of the Trinidad study to the more instrumental context of development research, and the result was the idea of 'communicative ecology', as discussed in Chapter 2. Rather than reduce media in development to the impacts and efficacy of a specific ICT intervention (which would thereby be treated as an independent causal variable), the idea was to map the broad range of communicative resources in the region to see how they did or didn't connect to communicative assemblages, and where there were potentials for more or different connection. This was an auspicious opportunity in that both UNESCO and the project participants themselves were primarily concerned to understand the relation between new and older media (specifically but not exclusively internet and community radio), rather than simply to make a case for one or another medium in development.

The Sri Lankan research was also a first attempt to develop strategies for integrating ethnography within media project development which Jo Tacchi and I next formulated as 'Ethnographic Action Research' (EAR, discussed in Chapter 6) (Slater, Tacchi and Hearn 2003). This was deployed in a subsequent and much larger-scale programme: ICTs for Poverty Reduction (ictPR), funded by UNESCO over two years (Slater and Tacchi 2004). This programme also extended the concern of the Sri Lankan research with the connections *between* media, and therefore involved radio, video and publishing as well as computers and internet. Moreover, the programme was self-consciously and consistently formulated as exploratory and as a learning process: UNESCO funded eight innovative ICT projects in four different South Asian countries (India, Bangladesh, Sri Lanka and Nepal), each designed to explore different aspects of media use in connection with poverty reduction strategies. In research terms we were equally encouraged to ask the questions 'What are media?' and 'What is poverty?', and to address these question to each of the eight locations and processes. Moreover, in a thorough implementation of 'EAR', UNESCO funded full-time researchers for each project who were trained and supported by Jo Tacchi and myself over periods of up to two years, as well as being both integrated within project development as key workers and supported by the UNESCO programme staff. This project is described from a methodological standpoint in Chapter 6.

The next big project, funded by DFID, was a comparative study of ICTs and poverty reduction in four countries (India, South Africa, Jamaica, Ghana). Although, like ictPR, this programme foregrounded open exploration of the connections between ICTs and poverty reduction, it was not located in projects and interventions (which I frankly missed); rather, each country team conducted ethnographies, over eighteen months, in one rural and one urban location, aiming to balance location-appropriate methodologies that would generate internally coherent research with strategies to support comparative analysis through choices of methods and analytical themes. However, the comparative dimension of this programme simply didn't fit into the present book, which therefore draws mainly on my own fieldwork in this programme: research in two Ghanaian sites, conducted with Janet Kwami in 2003–5.

Finally, a smaller project is discussed in Chapter 5, the only one undertaken in a northern location: a study of youth culture and technology use in Asturias, in northern Spain, funded by the Oscar Niemeyer Cultural Centre (CCON) (Slater and Ariztia-Larrain 2007, 2009). Its main contribution to this book was an opportunity to track the complexity and multilingual nature of scaling practices and scaling narratives not only of our young informants but also of our funders and of ourselves as researchers.

And then there was the one that got away: in 2010 I made exploratory visits towards a large-scale ethnographic involvement in the One Laptop per Child and per Teacher programme in Uruguay, a project that was dropped at the eleventh hour for political and legal reasons. However, my doctoral student, Daiana Beitler, was able successfully to carry out exemplary fieldwork which she generously allowed me to draw on, and my experiences of the Uruguayan story – both directly and mediated through discussion with her – have played a significant role in developing some of the arguments in this book. The Uruguay story involved connections between national/historical values, identities and projects (social inclusion, equality, education, modernization) and a new technological machine (the 'XO' laptop for children) that are very hard to see as other than 'macro' and transituational in a way that ANT deals with awkwardly. Beitler's work steered me even more strongly towards a concern with social forms and modalities (Chapter 3) than I'd been navigating before.

I am more aware than anyone other than my publishers that this book has been enormously delayed – life got in the way (family, illnesses, distractions); so did work, particularly the contemporary conditions of academic governance, not least at my own institution; and there were promising projects (Uruguay) that I held up my writing to include. The book is therefore based on particular research experiences that largely ended around 2007 (except for my mediated involvement with Uruguay from 2010). Although the literature I cite carries on to the present day, the empirical base could be considered historical, particularly given the speed at which digital cultures believe themselves to change. This is undeniable but also no bad thing: the book is located at a particular conjuncture and all the use of this material is, I hope, properly located in time as well as place. And that kind of specificity is precisely what the book is in any case advocating, rather than placing ICTs in a no-time or any-time as well as the usual no-place or anywhere. At the same time, I do have a suspicion that less has changed than readers might think (though this statement entirely depends on one's chosen scale – Strathern 2004 [1991]). For example, the shift over the noughties first to 'Web2.0' and then to social network rhetoric simply intensified older and familiar tropes such that the same themes that I outline in terms of 'network ethics' (the transformative values of connection) can still be traced, and in any case much that social network researchers are interested in now was already evident in Trinidadian use of ICQ instant messaging (or sexpics traders using Internet Relay Chat) in the mid- to late 1990s (and of course amongst 'social capital' theorists both in media studies and in development studies from at least the 1990s). I would also argue that the metanarratives that bothered me then – new media, development and globalization – had already solidified in roughly the same forms in which we encounter them now and which still bother me in the same ways.

However, a different kind of limitation to the ethnographies needs some comment. It will quickly become clear to most readers that this book is blinkered in one possibly disabling way that I could do little about: it is largely confined to studies of consumption and use. I have next to nothing to say about the design and production of technical objects and therefore ignore much of my own Science and Technology Studies inheritance, and equally ignore the political economy of media, at least in the narrow form in which it is conducted within media studies and media sociology. Nevertheless, I do invest a great many words in trying to figure out how communicative assemblages are configured, framed and implemented within development policy and practice, which should also be regarded as a moment of production. How disabling you find this absence will depend largely on your position on one of the central issues in the book – the extent to which our understanding of 'media' and 'ICTs' is ineluctably bound up with technological determinisms and with what I describe in Chapter 3 as 'bad formalism'. If one's aim is to trace the 'impacts' of given communications machines across the social field, then my avoidance of the moment of production is fatal; if the question is how communicative assemblages are constructed and stabilized within networks, then my account is partial but valid. My next project, to make amends, is centrally about technical design ('Configuring Light/Staging the Social', a study of light as material culture).

Back to Banalities: Redefining New Media, Development and Globalization

By this point the title of the book may strike the reader as misleading. I am clearly not about to offer a new theory of media, development or globalization, or their conjuncture, or in any other way to treat them as given objects about which one can or should generate realist theories; indeed, the aim is to avoid such framing like the plague, and to use non-northern research experiences both to contest the realism of these terms and to see how that realism functions to organize the field (and research into these fields) epistemologically, organizationally, politically.

This anthropological distancing or self-alienation from the common-sense terms of one's professional life requires reflection and fancy footwork both in the research itself and in the writing; both are essentially matters of strategic positioning in institutional spaces, tactical manoeuvring to carve out free spaces. By way of introduction, then, it makes sense to summarize some of these manoeuvres, and specifically to make a succinct case, for each of the three terms, for the strategy for asserting symmetry between participants to ICT4D processes.

New media[2]

Thinking about media, communications and ICTs has been dominated, with astonishing continuity, by the dichotomy that Raymond Williams (1978) put in the subtitle of his seminal book so long ago – the relation between media as technology and as cultural form. Williams saw – and evaded, more successfully than most – the reduction of communications to questions of impacts, to the question of which changes in socio-cultural life can be directly attributed to new technical means of communication and their institutionalization. This kind of question can take the crudest and most reductive forms in ICT for development, where the practical outcomes seem most urgent. What development gains can be directly ascribed to a particular ICT intervention? What blockages are clearly informational? On the basis of what measurable gains is the installation of a particular type of ICT facility preferable to digging a well or distributing anti-malarial nets? Answering such questions seems to rest entirely on specifying the generic properties of media, and how they can best be deployed in specific 'contexts' or locations ('best practice').

As discussed in Chapters 2 and 3, this problematic is often characterized in terms of the traps of technological determinism and a zero-sum intellectual game in which either human or technological agents are paramount, in which media are either tools or determinants of social development (Lister, Dovey, Giddings et al. 2009: 78–99). By contrast, my own first research in this area was governed by attempts to localize media objects, the way I had learned largely from sociology of consumption and then later from material culture studies. The question of media, in other words, was the question of difference: how the same resources were configured differently in different places, and how human users are configured differently through different object relations. We must start from the contingent and co-constructing assemblage of people and things rather than from the putative properties of objects.

Indeed, in many respects we already have good and sufficient resources for moving beyond the problematic of 'technology versus cultural form'. ANT, material culture studies, practice theory, assemblage theories, post-representational theory – all are concerned with the mutual constitution of entities through their connections, rather than with disaggregating them in order to attribute discrete and independent causal primacy to one or another. Properties are emergent and relational; it is as reductive to ignore the materiality of communicative systems as it is to argue that the technical structure of a medium trumps any specific act of communication. Neither materiality nor communication can be specified (and certainly will not be empirically encountered) independently of each other. This perspective underwrites, but was also partly enabled by, the ethnographic turn to specificity and contingency, again foreshadowed by Williams: the shape of a medium – as produced, as used – is a specific history of decisions, practices, choices, classifications, and not the generic unfolding of intrinsic technical or social properties across diverse social 'contexts'.

However, this kind of perspective cannot be fully realized unless all its implications are taken on board, unless it is seriously radical, and this seems to be more obvious when working in a context of development and North–South exchanges than when studying media in one's own world. Whereas development used to believe that modernization flowed ineluctably from the building of very large dams, now the very idea of ICT4D assumes that not only developmental gains but also integration into an emergent network society flows directly from the informational properties of digital media. In some respects, the very notions of media, new media and ICTs are essentially essentialist in the simple sense that if we start investigating communications with an unchallenged commitment to something called 'media', then we are already committed to seeing and acting on particular ways of organizing the world, to a logic inscribed in certain kinds of objects with certain kinds of properties that we can simply observe in different social locations or contexts.

At one level, the point I am trying to make here is not academically precious but extremely pragmatic: media essentialism – the positing of properties as intrinsic to specific communicative machines or institutions, independently of their social context; hence, claims about the impacts of these machines – is not simply a matter of intellectual error or a matter for paradigm shift; and it cannot be corrected simply through critique. Media essentialism is a fundamental aspect of certain kinds of governance and bureaucracy. A simple example: early in this research sequence, in first contacts with UNESCO, I was taken aside by a senior figure in its ICT policy and asked whether I was an advocate of 'telecentres' or 'community media centres' (CMCs). The question didn't make any sense until I understood that the two terms mapped out different bureaucratic divisions, regions, policies and forms of professional development: one (as far as I understood it) focused on inserting ICTs into local environments in combination with other resources that could support a range of business practices (e.g., alongside photocopiers, phone services and printing facilities); the other connected ICTs to a more explicitly community media tradition that prioritized things like information flows, self-representation and community deliberation. Each option involved definitions of media and their properties, models of development processes and paradigms of best practice for connecting them. These options not only embodied different, and differentiated, philosophies of development and media – each of which was solidified in the form of different communicative assemblages of ideas, skills, machines, institutions – but also the governance of different development apparatuses (one model was associated with African and the other with Asian programmes and UNESCO officers and offices, and with different networks of stakeholders and NGOs) as well as competition between UNESCO personnel. Which of course was precisely why I was taken aside and tested as to my allegiance. That is to say, telecentres and CMCs – as normative definitions of media, media properties and media practices and institutions – were part of projects to map and construct different 'technological zones' (Barry 2001, 2006), which were also political and managerial configurations. Less politely put, the very idea of 'media' was a vehicle for highly territorial turf wars between bureaucratic gangs (unfortunately another metaphor also fits: the territorial division of the world by colonial powers through everything from military borders to the gauge of train tracks). Distinctions between telecentres and CMCs, like the distinctions between media and new media, or between analogue and digital media cultures, constructed empires and zones of exclusion. Media essentialism in this sense was an integral premise of ICT4D management in that one organizes, controls and legitimates media policies across disparate locations by claiming to know about the properties inherent in 'the medium', uniform properties that are simply to be deployed (through 'best practice') in different places. Warranting the bureaucrat's very ability to specify particular properties of mobile phones or the internet was the underlying idea of 'a medium' or 'an ICT' as a particular known kind of object that could be defined above the level of its contingent occurrences, and which could travel anywhere with its properties intact. The job of the researcher, I was consistently informed, was to discover or confirm those properties around which media and their proper developmental use could be defined.

Hence, I could not understand or get a critical perspective on what was going on without moving beyond disputes about the specific properties of media to a consideration of how the very notions of media and media properties organized the field I was researching. And the urgency of this question was intensified by the fact that the framing of media was clearly more than just an interesting side issue in a world that was increasingly defined as transforming into an informational or network society: what was at stake was the very characterization of the future on the basis of claims about the properties of 'media'. Assemblage approaches to media (whether ANT, material culture, practice-based, Deleuzian or DeLandan) potentially release us from sterile debates about the properties of media, but rather more importantly they may help distance us from the role of normative definitions of 'the media' or 'new media' in the organization of communication and development.

Hence the recourse to infra-language: notions like communicative assemblages and communicative ecology, defined in Chapter 2, step back far enough, it is hoped, so that concepts of 'media' themselves appear as simply one kind of narrative through which some people organize themselves (and other people) in the field, and, in Latourian terms, do so by being 'empty', by aiming to trace associations regardless of the precise mixtures of things, forms, relationships and institutions we might encounter.

Development

The idea of 'development' has a doubled history. On the one hand, in its broad sense, development is a modern term that seeks to identify the deep structural logic or normative principles of social change at a given historical moment: a progression, a sequence, a direction, however mediated or dialectical, that tells us whether we are marching in step with history. This is the sense in which Marx's sequence of modes of production and their contradictions sought to ground a scientific rather than utopian socialist practice. Development in this sense identifies 'real processes' in relation to which analysts can mark divisions between those who are progressing and those who don't measure up to the modern, and it generates forms of knowledge and administration of those others.

On the other hand, development has a narrower meaning that translated this broad sense of development into an ostensibly technical relationship between North and South in the post-World War II period: 'development' refers to development industries and bureaucracies, a bewildering, mammoth and arcanely acronymed ecosystem of ODAs (overseas development agencies), NGOs (nongovernmental organizations), INGOs (international nongovernmental organizations), stakeholders, networks, governments, consultants, discourses, indicators, theories and best practices. The technical appearance of the development industry (as well as passionate attacks on that technicism) appears paradoxical, particularly to someone coming into it from outside: in order to claim to have knowledges that will allow it to accomplish 'development', the development bureaucracy has to make constant claims about the normative direction of social change and therefore to assume the old model of historical 'catch-up'. And yet it is supposed to deny this normative or teleological development pathway (i.e., the idea that there is only one path of modernization) and it normally has also to deny a sense of itself as constantly failing, at least partly on the basis that it doesn't know what is going on.

Earlier critiques of development tended to mirror the grand narratives of those they critiqued: for every Rostow (1952) laying out a metanarrative of normative modern development, there was a Frank, Wallerstein, Ferguson or Escobar for whom the development industry represented a uniform logic of underdevelopment, northern domination and the extension of state power. This book is instead indebted to more anthropologically grounded recent ethnographies of development – notably those by Maia Green (2000, 2003, 2009) and David Mosse (2004, 2005) – which round on the intensely experienced contradiction between institutionally necessary claims to knowledge and a constant sense that no one does or could know the future, or the logic of social change. This certainly accords with my own experience of situated conjunctures between new media, development and globalization. If anything, appeals to such grand and containing terms were ritual or gestural, ways of claiming certainty or negotiating agreement despite profound confusion, statements made so that one could go about one's business or appease a stakeholder, and they were often incorporated in highly formal documents and regulations in order to make processes manageable, accountable and ostensibly rational (Green 2009). Much of the time, new media, development and globalization were perhaps better understood as 'floating signifiers' or – more prosaically – as rhetorical 'fudging' and tactical ambiguity (Slater and Ariztia-Larrain 2009).

Terms drawn from media and information systems were clearly increasingly central in this game, particularly as much of the research was conducted concurrently with the mammoth process known as the World Summit on the Information Society (WSIS): this was a rewriting of 'development' in terms of knowledge, information, network society, ICTs, and so on, that started when the World Bank rebranded itself as a 'knowledge bank' in the late 1990s (McFarlane 2006b). At various points, the very notions of inequality and global power seemed to be redefined as 'digital divides' insofar as digital access was increasingly viewed as the only serious determinant of future development. Much of the history of development has taken the form of technical fixes (massive public works programmes, followed by the green revolution, followed by structural adjustment, etc.) of which new media, ICTs and global information society are merely the latest. Hence in one respect, there was a rerun of the oldest modernist mythology: a new technical engine of accelerated growth now defined development, and the aim of development in the narrower sense – the development industry, with a remit to close gaps – was digital inclusion, to bring North and South into the same development logic, within an at least basically fair international division of labour.

What are the issues of asymmetry in this case? In Chapter 4 I argue that there are two interconnected asymmetries in this picture of new media and information society as the new template for 'development' (in both broad and narrow senses: as template both for normative images of change and for the narrower development bureaucracy). Firstly, there is the extent to which a globalized information society is defined as a normative path, narrated from the North, that acts as a framework into which everyone must fit. Secondly, there is the ethical asymmetry that I have identified above in terms of network ethics: the extent to which the imagination of the future through the material culture and practice of new technologies is constrained and restricted to a narrow instrumentalism in the South. Crudely, the North is imagined through ICTs as transforming into new kinds of people and new forms of sociality; the South, by contrast, is simply provided with new tools to carry on being precisely what they were before (only, it is hoped, more efficiently) and to occupy a slightly more profitable, or simply less disastrous, position in the emerging new international division of labour.

Both asymmetries (northern theory/southern particularity; northern transformational ethics/southern instrumentality) share an underlying form: some people are development theorists who can define both the norms and visions of social transformation, and others are the facts or objects or – worse – 'beneficiaries' of these development narratives; they are *to be developed*. And therefore a tight focus on precisely how that developer/developed distinction is marked and maintained is all important (and too often lost even in the most critical development theories): the issue is not simply whether particular claims about new media and development are false, ideological, oppressive or performatively inscribed in practices; the issue is whose knowledges are frameworks and whose are mere beliefs, who gets to theorize social change and who has to locate themselves within others' theories (whether to conform or to critique)?

The very simple kind of symmetry to be asserted here is to define 'development' as all discourses and practices that seek to understand and act upon the future, to construct informed strategies (personal, familial, national, ethnic, global, etc.) for both surviving and achieving desired and valued forms of life in contingent and as yet probabilistic future conditions. This sense of 'development' includes its ethical dimension – understanding and acting on the kinds of agency and sociality that one can imagine in and through emergent socio-technical possibilities. Development in this sense is a matter of strategic thinking and acting, and on the basis of present values and of knowledges which are known to be provisional and contingent. If one cared to reach for grand theory, 'development' could therefore be considered an intrinsic and pervasive condition of modernity, of those social actors who need continually to reconfigure their sense of agency in relation to perceived social change.

Under this definition, most importantly, development embraces conditions of social existence across the social field: coolie labourers in rural India strategize futures quite as much as those global corporations, governments and NGOs who seek to intervene in their lives. Insofar as they all engage in the game of attempting (with tremendous uncertainty, fear and hope) to connect their own fortunes to provisional and risky understandings of where the world is going, how it will work, how they might act within these future states and how to achieve their own desires within these possible future states – insofar as they are involved in that game, more or less reflexively, they are all development theorists, development planners and development agents of analytically equal status.

Put more bluntly: the *normal* research experience was to be sitting in an interview or group discussion about poverty and communication and being intensely aware that the only reason we were all sitting and talking in the same space was because all of us – interviewees, project workers and stakeholders, myself and my academic community, UNESCO, DFID and the agencies and governments to which they were networked – *didn't* know what was going to happen, could *not* predict social change and development, had *insecure* and *partial* knowledge, and yet had nonetheless to *act*, to make and implement decisions about what to do, and to do so on the basis of what seemed like good reasons at the time. That's 'development' as I understand it; and the symmetry between participants is complete.

Globalization

'Globalization' is one kind of development narrative, a narrative of social transformation focused on increasing densities and speeds of interconnection. It is therefore closely bound up with ICTs as exemplifying, if not actually causing, an abolition of space through an instantaneity of flows. The tropes through which people were characterizing globalization in the early days of my own research interestingly conflated unimpeded flows of goods and of information: ICTs were seen as inevitably bringing about an economy that was both disintermediated and 'frictionless', a world of direct and deregulated connection that technologically mirrored neo-liberal aspirations to deregulated markets. Indeed, the information society was sometimes presented as if it were structural adjustment brought about, automatically and beneficially, by technological means. Certainly within the development industry, globalization was regarded as the assumed and unexplicated backdrop to all development policy and practice: the key to sustainable development is integration within increasingly densely interconnected and disintermediated markets; the only alternative – in this view – is to be marginalized and to descend into a Castellian informational black hole. As is usual, the most passionate (and activist) critics of globalization treated it in the same realist mode as its most passionate advocates.

In the context of North–South relations, and specifically development ones, this view of globalization involved the usual narratively driven asymmetries (Cameron and Palan 2004a, 2004b) in which globalization narratives were themselves globalized and all sense of their performativity was repressed: globalization presented as a kind of global tsunami or juggernaut, a crushing physical event that would engulf everyone and which would simply crush you if you were not prepared to profit by it (Slater 2003, 2008). However, these debates about globalization seemed to deflect from the most important issues, and the richest ethnographic data, which concerned the new media as material culture: what kinds of maps, connections, mobilities, could people imagine and enact through new media? It is certainly undeniable that there are major revolutions going on in the practice of space and connection. The problem, however, is what happens in trying to comprehend those revolutions by placing them all within the framework of globalization. To what extent does the idea of globalization impose a very standardized metric ('density' or 'speed' of 'connection') upon changes in spatiality and scaling that are far more heterogeneous as well as differently narrated and performed by different people? And in very pragmatic terms, what does it mean for research and knowledge production to have to refer everything back to this one narrative and framework for interpretation?

To some extent, dealing with the concept of globalization involves me in an attempt to assert symmetry through a pure ethnographic reductionism: the idea of globalization, I argue in Chapter 5, is based in an extremely abstract metrology (much as the old liberal/utilitarian concepts of satisfaction or utility or preferences were). Globalization is based on the idea of denser, faster, more immediately impactful *connections*, in which 'connection' – like utility – is a uniform and undifferentiated measurement that homogenizes apples and oranges, as it were. Trinidadian kids connected to US kids as quickly, densely, and so on, as the US kids connected to them, but this tells us next to nothing about the nature of those connections. What were the qualities, consequences, characters, of connection? How was connection differently mapped, represented, enacted? A social network analysis or descriptive mapping of densities would tell you very little about the difference between Trinidadian and American scaling practices. Moreover, to analytically prioritize network over actor is simply a reverse of the determination of networks by actors that ANT so successfully challenged. And, finally, the abstracting metrology of 'globalization' seems to reflect the distinction between syntax and semantics in information theory (Floridi 1999, 2010, 2011; Terranova 2004): we are invited to view the world as a Shannonian one of more or less structured or entropic data without regard for the meaning of the data that flow through information systems.

In the case of globalization we turn for an infra-language to Latour himself, and the concept of 'scales' and scaling practices, devices, representations: 'the global' and 'globalization' as an abstract measure of space is simply one kind of scaling, one way of mapping, representing and constructing different kinds of distance and proximity of connection. It is simply part of studying the making of associations. Moreover, scaling is clearly not a practice that belongs solely to northern modernists: we look at examples of Trinidadian, Ghanaian and Sri Lankan youth, for example, all very keen to imagine and position themselves within very distributed scales – global images – which they understand in entirely different and even clearly opposed ways. Everyone is a mapper or geographer just as everyone is a development theorist or a builder of communicative assemblages: as mundane social actors, we need to understand our connections in space as well as time, and most of us are much better and more complicated in our scaling practices than globalization debates give us credit for (Rantanen 2005). The infralinguistic symmetry asserted here is simply an attempt to situate all scaling practices and devices and categorizations within a uniform space. Symptomatically Chapter 5 is also, therefore, the one chapter that relies on a fieldwork story from northern Spain rather than from a southern 'beneficiary'.

Conclusion

This book arises at a point of convergence, and aims simply to 'make connections', to introduce diversity and dialogue rather than analytical or empirical generalities. It should be clear that the last thing we need in researching 'new media, development and globalization' is another attempt to theorize the whole. We will be looking instead at how new media are thought about and used in relation to development and globalization processes, and I hope this will be useful for people (including those in development work) to think more creatively, experimentally and concretely about what they are doing and could do with new machines for communicating. I also hope that ethnographic engagement with the ways in which people perform communication, social change and connection as lived experiences can demote the three terms of our title from their analytico-theoretical, abstract, universalizing thrones, and see what they mean in grounded, diverse everyday streets. And in an explicitly political vein, I want to explore what they mean within the experience of those who are normally the objects rather than the subjects of such universalizing concepts.

Overall, then, the aim of this book is to redefine new media, development and globalization for maximum symmetry and inclusiveness, so that each of them can travel wherever we need to go, and so that they can be owned by anyone – and applied to anyone. This is not a deconstructive exercise so much as an exercise in broadening terms sufficiently that they can bring everyone and everything potentially within the same frame of practice and reflection: cars and loudspeakers can find themselves within a 'media study' as much as the latest iPhone; a prestigious cultural centre in northern Spain is as much part of 'development' as a coolie in Tamil Nadu, and both are equally speculative development theorists; globalization embraces both the visions of Castells and the new geographies imagined by migrant labourers from Sri Lanka. Each is equally valid in constructing the three key terms in the book's title. Though it will require the whole book to make the case properly, its starting point is that a democracy of knowledge is urgent: many of the disasters associated with all three terms arise from a persistent inability or unwillingness to achieve a level of conceptual breadth that puts everyone in the same frame so that they can actually see and talk to each other. In this sense, 'making connections' is more than a matter of using media well.

2

Communicative Ecology and Communicative Assemblages

Studying 'the media' in the context of development makes us reflect more clearly on the issues underlying western approaches to the media, both academic and public. The concern is overwhelmingly with impacts, effects and social change. The media are pervasive, large-scale and highly visible institutionalizations of communication – and have been since the eighteenth century – and the question has always been: How do they relate to the experience of modernity and to processes of modernization? How do they change culture, sociality, governance, economy, for good and for ill? And what *can* they do? In development contexts, this concern is explicit because it is practical and managerial: can we – researchers, practitioners, funders, policy makers – demonstrate a direct impact of particular media interventions (projects, best practice, governmental and commercial media) on poverty, health, livelihood strategies, 'empowerment', and so on? Can we generate knowledges that can legitimate particular choices of resource allocation (why invest in computer centres rather than wells or anti-malarial netting?) and that allow us rationally to generalize from one development context (e.g., a pilot media project in Sri Lanka) to many or all of them (e.g., an ODA policy on digital media, or a UNESCO World Summit on the Information Society)? In cruder terms that are less frequently spoken aloud, the questions of

27

media in development are identical to the kind that have been asked about the media and modernity within the North for several centuries: What is the role and potential of the media in bringing about 'modernization', particularly at a time when modernization is increasingly associated with new media, creative industries and informationalization? Much of the research experience on which this book is based was funded at a point in time when the initial hype over new media and ICTs was paling, scepticism was setting in and claims were challenged. As a top DFID officer in West Africa informed me during a courtesy call at the start of my work in Ghana, 'We know bugger all about the impact of ICTs on poverty but we're throwing a hell of a lot of money at it. I don't normally talk to researchers but in this case I'll make an exception.' The role of knowledge was clear, narrow and instrumental.

At a superficial level, the problem with media impact questions is already well rehearsed, and will form a backdrop to the next two chapters. Firstly, to ask researchers to identify and measure the impact of 'the media' is to adopt a realist view in which 'the media' appear as given objects with given properties that can be specified independently of any particular social 'context'. As researchers, we are asked to find out what happens when we drop these objects into different contexts under varied conditions (e.g., differing local mediating factors or project organizations and approaches). This is clearly to assume that, for example, 'the internet' is an already known thing with properties that can be specified in the abstract but which may work out in different ways depending on 'context'. A major task for media in development researchers is to identify 'best practices' for situating a given technology, with maximum impact, in any context required. Secondly, however, the researcher is being asked to characterize the media as discrete and independent variables, ones to which specific events in the world can be unambiguously, and (with luck) measurably, attributed. This institutionalized imperative to map causal connections between discrete and known media objects and social outcomes is intensely managerial: it is not simply the (indisputable) desire to help and to make ICTs work more efficiently to better people's lives, and which depends on forms of knowledge and explanation, but there is also the need to manage empires of development projects and to ensure control, cost-accountability and formal audit. You get repeat funding if you can demonstrate social outcomes and outputs directly or potentially attributable to your media intervention; and the results of your intervention will (in theory, though rarely in practice) be generalized upwards to concepts of policy and best practice and therefore extended to other projects and regions. In all these cases, a certain *form* of knowledge is *de rigueur*; whether the term media 'impact' is voiced or is euphemized owing to intellectual embarrassment, its rhetorical form is objectified throughout development practice. As Maia Green put it, in development planning, 'development problems and solutions are represented through simplistic monocausal chains amenable to transformation via the transfer of financial resources. This, rather than naïvety about state power, probably accounts for the absence of any discernible relation between [development interventions and the reduction of poverty]' (2003: 128).

Both assumptions have undergone long critique from, amongst many quarters, deconstructions of technological determinism, material culture studies, consumption studies, Science and Technology Studies and – within media studies – co-configuration and domestication approaches (e.g., Morley 1986, 1992; or Silverstone and Hirsch 1992; Silverstone, Hirsch and Morley 1992; but see also Ciborra 2004 within the discipline of information systems) and latterly practice theories. As with any object encountered in cross-cultural contexts, we need to investigate how media are reconfigured in the very process of assimilating them into new social worlds, while at the same time attending to the reconfiguration of that context in relation to the media. Indeed the very meaning of social agency has been redefined from a zero-sum game between media structures and consuming audiences (a liberal view of constraint in which the freedom or power of either is always to the detriment of the other) to a narrative of how both agency and objects emerge together. My own first work in this area was of this sort: How was the Trinidadian internet different, and how did 'Trinidad' reconfigure itself in this encounter (Miller and Slater 2000)? As we shall discuss further in Chapter 4, simply demonstrating that northern narratives of cyberculture did *not* apply in Trinidad seemed a sufficient de-essentializing of a medium: rather than being one essentialized object unfolding in different places, there are many 'internets', including a number of different ones constructed by Trinidadians alone.

This approach involves studying 'the media' differently – in terms of their local, contingent construction and therefore in terms of their *difference* rather than their universality and given-ness. But it can still leave the idea of 'the media' entirely intact and in a realist mode: there are pre-existing objects out there in the world that can be studied and that can provide the unquestionable ground for defining disciplines (media studies, media sociology), political agendas (media society, network or information society) and – in our case – development institutions, programmes, policies and projects (WSIS, ICT officers, DFID). 'The media' – however ill defined – constitute a basic unit of analysis, and in this sense, 'the media' present themselves as an unexamined analytical commitment, an *a priori* that structures the field of knowledge rather than appearing within it as a challengeable postulate. The very idea of 'the media' is an organizing category, a classification through which we constitute (and manage, exclude, divide) knowledges and practices. To regard ways of organizing communications as 'media' is normative (there are – generally very confused – criteria for granting or withholding this social status from particular communicative assemblages) and performative (using the label of 'media' does not simply describe a type of communicative arrangement but rather plays a constitutive role in producing and reproducing, as well as excluding or controlling, different modes of communication). For example, Boyd-Barrett's (1977, 1982) discussions of the export of media professionalism to the third world are still exemplary studies not only of how specific media practices are globally disseminated through material arrangements (education, administration, training, programme formats and genres) but also of the dissemination of the very idea of 'media' in their modern and western sense.

Understanding this use of 'the media' to perform communications is politically urgent rather than academically pedantic: 'the media' and cognate terms (e.g., ICTs, information society, digital culture) do not simply name objects in the world, let alone objects with known and invariable properties. The aim of this chapter and the next, therefore, is to shift 'the media' downwards from an assumed analytical framework and realist belief in the existence of certain kinds of objects to be studied and managed; and to argue that we need to place the study of communication in a different kind of analytical frame that makes the fewest assumptions possible about what should and should not appear within that frame.

The Media Are Not the Message: A Story from Sri Lanka

Let's start with a really embarrassing research story. In March–April 2002 I took part in a 'monitoring and evaluation' study of Kothmale Community Radio and Internet Project (KCRIP). KCRIP was an extension of Kothmale Community Radio (KCR), a long-standing community radio project located in rural Sri Lanka, just south of Kandy, and funded largely by UNESCO but with an (ambiguous) institutional position within the Sri Lanka Broadcasting Corporation (SLBC, the national broadcasting service, a postcolonial legacy of the BBC). KCR was innovative and committed to exploring potential convergences of new and old media in increasing its role in the community, hence its recent addition of an internet project. The UNESCO information officer who commissioned the research (W. Jayaweera, who will feature importantly in Chapter 6) was himself a Sri Lankan who had been a radio broadcaster with a commitment to community radio going back twenty or more years. He was concerned that any 'monitoring and evaluation' research should be appropriately sensitive to the complexity of the project and community. He was therefore open to a broadly ethnographic approach, which I proposed under the code name of 'communicative ecology' (see below). Rather than study the 'impact' of the internet and the ICT4D intervention on Kothmale, we would instead explore the ways in which the new media were entering into the wider communicative processes of the locale, including the older media (radio) that KCR had long practised. We would do a broad mapping of communication in the Kothmale region (of its 'communicative ecology') into which we would fit KCRIP, not as a privileged object to which we could attribute impacts but rather as new communicative resources and arrangements that either connected or failed to connect in various ways to existing 'local' communicative practices.

At the same time, as the UNESCO officer was intensely aware, 'monitoring and evaluation' has a crucial function in legitimating project investments. It means, firstly, measuring the impact of projects in order to cost-account the resources invested in them, generally with an eye to success in the next funding round; and, secondly, trying to generalize 'lessons' or 'best practice', both to improve the project and to apply its model in other contexts (thereby also increasing the prestige of the project and of stakeholders, including the UNESCO team itself within UNESCO and within the wider development community). Indeed, our UNESCO officer, located in Delhi, was responsible for an empire of ICT projects stretching from Dubai to South Korea. We were therefore asked to include a survey in our study in order to produce conventional metrics – *numbers* – that count up standardized things and their relationships (e.g., between radio programmes and health information), things and relationships that could be counted anywhere in the world and therefore could be compared numerically. Figure 2.1 presents an excerpt from the questionnaire I prepared in London, having never before set foot in Sri Lanka. It went through several iterations, by email, with comments from local project workers and collaborating researchers. But it is in fact a bog-standard media studies instrument: it aimed to measure the use of a conventional list of conventionally conceived media – newspapers, radio, internet – although I pushed the definition of 'media' to include transport and mobility – movements of people to Kandy and Colombo.

The standardized survey was administered within looser, more ethnographic interviews that took place in people's houses, and indeed we largely used the survey opportunistically, as an excuse to get in people's doors and have much longer and more interesting conversations with them. On this basis it took at most two days of fieldwork before we realized that the questionnaire was based on our utter ignorance as to

		How many members have done the following in the last month?	...last year?	Where did they do the following?
a	Sent or received a letter			
b	Listened to radio			
c	Watched TV			
d	Read a newspaper			
e	Made a telephone call			
f	Read a magazine			
g	Used the Internet			
h	Read a book			
i	Used a computer			
j	Used a mobile phone			
k	Sent or received an email			
l	Travelled to Colombo			
m	Travelled to Kandy			
n	Travelled to XX [neighbouring town]			
o	Looked on a website			

Figure 2.1

what counts as 'a medium' in upland Sri Lanka. I had produced a conventional northern list of media that simply did not include what every one of our informants knew commonsensically to be the key communicative assemblages in their lives, of which two in particular stood out. The first of these missing media was 'roads', or, more precisely, mud. I had included 'travel' in my survey (and was really pleased with myself), but not the *media* of movement, whereas all conversations about communication in our region started from bus schedules, the costs of travel and the problems of coordinating people's physical movements, and weather (e.g., the very existence of roads was a seasonal matter) (see Morley 2007 and 2008 for a recent discussion of 'non-mediacentric media studies' that strongly focuses on transport). Indeed, the most common communicative tasks concerned the coordination of movements of people and messages across numerous technologies and people.

Even more crucially, the importance of roads reflected a valorization of physical co-presence that I simply could not have understood in advance of doing some ethnographic work: as we will see in a moment, the local and the face-to-face were *so* important that – it could be argued – the entire purpose and meaning of 'the media' for local people was to accomplish or to simulate co-presence. The very *purpose* of phones or radio or internet was to a large extent to coordinate the real or imagined assemblage of people and community. Hence, to talk of roads or mud as 'media' was not a tricksy ANT-ish or McLuhanesque move; it was simply to recognize the paradigms of communication in terms of which people understood and valorized new media technologies and might integrate them into their communicative assemblages: numerous interviews involved complex accounts of how different 'media' (phones, roads, buses, mobiles, radio, other people's movements) could be linked to engineer the visit of a friend or relative. *That* was the communicative ecology into which both KCR and KCRIP fitted.

Secondly, everyone knew that the most common local media experience was provided by *loudspeakers*. Their omission from my list was more embarrassing because once you *saw* them, loudspeakers looked like a medium in the most conventional sense of the word: a technology that mediates communication and orders it through cultural forms and institutional arrangements for the production, circulation and consumption of symbolic material. Two examples were frequently cited and observed. Firstly, if you want to spread health information or political ideas or mobilize party political or trade union activity in upland Sri Lanka, you mount loudspeakers on cars and send them out with a map of regional health or election districts. This is a stable broadcast medium, operated routinely, that includes all that 'a medium' should: connected technologies (car + speaker + mic + maps + road); logistical and communicative skills specialized to this medium, and learned over time, including highly skilled actors who approximate to media professionals; and an organizational form that configures communicative practice within institutions such as hospitals and trade unions. To borrow ANT-ish idiom, loudspeaker cars were clearly the heterogeneous engineering of a stabilized communicative assemblage that was black-boxed for locals but was omitted from the approved list of 'media' with which I had arrived from northern media sociology.

The second loudspeaker example – loudspeaker events – turned out to be directly crucial for our own research. These events involved erecting a stage and loudspeakers in the central square of a larger town, and organizing a varied programme, several hours long, of music (live and recorded), contests and competitions, performances, advertising, speeches, and so on. The central figure was the announcer, an MC who managed the whole show, and who often had considerable status and celebrity in the locale. These were complex and expensive events to organize and finance, and often involved sponsorship deals and tie-ins with commercial radio and local businesses or even national advertisers. They were live events, though they were often also mounted as outside broadcasts on radio.

My omission of loudspeaker events was serious enough in leaving out a popular communicative assemblage with a symbolically significant position in the communicative ecology of the area. Had we limited research to my survey – which is not uncommon in development monitoring and evaluation – we would have seen Kothmale from the perspective of northern media studies rather than local communicative practices. But the importance of loudspeakers in Kothmale presented a still more profound challenge to the notion of 'media': in local communication the relation between loudspeakers and radio, and then internet, is better understood as a continuum than as the coexistence of separate media in one social space, each with its separate effects or impacts. Loudspeaker events were often sponsored by local radio stations plus other commercial sponsors, and broadcast live to various distances. KCR relied heavily on broadcasting local events of this sort. For example, the April *puja* that year (a deeply important event for the majority Buddhist Sinhalese communities) involved a local gathering through the night ending in a drumming competition in which KCR broadcast local drumming as part of a national programme that linked drumming villages all over Sri Lanka. The relation between local event and radio broadcast was complex and inextricable: participants' general sense was not that they were staging a local event for radio broadcast but rather that radio allowed a wider audience to participate in the local event, as well as to demonstrate the high quality of the local event to a wider audience (the aim was to show that local drumming, local radio, local parties, local worship, were best).

Conversely, radio stations – commercial ones as well as the community KCR – largely secured their all-important local popularity more through their participation in local events than their airing of international pop music genres, national news or any other aspect of the 'wider world'. And some of the legitimation deficit of SLBC could be attributed precisely to its national public service framing, which did not connect to the moral status of locality. Moreover, there were many other connections between loudspeaker events and radio that blurred the boundaries between them as separable 'media', the most important being the most practical: KCR staff – who worked for KCR on a voluntary and largely unpaid basis, some of them for many years – relied on being hired for loudspeaker events in order to reach a nearly adequate income, hence loudspeaker events subsidized their community radio activities, and through them sustained KCR itself; conversely, there was a virtuous dynamic between celebrity accrued through community radio announcing and being hired and paid for DJing loudspeaker events. In other words, the very idea of a media 'career' involved a far more complex assemblage than could be contained within my northern classifications of existing media. Moreover, tellingly, announcers themselves considered the skill-sets involved in loudspeaker events and radio to be identical, which indicated something both about their view of the two(?) media and about the cultural forms that made up the generic content of each.

Loudspeaker events were therefore essential in understanding KCRIP in terms of finances, cultural forms, careers, communicative skills and much more. Imported categorical distinctions between 'media', defined as discrete objects in northern cosmologies (and as a basis for ascribing impacts separately to each media entity), simply obscured the ways in which communication was organized here. But this continuity between loudspeaker events, community radio and commercial radio also exemplified, and reproduced, a still deeper order, what has been described as village ideology (Brow 1996). The underlying belief, and the basis of the project of Sinhalese nation-building for several postcolonial decades, was that the village forms the moral core of all life, and that Sri Lanka is properly a 'nation of villages' (Brow 1996: 23). Indeed, KCR – a project initially linked to a large-scale hydraulic project (Kothmale dam), as in so much of Sri Lanka's history as a 'hydraulic civilization' (Wittfogel 1956) – could be interpreted as a typical project of reconciling massive national technical interventions with village communities. In terms of 'communicative ecology', this moral status of the village endowed the ideas of co-presence and locality with a moral and existential priority through which all other communication was viewed: for example, radio extends to distant others the privilege of sitting in on our village events (you can hear how good our *puja* drummers are); websites allow distant others to glimpse our landscape and our temples. Commercial radio got its legitimacy and popularity from local anchoring (as in the *puja* drumming or sponsoring loudspeaker events), and KCR was most warmly approved of because the voices were local and listening to a programme was described as like sitting at home with friends (and certainly not like joining a global culture through commercial radio). Similarly, internet users at KCRIP generally designed websites intended to show to the world their local beauty spots and temples: the internet was not a vehicle for bringing Sri Lanka into a global space, but rather afforded foreigners the privilege of being able to see their village. Looked at this way, the loudspeaker event was not a pre-medial, 'local' or rudimentary assemblage, let alone one to be superseded by 'new media'; it was rather, for people in Kothmale, the paradigmatic form of legitimate media, the *ur*-medium, the exemplar to which newer media – such as those we were studying – had to approximate and connect if they were to be either intelligible, popular or legitimate.

The power of naming

One response (in fact my initial one) to the omission of loudspeaker events from my survey would be simply to *recognize* them as 'media' and add them to the approved list and to the survey. As noted, once visible, they *looked* like media; and conferring that label might have a political efficacy within development communications in valorizing local communicative structures by according them official status as media (clearly not just a great honour but also a potential route into funding). However, this would render invisible to research the role of this labelling in moulding the communicative ecology of the area: I could not regard the 'media' label as mine to grant theoretically in that it was a normative and performative ascription made and disputed by the actors themselves. And of course my own presence in Kothmale as a researcher was essentially to negotiate the medial status of internet and radio at UNESCO's behest – I was being funded to help produce the internet/ radio as a medium and assess UNESCO's success in this stated aim of its funding.

No Sri Lankan we interviewed categorized loudspeakers or roads as 'media', and most Sri Lankans largely shared with me the same amorphous labelling of 'the media' that I shared with media studies and with development agencies: a list of technologies and institutions (as on my questionnaire) whose consecration as 'media' rests on a largely unexamined history. At the same time there was a lot of definitional work going on around 'the media'. As noted, UNESCO was itself trying to stabilize media notions, and not least through my research: the *point* of the project and the research was to look at relations between new and old media in which UNESCO and KCR were invested, and at new formats that specifically aimed to stabilize a new media hybrid. For example, KCR was internationally associated with a new radio format called 'radio browsing' in which listeners sent in questions and requests for information that the announcer and invited guests researched online, often during the broadcast itself. This was a radio–internet hybrid in which the old medium of radio was seen as popularizing and mediating the new medium of internet. This concern with media definitions and hybrid formats that might challenge them had to do with pressure on UNESCO officers who were developing bureaucratic niches, careers and projects to demonstrate generalizable best practice. This pressure (and potential) was intense in the case of Kothmale because it had an exceedingly high international profile at that time within global ICT4D networks and amongst community media activists. Media labels, and the naming of media, were therefore crucial to the management of development practices. For example, 'radio browsing' was almost like KCR's 'brand' and the signifier of its distinctive identity. Could 'radio browsing' be stabilized as an object through which a model of media convergence could be developed and extended outwards through UNESCO's Delhi communications office and then throughout the ICT4D field, with ensuing definitions of projects, best practices and funding programmes? Media labels as normative stabilizations of exemplary 'best practices' would allow development workers to rationalize, legitimate and expand their policies and programmes.

At another level, a central issue for the entire project, and central to the research, was the position of the radio announcers at KCR. These exceptionally dedicated people were committed to 'community media', which, as we have seen, they funded largely by doing loudspeaker events (which were not classified as 'media' by anyone). At the same time they felt pressures to break through into more conventional and better-paid 'media' careers at SLBC or in commercial radio stations, partly as a result of long-term burn-out and partly owing to increased pressure of family commitments and obligations as they got older. But this break-out into 'the media' was impossible because of the dubious status of KCR as a medium: neither their community radio nor their loudspeaker work counted as 'media' experience, nor did it translate into the kinds of personal connections and networks required to break into 'the media'. Their serious, self-sacrificing and long-term commitment to KCR both was and wasn't 'media', and on this rested their ambiguous, frustrated and in the end impossible position within the field of Sri Lankan communications.

The negotiation of 'media' as a social status was a decisive part of the story to be told. Three more stories from this fieldwork will illustrate a further point about why the label 'media' needs to be kept *in* the research frame: naming (or not naming) communicative assemblages as 'media' can have variable functions and very different outcomes.

Firstly, here as elsewhere, people largely did not talk, unprompted, about 'the media', or relate to them as discrete objects; they talked about the interests, projects and tasks they were pursuing – their practices – and these might or might not include consecrated media (see Toft 2011); or rather they assembled various communicative resources but the notion of 'the media' played variable roles. Again, this could be crucial in understanding the assemblage we had actually been sent to research. For example, in Kothmale, people talked a lot about specific communicative flows such as the circulation of music, which was highly valued. A plethora of resources were recognized as interconnected nodes in this flow: KCR and loudspeaker events clearly had value for accessing traditional music; commercial radio, by contrast, connected ambiguously to it; new resources such as the CD-burning shops then springing up all over were clear extensions to the existing circulation of cassette tapes and domestic consumption that were core to music culture. An exemplary figure was a local cultural intermediary who called himself the Sri Lankan Elvis: a fifty-something rockabilly fan who traversed radio, loudspeaker events, parties and much more with his battered box of tapes, supplying cultural resources, for years, like a medial rag-and-bone man with a burning mission to localize his music in Kothmale.

A second example is what might be described as a temporary or evanescent medium. During this research, everyone – from the villages through to the higher reaches of UNESCO – repeatedly narrated one exemplary moment in the life of KCRIP: instead of having to wait a week to get their final exam results by post from Colombo, secondary school students were invited to convey their exam number to KCR by foot, post or phone; the staff could then look up their results online (for the first year ever) and broadcast them over the radio, using the exam number to maintain anonymity. Given that young people and their families believed that their future lives depended entirely on educational credentials, cutting out a week of desperate anxiety through new media demonstrated the developmental power and benefits of the internet. KCRIP staff, meanwhile, repeatedly told this story to clinch the argument that the popularity and spread – the impact – of new media depended on public demonstrations of dramatic practical efficacy: clear and attributable impacts of discrete media. And in this case, moreover, they had demonstrated the efficacy of combining new and old media, radio and internet, which was KCR's signature assemblage.

However, the alternative lesson that could be drawn from this episode concerned the practical demonstration of complex assemblage and coordination that went beyond radio and internet convergence; and clearly these two media labels alone could not capture the range of things that coalesced, temporarily, into a highly effective and valued system: chains of people delivering messages by word of mouth, post, roads, phone; institutional arrangements both in Colombo educational departments and in the Kothmale region; and so on. Both UNESCO and KCRIP had institutional interests at stake in reducing this assemblage to the adding together of two 'media', 'radio plus internet', despite the fact that the more complex kind of assemblage represented by this exam information system actually permeated KCRIP and constituted its signature way of working. Yet they – like any media researcher or practitioner – specified their assemblages in terms of the approved media forms and labels, thereby themselves rendering invisible the wider assemblage they had in fact mobilized. They were a 'media project', so they were committed to narrating this story of assemblage as a story about 'media'.

The final example goes to the heart of the power of naming. In this case, an evanescent or ersatz 'medium' was in fact 'named', but in a utopian mode that demonstrated how the term confers social status. The KCR internet project (KCRIP, which was basically the usual countertop of computers lined up facing a wall) was on the other side of the radio studio, so that announcers looking through the studio window could see and communicate with computer users. There were also speakers on the computer centre side of the window so that people in that room could hear the broadcasts and watch the announcers. The following story, or parts of it, may be apocryphal, but we were repeatedly told that one day a computer user who was holding a voice over IP call with a friend in Dubai (where huge numbers of Sri Lankans do migrant labour, often without returning for decades) decided to hold his microphone up to the radio speaker so that his friend could hear the traditional Sri Lankan music that was being broadcast. Instant internet radio. Apparently the next evening a computer user was talking to someone who worked on a military base somewhere else in the Middle East, and this time he connected his microphone to the PA system at the base so that Sinhalese folk music was broadcast from KCR to the entire military establishment.

One of the people who told me this story was Kumar, who was one of the most talented, famous and versatile of the KCR announcers, but who was doubly disadvantaged both as a radio volunteer with little pay and no career structure (and certainly none equivalent to his skill and experience) and as a Tamil. On my last night in Sri Lanka, indeed on the way to the airport, Kumar goes into a rhapsody on the theme of media skill, technology and assemblage based on this 'internet radio' story. He says that he wants desperately to start an internet radio operation at the station. 'We have to do globalization,' he says, 'we really have to do globalization.' With internet radio they can connect up with all the Sri Lankans abroad, and they can bring world music and news into Kothmale. They can be global without being any less local. He dreams of taking requests from Sri Lankans in Dubai to play local music; he equally dreams of showing people all over the world how bloody good he is as an announcer. This dream melds into another: Kumar conjures up a late-night radio show, a graveyard shift from 10.00 pm to 2.00 am: the station will be dark, he says, no one to disturb me or interfere, and he can sit alone in his booth talking to the world. I will get an email from Mr Don in London and from Mrs Jo in Australia and I'll talk about it and play your music. I can make money from advertising because I am a good businessman and I know everyone in Gampola – I'll show SLBC that the programme can pay its way. I can speak Tamil and Sinhala and English and Hindi and (when very drunk) German. And I can experiment and experiment and experiment. (A version of this story appeared in Slater and Tacchi 2003.)

'Internet radio' in this story is not so much a technical term or official medial identity; it is more a way of recognizing, imagining, extending and valorizing Kumar's joy and skill and pride in connection, and giving it a meaning and status beyond the mundane everydayness of announcing and running loudspeaker events, and of being a Tamil constantly fighting for social legitimacy. It's a utopian dream of pure freedom through pure connection. His story, like that of all the announcers in KCR, represented a complex relationship between emergent media practices, existing official structures and definitions, and attempts both to legitimate themselves through those structures and to overthrow them completely. That is to say, in a rather Bourdieuian vein, the power to name media, to consecrate communicative assemblages with public and normative definitions, is part of the contestation of the field of communications and of interventions in this field, of the ways in which actors calculate and position themselves in such fields.

The problem with 'the media'

The most obvious lesson to draw from my survey gaffe in Sri Lanka is pretty simple: do the ethnography *before* you write the questionnaire. That gives you at least a sporting chance of asking intelligent and intelligible questions based on locally meaningful categories. Attempts at standardized enumeration should at least open a dialogue between the communicative categories of the researchers and the researched (what are *their* terms for media, communication, information, etc.?) with a consequently more equalized basis for moving between one communicative ecology and another. My bad survey standardized one media cosmology as a template to impose everywhere (which is what I was institutionally asked to do); the alternative would have been to find more open and mobile categories that could accommodate diverse organizations of communication. Or, more simply, to look at what's going on before asking about it. In this case, without the ethnography we would have produced a picture of home, not of Kothmale.

The second lesson to be drawn is that a 'medium' is not a thing but a classification, and hence a social status that is ascribed, contested, disputed, aspired to – or, in Kumar's important case, it is a vehicle for reimagining the social status of different modes of connecting. It is therefore a performative term in a straightforward sense: to call something 'a medium' is part of constituting social phenomena, not simply describing them, and this performance of 'media' has a particular political valence in North–South development contexts, especially when North–South relations are dominated by narratives of transformation into an 'information society'. For me as a researcher to decide, theoretically, whether or not a particular assemblage is 'a medium' is to enter into that performative game, which is precisely why I was funded to go to Kothmale in the first place.

Hence the third lesson to be drawn is that I no doubt used 'media' as an analytical framework partly because I was connected to a managerial project, a UNESCO commission, rather than starting from the questions of communication that arose in Kothmale. My approved media list integrated me within a project of 'monitoring and evaluation' in which my role was essentially to assess the impact of 'a medium' on 'beneficiaries', and to do so in such a way that any impact could be, firstly, causally attributed to a development intervention; and, secondly, generalized to other development contexts.

That is to say, the ability and the need to treat 'the media' as a taken-for-granted framework is crucially linked to managerialism, bureaucracy and power. As we noted at the start, the very requirement (on me, on project workers, on various rungs of the UNESCO hierarchy) to produce standardized and generalizable knowledges on the basis of conventionalized and effectively universalized categories ('the media' *are* television, radio, internet, etc., and we *know* what these objects are) is intimately connected to the need to do things like make investments, coordinate policies, produce evidence of effectiveness, argue for more money, extend one's domain of bureaucratic governance and control, and so on. Development agencies like UNESCO play a major role in stabilizing objects like 'the internet' through their policies, funding, conferences, publications, and so on; but they also *require* and depend upon the stabilization of such objects in order to rationalize their own practices and organization. In the end, the reason I am embarrassed by this story is not the first or second lesson drawn from it, but rather this third one: my agreement to produce this kind of survey integrated my research into precisely this kind of managerialism in which knowledge is produced as functional by virtue of uncritically acting upon and making real the categories in which a bureaucratic process was already heavily invested. The very use of the idea of 'the media', in that context, placed communicative assemblages into what Wilk (1995) has called a 'structure of common differences', a grid of standardizing categories through which various agencies, academics and a general population can see the world of communication from the standpoint of ever-renewed modernization.

Communicative Ecologies and Communicative Assemblages

What larger analytical frame could we deploy to encompass the whole picture, including the performative role of media concepts themselves? My survey gaffe in Sri Lanka was all the more embarrassing because the research had actually been organized through a concept I conjured up in 2002 specifically to avoid these kinds of problems: 'communicative ecology'. The concept was defined in the research proposal for this and some subsequent projects in the following terms:

- 'the whole structure of communication and information flows in people's ways of life'; and
- 'the complete ensemble of (symbolic and material) resources for communication in a locality, and the social networks which organize and mediate them'.

The aim of this research strategy was to move as far as possible from studying the impacts of a medium to an ethnographic investigation of how people constructed stabilized ways of communicating, and to start from asking what counts for them as media, communication, information, connection, and so on. The research strategy was therefore construed as a broad mapping of the organization of communication without any prior commitment to specific kinds of entities, such as media, or to definitions of people, practices or place. In order to make maximum space for actors' classifications to appear as research topics rather than analytical frames (including the classifications of UNESCO, my academic colleagues and myself), 'communicative ecology' was intended as a maximally empty and banal concept which said nothing but could accommodate anything, along the lines of an 'infra-language' as proposed by Latour:

> [U]se the most general, the most banal, even the most vulgar repertoire so that there will be no risk of confusing the actors' own prolific idioms. Sociologists of the social, as a rule, do just the opposite. They are keen to produce precise, well chosen, sophisticated terms for what they say the actors say. But then they might run the risk of confusing the two meta-languages – since actors, too, have their own elaborate and fully reflexive meta-language. . . . ANT prefers to use what could be called an *infra-language*, which remains strictly meaningless except for allowing displacement from one frame of reference to the next. In my experience, this is a better way for the vocabulary of the actors to

be heard loud and clear. . . . [A]re the concepts of the actors allowed to be *stronger* than that of the analysts, or is it the analyst who is doing all the talking? (2005: 29–30)

We might see this as paralleling Polanyi's reformulation of economics: like media studies and media sociology, conventional economics defined itself by committing itself to a specific object – rational choice. To move, as Polanyi did, from defining economics as the study of 'human behaviour as a relationship between ends and scarce means which have alternative uses' (Robbins 1935: 15) to the study of 'the substantive provisioning of human needs' (Polanyi 1957) is – like a move from media to communicative ecology – to open the research to any practices (substantive or classificatory) through which agents might constitute their own field.

At one level, the idea of 'communicative ecology' is simply a recognition that, in any actual situation, the media are always mediated (or re-mediated). It makes little sense to treat any medium as an independent variable to which one wants to ascribe discrete effects. Firstly, they are mediated through social practices, purposes and relations. Secondly, they are mediated through a media mix or media repertoire – everyday life is made up of many different communicative resources that messily combine or conflict, that are networked with some entities but that block others. To be a skilful communicator is generally to be able to orchestrate a range of resources into practical and sustainable action.

This is similar to Bausinger's (1984) notion of media ensembles, as cited by Morley: 'Much as Bausinger argues that, rather than studying the use of media technologies one by one, we should pay attention to how they function in concert, as "media ensembles", English-Lueck insists that these people should not be seen as simply owning or using individual devices but as operating in particular "ecosystems of technology"' (Morley 2007: 206). Morley uses these notions, fruitfully, to argue for a 'non-mediacentric form of media studies' which 'decentres' the media 'so as to better understand the ways in which media processes and everyday life are interwoven' (2007: 200). As he notes, it is a perverse fact that we cannot get at this interweaving if we are wedded to specific media as objects of study. Similarly Toft (2011), in studying social movements, asks that we start from the communicative tasks that actors are trying to accomplish and then look at the tools they use to accomplish them, as in my circulation of music example above.

In fact, over the past decade or so, media studies (including media research within sociology and anthropology) has become increasingly and profitably restructured in terms of theories of practice, as well as closely related theories of mediation and mediatization (e.g., Askew and

Wilk 2002: 10; Bräuchler and Postill 2010; Couldry 2004a, 2012; Couldry and McCarthy 2004). These positions are obviously closely related to mine, particularly in requiring that research embrace the entire social life of systems of communication (technologies, institutional forms, everyday use and consumption, textuality, etc.) and fully embed them in wider social relations. Practice approaches have a clear commitment to defining communicative arrangements from the ground up, in terms of the place of media in lived experiences, ways of acting and relating, and so on. Moreover, in the case of Couldry, the interest in practices actually arises from an extremely effective critique of different forms of media-centrism, the tendency to assume the social centrality of media in stereo-typical forms which has been disabling for media theory (Couldry 2004b). Two forms of the 'myth of the mediated centre' loom largest in Couldry's account: on the one hand a functionalism that assumes a sta-bilized social order, a core social reality, that is both represented and effectively reproduced in media; and on the other hand a media studies focus on the largest and ostensibly most powerful media (basically, broadcast media) on the grounds that they promise the best chance of accounting for – again – a mythically cohesive social order. Both mythol-ogies short-circuited proper investigation of how communicative flows are stabilized and then how they become effective or important in the other social processes they are part of. 'Practice' is a good way of keeping open (to both theory and investigation) the questions of what is being assembled and on what it is having an effect. The concept of 'media' (and the media's own seemingly infinite sense of self-importance) should not lead us either 'to give undue prominence to media . . . in explaining social phenomena' (Couldry 2004b: 186) or to take as our analytical task to explain the production of a mediated social centre that is itself mythical. At one level, Couldry simply and correctly leads us back to what I have been treating as an ethnographic question: rather than start-ing from theoretical presumptions about the self-evident importance of the media in producing a self-evidently coherent social order (and an increasingly 'mediated' one at that), we need to start from open questions about the importance of media in people's lives (Couldry 2004b: 187). He then offers, in many of his contributions, excellent guidance in how to study the media in terms of practice, once one has accepted that 'the media' are what one is meant to study.

Unfortunately, however, that way of putting things already starts by presuming 'media', and moreover that 'our research *can* take for granted a mediated environment (in certain parts of the world at least . . .) that is *supersaturated*' (Couldry 2004b: 187). (The non-media-saturated other parts of the world play no further role in this approach and the fundamental question for Couldry remains the nature of the modern

West as a 'media society', a point to which we will return below.) The problem is that while Couldry very effectively dismantles the functionalist myth of a social centre, and he makes a good case for shifting our attention away from centrist media, he still retains an unexplicated loyalty to the very idea of 'the media' as an unexamined organizing concept that can simply be taken for granted; indeed one that can, without argument, provide an object around which to define whole academic disciplines (media studies, media anthropology and media sociology). There are clear signs here of a stalled or incomplete revolution: the idea of 'media practices' obviously and rather tautologically assumes precisely what we've argued is a conflictual and contingent outcome – the existence and social status of things called 'media' in the first place. If we start from a commitment to specific privileged objects – and even name our discipline or sub-discipline after them – we've already short-circuited the research, and (in the case of development, but probably other policy areas) we have already allied ourselves with other institutional agendas that are also already committed to the existence of these objects. If, as in Couldry's case, our aim was to decentre 'the media' in both academic and media accounts of western society, then this is a somewhat perverse strategy to adopt.

Couldry (2004a, 2012), for example, defines media practices as any practices oriented to or related to the media. This promisingly and correctly ensures that the researcher looks at all practices that may be relevant whether or not they are labelled as medial by social actors, but it does this tautologically by assuming the very object whose emergence it needs to explain: what is a medium, and for whom, and under what conditions? What ways of organizing communications does it, and doesn't it, represent? More precisely, the notion of media practices is tautological once it is taken out of the context of a northern world that can unproblematically assume a list of objects with medial status, and that takes its own increasing mediation (the increasing importance of 'practices oriented to the media') as given and as constitutive of its own modernity (see next section). But this is to assume, in a very ethnocentric way, that only 'the media', and practices related to them, are of concern in studying communications. Communicative and technological ecosystems are clearly ensembles of much more than just media, and the specification of certain assemblages as 'media' is consequential, constitutive and needing to be open to investigation rather than built into our definition of the field (and academic discipline) itself.

Hence while 'media practices' correctly broadens the scope of research, it refuses to give up 'the media' as its basic and unquestioned unit of analysis, and as self-evidently setting the central social analytical questions for research, which was Couldry's original aim. Some of the problem comes out in a related media studies debate, over the notion of 'mediation'. One way of beating a path out of narrow media studies is to adopt as a central analytic the idea of 'mediation', which offers both an overarching, indeed Hegelian, view of social process and a very specific question about the nature of modern societies: a concern with the extent to which we increasingly live the social through 'the media' or to which the social is itself mediated. It is a perfectly good question, but not the only one in town, let alone down South, where quite other questions about the nature of communications might be asked. The question we might ask about western media studies (as we will in the next section) is why the broader definition of mediation (how the socio-technical means by which people are connected and reproduce specific types of practice and relationship) gets narrowed to a question about 'the media', in which 'the media' are accorded a central or paradigmatic role in mediation, which Couldry effectively critiques (particularly in debates over 'mediatization' [Couldry 2008; Hepp 2009; Livingstone 2009a, 2009b; Lundby 2009; Schulz 2004]). It is this that smacks of western academics treating their local social problems as if they were universal (see the injunction that the media should be treated as 'good to think' the big social questions, rather than as important in their own right in Abu-Lughod 1997).

It could be argued that my own methodological ruse begs a similar kind of question: 'What is communication, and how do we identify it?' And, depending on how I answer that one, the idea of communication either becomes so broad as to be meaningless or else just as prescriptive (if less often performed) as the idea of 'media'. One response is Latourian, and was suggested in the previous chapter: terms like communicative assemblages and communicative ecology are offered not as theories or as labelling objects in a realist mode but rather as tactical research manoeuvres; they are not to be institutionalized or reified but to be deployed only so long as they work in their intended aim of ensuring a space for symmetry between the researchers' and the informants' cosmologies. Hence, if UNESCO had seriously started building its policies around 'communicative ecology' concepts, I'd have had to come up with a new idea for my next research project.

However, there is another kind of answer, discussed in the next chapter, which treats these terms in a different, and even anti-Latourian, way, such that 'communication' becomes important as a more general heuristic: for example, Bourdieu (1990) analyses his Kabyl house as an assemblage that embodies, performs and symbolizes a gendered division of labour as well as other cosmological structures. Should we regard the house as a communicative assemblage? We could, for example, argue this in terms of Bateson (2000 [1972]): the world can be heuristically understood as informational because it is patterned and structured; the world *is* a communicative assemblage in information theory. During fieldwork in rural Bangladesh, a group of girls drew a map of their village indicating where they could or could not walk unaccompanied by a male; they could easily treat the layout of the village as an information system that conveyed risk and safety. Moreover, it was intended to do so. We will pursue this further in the next chapter. For now I'll take refuge in a pragmatically ethnographic answer: just as with 'media', we are concerned to find out where, when and how actors identify and classify communications, including what is a communication, a communicator, a means of communicating, and so on. This includes ways in which modes of communicating are stabilized, and ways in which communications are or aren't differentiated as specialized activities, roles and institutions (such as 'media'), and with what consequences. It is an empirical question as to whether a house or a village should be treated as a communicative assemblage, but we could learn a lot by applying this heuristic.

Communicative assemblages

In this research strategy, communicative ecologies do not contain media, they contain 'communicative assemblages'. As the terminology would imply, this was developed in relation to actor-network theory and I will elaborate on it here with reference to ANT. The other major influence – material cultural studies – will be developed more in the next chapter.

The idea of a communicative assemblage should focus attention on the heterogeneous and skilled engineering of stable or routinized systems for accomplishing communication. It should also focus attention on how, whether or when actors recognize or classify assemblages, and the part this plays in the engineering of them. In now classic ANT fashion, this strategy is concerned with tracing the making and stabilizing of connection and association, and treats the finished form of an entity as a provisional accomplishment rather than a point of departure for research. The black-boxed form of an entity, like a medium, is the condensation of a network; it can always be expanded or 'redistributed' back into the network of connections that sustains it (Latour 2010).

We could in fact use various terms – assemblage (or *agencement* [McFall 2009]), system, network, institution – each of which would emphasize different aspects of the phenomena. 'Communicative assemblage' focuses us on the very practical and contingent nature of heterogeneous engineering, suggesting the kind of mundane *bricolage* that goes into conceiving, constructing, maintaining, repairing and operating communication systems out of the socio-technical materials to hand (and suggests as well the crucial distinction between formal definitions of a regulated system and the informal, unofficial performative understandings through which it is actually operated and stabilized (Angell and Ilharco 2004; Avgerou, Ciborra and Land 2004; Bowker and Leigh Star 2000; Suchman 2007). 'Communicative system' captures the desire for stabilized and reliable communication channels that skilled communicators can use routinely; it labels, as it were, the provisional or posited achievement of the work of assemblage. Finally, 'communicative network' points us towards constitutive properties of connectedness itself, and the ways in which the properties/affordances of all participants to a process are contingently emergent from the ways in which they are interconnected; hence, network – though worn out by over-use, and too shared with actors to work as infra-language – foregrounds ontological issues which have opened up radically new analytical, as well as political, possibilities.

Any or all of these terms challenge an ICT4D that starts from the taken-for-granted categories of 'media' or 'new media' or 'ICTs' as given objects (even ones with disputable properties) on at least three major grounds.

Firstly, communicative assemblages are complex interdependencies; although some elements may be made to stand out as decisive (the computer, the cellular mast, the human user, the vision of information society), no element 'works' or has the medial properties that characterize it for participants without being connected to other elements (roads and buses, travelling teachers, skilled announcers, circulating concepts of 'community radio', UNESCO policy makers and funders). I cannot access the internet with the pen I am now holding; but I can if I write down a message, hand it to a friend who is going down the road to an internet café and who is able and willing to do me a favour. There may be more or less redundancy in communicative assemblages; there may be optional, alternative or replaceable elements. And all skilled communicators have a plan B. Nonetheless what makes for communication are routine connections and paths of circulation. The heterogeneity of this engineering is crucial from a pragmatic as much as an epistemological point of view: 'symbolic' elements like the classification of an assemblage as a medium are as crucial to making it work, and work in particular ways, as having a fibre-optic cable or literate users. That is to say, the symmetrical inclusion of the material and symbolic is as empirically important as it is an epistemological position on the relation between nature and culture.

Secondly, assemblage or *agencement* encapsulates the ANT stress on agency as relational, as the obverse of the pattern of interdependencies (the 'network') that formats it, and this has a particular analytical and ethical force in the context of development, and particularly in ICT4D: it makes it impossible to understand the function or impact of media in terms of tools that are used by agents. Agency is not about the efficacy of given objects in achieving ends that have already been defined by an actor, but rather it is a story about the way in which connection works. If entities – human or medial – have properties only in and through their patterned interconnection, then it makes little sense to talk either of media having 'impacts' in 'contexts' or of humans being 'empowered' when provided with medial tools to achieve their already defined ends. In ANT as in material culture studies, we start from a co-configuration of human users and material tools that distributes agency through their interaction. This poses a particularly fundamental challenge in the context of development theory and practice that – even in its most pro-gressive moments, such as empowerment or capabilities approaches – finds it hard to think productively about agency. If the capacities and properties of actors, including human ones, are relational, then it is crucial to focus on the nature of the persons who emerge from these processes. Inventive cases such as Kumar with his 'internet radio' suggest agentic creativity and the crucial ability to imagine future skills and personhood, but any communicative act is knowledgeable and skilled in the sense that people need to elaborate knowledges of what they are trying to do and how to use means at hand to do it. Moreover – and against the somewhat rationalistic view of the actor that sometimes comes out of ANT – thinking about oneself as a communicator as part of different communicative assemblages involves skills in etiquette, empathy, body management and other 'social skills': communicators need to be technologists, poets and priests all at once; they are involved and altered in all aspects of their agency.

Thirdly, although there is always improvisation in communications, the idea of communicative assemblages is meant to focus research on how communications can be stabilized, routinized or institutionalized, including stabilized by according public and social status to particular assemblages as media or objects of media policies. The issue of stabiliza-tion, and black-boxing, has been central to practice theory (Knorr Cetina, Savigny and Schatzki 2000; Schatzki, Knorr Cetina and Savigny 2001; Shove 2005; Shove, Hand, Ingram et al. 2007; Warde 2005) but oddly marginalized in media practice theory. Yet so much of the politics and policy around communications concerns the ways in which assemblages might be named, reified, naturalized, taken for granted, both within everyday life and in formal and official configurations, and the ways in which control over these stabilizations is exercised and contested. The ability, for example, to give a black-boxed, assumed and infrastructural status to, say, websites as a means of accessing health information in a development context is the endpoint of precisely the complex history of defining 'a medium' that needs to be unpacked.

Communicative ecology

In my own research the idea of 'communicative ecology' was itself an attempt at heterogeneous engineering: it aimed to enrol various actors (academics, practitioners, funders, development agents) into a research strategy that tried to frame research ethnographically but covertly, without using the word 'ethnography' (which still sounds prohibitively expensive and unconventional to development agencies); and a strategy that would be seen as relevant and useful but without relying on the notion of 'impacts' (whereas ethnography is frequently seen as 'academic' in the pejorative sense of other-worldly and irrelevant). I would not have used this phrase otherwise.

The core ethnographic move was away from the search for causal attributions and towards the presumption of holism: that any element of a culture needs to be understood in terms of ever-wider relations and practices to which it connects. Loudspeaker events made sense of radio and internet but themselves needed to be understood in terms of such things as announcers' careers and family commitments but also the meaning of village and locality within Sinhalese morality and nationalist projects. Holism in this sense is not *wholism*: there is no presumption of a homogeneous, coherent or consensual culture or way of life; only the presumption of a density of interconnected mundane practices. Not only are assemblages heterogeneous, but so are the assemblages of assemblages that make up intelligible ways of life.

In line with ANT's 'flat ontology', ecology is not meant to suggest a context, environment (as in 'media ecology'), 'culture' or other container or macro-structure within which media practices take place. Nor is a communicative ecology an established 'place' or location (as in, 'We will study the internet in Sri Lanka,' or, 'We need to see how the internet is configured locally'). Rather, the focus is on emergence: what we can refer to as communicative ecology is nothing more than the result of all the assemblages and interactions that we trace. By the same token, a communicative ecology is not meant to invoke a homogenized or coherent space, by virtue of, say, the spread of 'digital culture'. Communicative landscapes are generally messy, contradictory and often don't work very well. Achieving interoperability between my work-based electronic diary and messaging systems and my home-based systems for coordinating with partner and kids is apparently impossible and generally verging on disaster. Having said all this, in the next section and the next chapter we will look at how media can be central to making places and policing their boundaries: that is to say, a communicative ecology can certainly take various territorial forms (as Barry [2001, 2006] analyses through the idea of 'technological zones'). Moreover, for me to say – as I often do – that 'I researched the media in Sri Lanka' – presuming an object and a place in which to find it – would be completely intelligible to most people. We just need to factor in precisely what *makes it* intelligible.

'The Media' and (Western) Modernity

I've argued that I cannot legitimately re-label communicative assemblages such as loudspeaker events as 'media' because 'the media' is a normative and organizing concept. That begs a question that is crucial to thinking about communication in a development context: What kinds of projects and purposes is the idea of 'the media' attached to? What work is it meant to do? And what are people trying to do through it? In this section, I want to take up a very small part of that question – What role has the idea of media played in modern western thought, particularly in academic thought? – and to argue that the idea of 'the media' has played a normative role in that it is one of those key terms through which the West has grappled with its own specificity: its modernity and (supposed) exceptionalism in relation to other places. This is one reason why the term is so consequential when applied to other places.

Symptomatically, 'the media' is a very difficult object to define, despite the fact that several disciplines are premised on their existence as objects of knowledge; indeed scholars often ritually begin their texts by acknowledging the vagueness of the term, before carrying on regardless, on the basis of its self-evidence or of a technical definition (Lister, Dovey, Giddings et al. 2009: 80–94). Media might signify:

- material (what an artist works 'in' or 'on', and 'through' which meanings are expressed or experiences are stimulated) (Williams 1977);
- or technical mechanisms of mediation (the television, the cinema, etc.), though this is itself often metaphorical in that most 'media' involve numerous technologies (e.g., a chain of technologies in order to take, then print, then circulate photographs or films);
- or technology plus media institution ('the press' is not just printing presses, but their concentration in a few mass producers of meaning, with attendant division of labour and skills such as the production of professional journalists, editors, proprietors, etc.);

- or finally, most broadly, a more generalized social phenomenon (the press = technology + institutions + formation of particular kinds of audiences).

In a usefully exhaustive genealogy of the terms 'media' and 'mediation', Guillory (2010) sheds some light on this confusion. The distinction between older 'arts' and modern 'media' is obviously not intrinsic, and the transition from an art to a medium is instructive about western modernization. In the abstract, any art could be accorded medial status, and '[t]he very fact of remediation . . . suggests that pre-modern arts are also, in the fully modern sense, media' (Guillory 2010: 322). The important question is: under what circumstances does a communicative practice take on a 'medial identity'? Hence for literature to *not* be classed as media, and to be studied in literature rather than media studies departments, conjoins a Bourdieuian hierarchy of distinctions with a distinction between pre-modern and modern communications: as we have noted, 'medial identity' is a social status that needs explaining. The underlying issue for Guillory appears to be one that is definitive of modernist culture in general: a problematization of the medium of expression such as to make it visible behind the message. For Guillory, the crux is an early modern move from rhetoric to communication; in the latter case the aim is not persuasion but expression of true meanings, as a result of which language becomes visible as a medium of thought: it can be transparent or opaque, can get in the way ('mediate'), and can fail and need revision. This concern, in Guillory's argument, can take an exceptionally totalistic form – 'mediation' in the Hegelian sense) – which concerns the entire relation between word and world; or a narrower form concerned with specific materials of expression – 'media' (see the related discussion in Williams 1977: 158–64 in which 'media' are initially defined as 'intervening and in effect causal substances'). What is important here is that, according to Guillory, neither media nor mediation was connected to the idea of communication and to this problematic of language until the late nineteenth century: 'The emergence of new technical media thus seemed to reposition the traditional arts as ambiguously both media and precursors to the media' (Guillory 2010: 322). That is to say, the specification of 'the media', the construction of this social status, did not simply remediate but reconfigured the whole field of communication. Guillory indicates how the very idea of media, and its selective use, is emergent from a particular history, one in which western modernity is concerned with its own specificity and with distinguishing it from pre-modern communication. In specifying its own communicative resources and dangers it organizes all the others.

However, Guillory's account is largely internal to intellectual history, whereas we can give the genealogy of 'the media' a more explicitly socio-historical rendering. 'The media' is one of those terms through which the West has narrated its modern experience and transformation to the extent of providing – at any given historical moment – a diagnostic description of the kind of society it is becoming: 'media society' – like consumer culture, market society, industrial society, mass society, information society – takes its meaning from narratives of decline or progress in which the media figure or prefigure forms of community, sociality and social order. The media are themselves the material culture of modernity. Moreover, as Raymond Williams carefully charted long ago in *The Long Revolution* (1980 [1961]), media as a focus of western modernization is intimately connected with the two other main designations of modern transformation: democratic and industrial revolutions. The linkages are most dense – as, again, Williams himself stressed throughout – around the ideas of masses, mass culture, mass media, which foreground the constitutive worries of the modern West: what happens when people are released – economically, politically and culturally – from the intimate regulations of the *ancien régime*, based on personal, face-to-face regulation, connection and communication, into the individualized freedom/anomie of markets, elections, cities, industrial labour and sovereign private consumption. 'The media' are both emblematic and explanatory of the modern; they are one of 'our' ways of telling the story of the West's historical specificity and difference from what came before it or stands outside it. (For Williams' critique of the concept of 'media' as a reification, see Williams 1977: 159–60.)

And 'the media' that are selected out for this narrative are emblematic and explanatory in relation to this specific kind of story, this tale of modernity, whether it is told as downfall or enlightenment: press, radio, television, and finally (though surprisingly slowly) the internet. All are matters of public concern (and governmental regulation) in relation to questions of power and control over aggregated publics, of new forms of order to replace those ascribed to 'traditional' society. They are prone to industrial organization of production and distribution; concentration of ownership and control; mass broadcast distribution on a one-to-many model; and therefore symbolize, again, either incipient mass manipulation (e.g., propaganda) or another liberal mechanism (like markets and elections) for devolving choice to sovereign individuals (albeit by rather indirect routes).

John Thompson's *The Media and Modernity: A Social Theory of the Media* (1995) illustrates some of the issues extremely well. The book starts from a definition of the subject that is entirely compatible with the one adopted here: Thompson is concerned with 'transformations in . . .

the social organization of symbolic power' (1995: 4), building on a properly abstract definition of communication as 'a distinctive kind of social activity which involves the production, transmission and reception of symbolic forms, and which involves the implementation of resources of various kinds' (1995: 18). These resources include a 'technical medium', defined as 'the material substratum of symbolic forms', and the skills/cultural capital to enact these codifications and decodings. There are forces and relations of communication, as it were; and we might look at the ways in which these forces and relations are 'institutionalized' (an interesting alternative to the notion of media 'practices'): 'a relatively stable cluster of rules, resources and social relations' (1995: 12) governing production, circulation and consumption.

However, Thompson then specifies this general notion to a specific narrative of western modernity, specifically to a concern with the emergence of mass communication as an ordering institutionalization. While he acknowledges that 'mass communication' offers a bad description of new media forms, the term has to stay precisely because it addresses the fundamental and constitutive concern of modern self-reflection with a revolution in communications that – much as in Williams' account – transforms symbolic power in relation to and along similar formal terms to industrial and commercial transformations. In order to focus on this particular narrative of mass communication, Thompson highlights particular features that distinguish mass communications from face-to-face interaction, and here is where the problems start. Although he acknowledges a 'material substratum' or 'technical medium' (in Williams' sense of the material on or through which someone works to express something or construct a symbol) in face-to-face interaction ('Even the exchange of utterances in face-to-face interaction presupposes some material elements – the larynx and vocal cords, airs waves, ears and hearing drums, etc.' [1995: 83]), this is not of the same order as those assemblages that we normally put on our lists of self-evident 'media' (TV, radio, press, etc.). Hence, face-to-face communication appears as a pristine form of interaction into which the technical intrudes. The reason is that the face-to-face is defined in opposition to the modern experience of decontextualization, in which, because symbolic forms are materialized and detachable from social contexts of production, they allow for the distantiation and one-way communication with which modern thought has been so obsessed. The concern is to understand how western societies came to be so mediated, media-saturated and media-structured. That is to say, the very way in which a medium or mediation is defined is integral to the telling of that particular story.

This provides one of the best available accounts of the way in which the idea of media, and particularly mass communication, played a role in defining western modernity, its problems and accomplishments: the media as institutionalized technical distantiations from the face-to-face are one of those lines in the sand that the West draws between itself and its others and its past (and through which it reincorporates them, on its own terms, as in Guillory). Whatever distinguishes modern western communication, it is certainly not technical mediation – that is always present – but rather a particular problematization of mediation that distinguishes the modern from the pre-modern, the West from the rest. What is far more problematic is to use this definition of the media, devised to tell this very particular story of western exceptionalism, to make sense of – let alone regulate developmental relations with – the rest of the world. It is worth taking this up at the level of the media definition itself, which I will do with three points.

Firstly, the material or technical element of face-to-face interaction cannot be equated with the notion of a 'material substratum', with the larynx or airwaves that allow sound, for example. Rather the technical is always present, just as it is in more 'modern' mediations. As we saw in the case of Sri Lanka, the very achievement of co-presence, the ability to be face-to-face, doesn't happen by accident and normally involves skilful coordination of people and things: the fact of being face-to-face is a technical accomplishment to be explained. As is maybe clearer in less 'modern' places, accounts of how people come to be co-present involve, for example, modes of transport, different time-space calculations based on factors like weather and mud; an account of the technical staging of the conversation (on the road, in my house, etc.). Messages have to be moved to be communicated; in most instances this involves the transportation of the messenger, and therefore the coordination of multiple technical systems. Face-to-face interaction is not an *ur*-form of mediation, or a point before technical intervention; it is itself a technical accomplishment.

Secondly, Thompson wants to be able to assume that face-to-face interaction involves little space-time distantiation, little distance from an original social context of symbolic production. This very much depends on what is meant by face-to-face communication or co-presence, both of which are often hotly contested. For example, much face-to-face communication does not involve pristine co-presence but depends rather on chains of intermediaries, messengers or other systems of physical distribution of messages. Rumour (see Burrell 2012) would be a good example of this, or marketplace communication. A nice reversed example from Sri Lanka: a local telephone booth operator offered a service that converted email into face-to-face communication – messages were received via his email account, printed out and then delivered to people's homes and read out by a messenger. Consider also religions, which involve constant discussions as to who can mediate the word of God and how, and whether different forms of face-to-face communication (confessionals, prayer, retreats, etc.) can be legitimately regarded as alternative technical arrangements for communicating with the divine (Miller and Slater 2000).

Thirdly, Thompson – like most in this tradition – wants to regard face-to-face communication as in principle two-way, in contrast to the one-way broadcast model that defines western mediation. This is a very weak assumption in that it ignores the ways in which any communicative assemblage, as a structured process, involves forms of power. To give a vivid example of face-to-face communication that clearly works on a broadcast model: traditional Ghanaian political processes are structured through the figure of the *okyeame*, the royal orator who speaks for the chief (Yankah 1995). Chiefs do not speak directly with anyone but the *okyeame*, who then 'broadcasts' his views through heightened and ritualized rhetoric that has a formal, public character. Any encounter with the chief is physically face-to-face, but communicative co-presence is in some doubt as he never speaks directly to anyone but is, rather, mediated. That we can look at less 'exotic' communicative structures in precisely the same way is central to Meyrowitz's use of Goffman to treat face-to-face and 'mediated' communication symmetrically as 'social situations' or interaction orders in which the key issue is 'patterns of access to information', and in which the decisive theoretical move is to think of social situations as 'information systems' (Meyrowitz 1986: 37).

I am belabouring these points in order to indicate how the notion of media, or mass communication, functions here: 'media' are defined in order to bring to the fore precisely those forms of mediation – mainly press, radio and television – through which the West tells the story of its specific achievements and tribulations. (Thompson, like most media studies, largely leaves out of the story other possible media such as photography that do not have a canonical place in this narrative.) While it makes clear common sense to argue (as does Thompson, but also Silverstone) that 'use of communication media involves the creation of new forms of action and interaction in the social world, new kinds of social relationship and new ways of relating to others and to oneself' (Thompson 1995: 4), and that one can make this claim without necessarily courting technological determinism, nonetheless this kind of position still seems entirely bound up with a story about the progressive technologization of communications, and a sense that 'we' are becoming a more mediated society. It is hard to see how terms that emerge from the West's sense of its own problematic modernity, and which rest on differentiating its mediatization from the face-to-faceness of the rest, can help articulate communications in other places. Once again, I think Latourian infra-language is more helpful: a mediation is not a particular kind of machine, or the intrusion of communicative machines into social relationships, but rather anything that makes a difference, that is more than an intermediary, and therefore is not simply something that gets between other things, transmitting or distorting, but rather something that acts as an agent within a larger assemblage.

Connections and Exclusions: Communicative Algorithms

I want to end this chapter with a more graphic juxtaposition between 'communicative ecology' and 'media' as analytical frameworks, this time from rural Ghana. Adopting an infra-language that asks one to look at communicative assemblages as complex connections allows one to see where and how the idea of media makes *disconnections*, exclusions and divisions, and how it can naturalize these exclusions by anchoring them in supposedly self-evidently real and discrete objects ('computers', 'the internet') which are also the objects of extensive bureaucratic discourse and practice. Put more bluntly, I am treating the notion of 'media' as providing an instance of Bourdieuian symbolic violence in a development context: power exercised through naturalized categorizations. This is a story about how 'media' concepts *dis*assemble and cut networks.

Cutting the network in Korapo

My rural fieldsite in Ghana comprised two villages at varying distances (about 20 minutes and 45 minutes by bus) from the district capital of the region, which we will call Korapo. The region, which lies in the southern third of Ghana, and to the west, is overwhelmingly agricultural, centred on smallholdings for the production of oil palm and cocoa. The villages were not yet electrified, though the region was gradually moving onto the grid, and this was eagerly awaited throughout the fieldwork period.

In the district capital, also called Korapo, on the ground floor of the regional government offices, was an exceptionally well-equipped computer centre with about twenty well-specified computers and an internet connection (ISDN) that was seriously fast and reliable for its time. The centre was the initiative of the charismatic, dynamic and young district executive officer (DEO) of the region, who in fact came from one of our research villages, and who was expected to have a major national political career ahead of him. The centre was paradigmatic of his visionary status, bringing the future to Korapo partly through his creative opportunism in attracting major funding, in this case from the UNDP (United Nations Development Programme) and HIPC (Heavily Indebted Poor Countries initiative – debt cancellation money). Moreover, the centre had a growing national profile in that it was the first of what were to be similar centres to be built in every Ghanaian district capital, and on which a major portion of their debt cancellation money was to be spent.

The computer centre was almost always completely empty except for a couple of local bank employees who were being taught to do spreadsheets, and for the occasional school class that was transported with enormous difficulty from outlying villages, like our fieldsites, to be in the presence of the computers for one visit per year. The children, and teachers, could do little more than witness an incomprehensible machine or totemic object, which they could not connect to any practical or embodied knowledge, and to which they were related through the deadening notion of 'computer literacy'. It was in any case unclear what the centre was for, or what a computer or internet connection was for, except in the most nebulous sense that computers and internets were things that one had to introduce in order to 'develop' and to be seen to be developing. The self-evidence of the machine and its benefits was constantly acknowledged; where necessary, this formal acknowledgement was buttressed, as in most development contexts, through reference to exciting possibilities, all cited in the form of pilot projects known to exist somewhere that somehow might be generalized to other places such as this one (e.g., getting doctors in Cape Coast to diagnosis illnesses remotely via email or SMS).

As a communicative assemblage, the computer centre clearly did not connect to any local networks; instead it connected upstream to current discourses on information society and ICT4D, as mediated through development agencies, national government, the media and the personal experiences (often abroad) of the more privileged Ghanaians for whom the computer and internet were self-evident and already complete entities. The very idea of a computer *centre* spoke volumes: it was not designed to connect outwards, either to people or to other objects, to the extent that for a long time even the printer was not hooked up and no photocopier was available. The computer was an autonomous entity both practically and iconically. We could summarize the patterning of the centre as follows, where the terms in inverted commas represent entities that are black-boxed and understood as disconnected/self-subsisting:

If you come to the computer 'centre', you can access something called 'a computer'; you can take computer 'literacy' courses and use 'the internet'; you can get 'information', and take it 'home' with you.

We could also represent this in the form of what might be called a 'communicative algorithm':

Access to 'computers' = an ICT

– a formula in which the left-hand term could be expanded into a range of actions and entities that connect people to computers but which play no substantive part in defining the assemblage (that are intermediaries, rather than mediators, in Latour's terms) and in which all values and affordances are already contained in the term to the right.

The socio-technical closure of the computer around normative definitions of 'a medium' and its promised impact (Ghana will leap from an agricultural economy to an information economy in the next fifteen years) was an actively exclusionary process. On the one hand, the idea of a 'medium' partly served to assume the existence, and agreed identification, of an already stabilized object with known properties that was already presumed to be manageable and predictable within development policy and practice. That is to say, to label things as 'media' or 'ICTs' or 'computers' or 'internets' was – through the power of naming – a way of stabilizing arrangements and making these objects manageable and accountable. This was despite the fact that most people conceded privately that this was far from the case and that there was little knowledge at all as to what ICTs were or were good for or how they could be properly linked to development – there was as much empty rhetoric here as anywhere else about the coming 'information society'. Moreover, this stabilization was conducted in terms of normative views of the ICTs in question that could only make sense in contexts other than Korapo: the norm of an individual user with direct hands-on access to a machine and the 'literacy skills' to use it knowledgably in order to activate recognized cultural forms like spreadsheets and word-processed letters (such as the bank employees were busy with).

On the other hand, if this idea of a 'media centre' was linked to (and indeed only intelligible in terms of) northern norms of ICT use, these media categorizations were also ways of marking exclusions and differences from local forms of communication, constituted ways of *disconnecting* and disassembling. For example, the context of this research was the run-up to the UN's WSIS, which was defined around new media and the information society such that radio and community radio were excluded, and computers as new media were deliberately *disconnected* from these popular older media around which considerable political and medial experience had accrued over the years (as in Sri Lanka): the community radio activists in Ghana were not even invited to WSIS pre-meetings or the culminating jamboree in Tunis in 2005.

We might relate this dialectic of connection and exclusion operated through definitions of media to Andrew Barry's (2001, 2006) notion of technological zones. Political entities and territories, he argues, are partly constructed through socio-technical extension: for example, ensuring the interoperability of things like railway gauges and information systems is part of political integration and control such that – in true ANT style – we not only cannot regard technology as politically neutral, but we also need to regard politics as intrinsically technical and technological. Defining 'media' to make some connections and break others is deeply related to this in that the warrant and intelligibility of these alignments may depend on grouping them under media categorizations. While it may be the case that satellite footprints don't acknowledge territorial borders, it is also clearly the case that, for example, moving a whole country from Microsoft to open source software (Schoonmaker 2007) may well be instrumental in creating new borders and alignments, or that cutting radio off from new media demarcated possibilities of political participation and naturalized them in terms of supposedly intrinsic properties of the media themselves (and their supposed causal power in explaining the future of development). And of course in this particular instance, the separation of the computer centre from existing communicative assemblages and its attachment to global new media agendas was clearly an exercise in empire building on the part of the district assembly: it could align itself and its DEO with the most progressive and advanced political forces then assembling.

However, there was also a much cruder kind of exclusion being effected through the idea of new media, one closer to Bourdieuian symbolic violence than to Barry's technological zones. Most memorable was an interview with the chief education officer of the district, a well-heeled middle-aged woman who clearly resented being posted to the sticks. She spent most of the interview – until we stopped her – trying to connect with myself and my research partner as elite- and northern-defined, largely by regaling us with terribly amusing jokes about how stupid the villagers were and how ridiculous it was to provide computers to people who spent their days trudging around in mud. Her computer sat proudly and ritually on her desk, and her senior staff attended as an appreciative audience, laughing and supporting her narrative at every opportunity. This was clearly not the case of a reparable failure to connect; it was the deliberate use of the very notion of a medium to enforce disconnection and exclusion, to regard everyday life in Korapo as a communicative wasteland, a *tabula rasa*, an informational black hole (to quote Castells, as she might have done, approvingly). And it was to do so with the full normative might of definitions of 'new media' that had garnered a decisively central role in all narratives of the future. From this perspective, the DEO's success in bringing this new medium to Korapo was a real triumph, but prestigious for all the reasons that would also render this technology disconnected and useless.

The education officer's (or indeed Castells') ability to see Korapo as a communicative *tabula rasa* or informational black hole waiting to be filled in (or marginalized) by new media depended precisely on an exclusionary idea of 'media' which could then be defined as absent from these villages. There was of course plenty of communication and communicative assemblage going on in Korapo; it just didn't fit the official categories. It is therefore important to see, even briefly, what was rendered invisible by this process of building defensive walls around a prestige medium. This might also give us a sense of what the computer centre *could* have connected to had it not operated with this idea of media as a discrete and already-known class of objects. And, frankly, it also gives an idea of how sophisticated the communicative engineering was amongst the stupid villagers as compared to the limited and disconnected engineering of our elite education officer.

Indeed we might start with several interesting ways in which people in our fieldwork villages had a more complex approach to communication than depositing a lot of computers in a room in the government offices. Firstly, migration, personal movement and connection: Korapo was an entirely typical case of Ghana's massive internal movements of people over their life course. For example, the area contained very large numbers of in-migrating settlers, largely tenant farmers, who had arrived from Volta and other regions in the past thirty years in response to labour shortages and land availability, and who maintained personal contact with home villages and kinship networks. We can add to this the regular movement of young people to family in Accra, Cape Coast and Kumasi for education and jobs, which is often talked of as a normal biographical stage; as well as the equally typical visits of urban relatives to village family, often for several months, particularly when there is a funeral in the offing. This personal connection through physical mobility has a clearly contradictory impact. On the one hand, there is always a sense of connection to the population centres and sites of modernization, and a constant effort to use available resources to maintain connection. A baby in our remotest fieldsite was named Clinton, its mother having seen the great man speak when he visited Accra during her own stay there, some time ago, as a teenager. On the other hand, the same degree of regular contact intensifies the sense of backwardness and threatened or impending disconnection: for example, ICTs, in the sense of computers and the internet, are seen as machines which will *increase* the advantages of urban over rural youth, irreversibly widening the gulf between them; while every month without mobile phone coverage is a further step backwards. In either case, the *default* condition of Korapo residents is a complex connection managed over time and the life course, across technologies and at various scales from district to major cities and to foreign lands.

Secondly, 'light' was the facility most often demanded by people in the course of discussions of media and communications. In the Ghanaian English of Korapo, 'light' meant 'electricity', with the named advantages of refrigeration and TV. However, it also simply means light: electrical illumination. Particularly in conversations with young people (who generally had direct personal experiences, through personal movement, of the urban, or experiences mediated through mobile friends and family), 'light' was considered as a medium in a straightforwardly McLuhanian sense (McLuhan and Fiore 1967: 16: 'its real message is the way that it extends and speeds up forms of human association and action'): it is a technology that affords particular forms of sociality, observable experience and communication (such as hanging out with friends after dark). Local media theory or communications theory in Korapo, then, was articulate and sophisticated, but concerned 'media' other than computers.

This also applies to my third kind of evidence for Korapo being a communications-rich ecology rather than an informational black hole. A somewhat ironic piece of evidence: our most remote village was actually the centre of a moral panic about media that had particularly engulfed local teachers and religious leaders. A local entrepreneur ran a kind of video cinema on a diesel generator hooked up to video and DVD players and a fairly extensive collection of the normally demanded video fare (no different from taste in Accra): Asian kung-fu, Nigerian romances and witchcraft narratives and a minority smattering of Hollywood. The place was considered both popular among and dangerous to youth.

There were other conventional media – TVs hooked up to generators; some video games on the main road to Cape Coast; a kid with a GameBoy (but no batteries) in our remote site; travelling peddlers selling some books and old religious pamphlets. But above all there was radio, which was ubiquitous, constantly on and – since political and regulatory liberalization since around 1999, and the rapid spread of local-language broadcasting – symbolically hugely important as a dependable public voice, focus of communal identification (in an Andersonian sense [Anderson 1986]) and primary source of news and information. As in many other places, these media constitute communication systems, often interlinked (e.g., the video cinemas are serious businesses involving linkages at an international level, as well as local publicity through word of mouth and posting of schedules, response to demand as well as moral censure, etc.). At the same time, however, they frame other media, as well as what we would here call the overall communicative ecology: film representations of urban modernity, in Lagos or Mumbai and occasionally the US, intensify the sense of contradiction between knowledgeable connection and actual 'backwardness' much as personal migration does – people 'know' from a vast range of media what the modern world is all about, but are excluded from it. But of course all this is *old* media, not new media, not computers or the internet or information society; and if we – like both the DEO and the education officer – discount all this, then and only then could Korapo be deemed an informational black hole.

While all three of these – migration, light and 'old' media – testify to the complex scene of Korapan communications, most important is the daily mobilization of heterogeneous resources which is central to the reproduction of everyday life, and which requires – for all manner of reasons – complex coordination of activities over distance. These assemblages are often highly complex, and involve a wide range of interconnected people, objects and events, as well as an economy of effort that often results in many different communicative events and goals being combined within the same or overlapping systems. I will explicate this through an example which is a synthesis or composite of an analytical type extracted from a range of fieldwork: Ghanaian women are, famously, almost universally traders, and in rural Ghana this can both require virtuoso coordination of distant connections and garner distant resources and opportunities. A woman like 'Sarah' (my composite character) might have a small shop, stall or table selling either a range of goods (groceries, cosmetics, some vegetables, all sourced from a wide range of contacts) or a specific commodity (e.g., smoked fish). This can involve coordinating spatially dispersed actors (suppliers, distributors, customers), temporally distributed activities (deliveries, market days, holidays, etc.) and goods (not just the traded commodities but also forms of monies and credit, as well as reputation, good will, etc.) – and of course price information, because with this dispersion the dangers (and opportunities) of arbitrage are fundamental to economic practice.

At the same time, Sarah is by virtue of all this commercial coordinating activity rather well connected and skilful at making connections. The following kind of description is therefore very common in field notes (this is again a composite rather than an actual quote, designed to bring together the range of features routinely encountered):

I send younger son by tro-tro [privately run bus] to Korapo with cassava and messages; he gives messages, face-to-face, to elder son in school, and phones my elder sister in Accra to arrange delivery of perfumes by next truck and to find out if elder brother from London is coming home for Christmas; younger son is to return with soap, charcoal and the daughter of my third cousin once removed . . . etc., etc.

As with Sri Lankan loudspeaker events, I was tempted to label Sarah's operation as 'a medium' in that it is routine and stabilized, skilful, and coordinates a range of people and technologies to systematically secure a flow of information and communication. Sarah would do this every market day, week after week, no doubt adapting and selectively mobilizing bits of her assemblage depending on the tasks at hand that particular week. We can schematize Sarah's assemblage in the form of another communicative algorithm:

> Mother + son + road/tro-tro + phone kiosk + market day + extended kin networks accessed by phone = an ICT.

While this is overly linear, it represent linkages that one can understand as stable, durable and recognizable. It typifies a way of doing communications (in fact quite lot of communications). It also makes a standard ANT point that things have properties through their interconnection. A telephone is not a telephone without a tro-tro to get you there. A tro-tro is not a tro-tro in any meaningful sense without a passable road, petrol, mechanics, and so on. Hence, the telephone as a medium is simply, crudely and unavoidably dependent on spare tyres for a broken-down bus. We may make analytical distinctions between telephones and buses, but in this case we should not make strong practical distinctions: the categorial distinction is only part of a wider practical configuration. In this case, even less than in the case of Sri Lankan loudspeakers, Sarah does not call her assemblage a medium (though there is no principled reason why she shouldn't); but more decisive is how her assemblage is viewed by those for whom 'media' are a central normative and performative issue. When the education officer was ridiculing the casting of the technological pearls of new media before the swine of the villages, wallowing in their mud, she was of course talking about Sarah.

Reconnecting

The point of this story is not that Sarah's communicative assemblage made connections and the computer centre did not. Although the computer centre's 'medium' was perceived as a stand-alone object with inherent properties that would emerge if you knew how to use it, it took this form precisely *because of* its connections to prestige technology and development discourses, to the experiences of individualized use of ICTs in northern life, government offices and internet cafés, and to academic and policy framings of ICTs. It connected to plenty of networks, but unfortunately not to the ones in which it was supposed to be an actor.

There was a painful irony involved which was not lost on many participants. The charismatic DEO who was driving this initiative had earned his reputation largely through the creation of an agricultural education extension system – based just down the hill from the computer centre. This programme was *defined* as a system for connecting information to localized communications by sending extension officers out to communities to give seminars and training, to organize demonstration farms and model plots, to distribute informational posters and – most importantly – to build up relationships with the people by physically going to the villages and staying there. There was great pride in major revisions of traditional agricultural practice (e.g., the extension officers were linked to a fertilizer scheme that depended on changed tilling techniques; everyone agreed that the result was dramatically increased yields). And similar and connected communicative assemblages had been established for health campaigns, for example for polio vaccinations. Whereas this extension programme was conceptualized in terms of complex and opportunistic connection using all known means, the computer centre involved a pristine closure around the prestige object to the extent that the same extension workers – housed just down the hill from the computer centre – had no access to it. Defining the centre around new media was straightforwardly exclusionary. Despite the DEO's success with the agricultural programme, his introduction of one of the best computer facilities in sub-Sahel Africa at that time was based on the entirely opposite principle of disconnection and disjuncture: the computer/internet was a specific *medium*, understood to possess attributes independent of any context or connection, a stance only possible because of its connection to global prestigious discourses of new media, development and globalization.

This particular irony was not lost on the very able, open and hardworking young man who ran the computer centre and who was increasingly frustrated by the futility of what he was doing and the need to make connections much like the extension workers had done. We had several late-night conversations about this and about how to relate our research to his situation. One simple story stands out. The computer centre clearly fulfilled no informational or knowledge role insofar as it was defined as a 'centre' that children physically had to visit, and they could only visit once a year at best and for no particular practical or intelligible purpose. In contrast to the massive unused information capacity of the centre there were virtually no resources in the village schools, which had no books, often no paper or pens and sometimes no roofs.

At the same time, we knew that at least one of the school teachers from our most remote fieldwork village, a woman who was exceptionally active in community initiatives, went to Korapo at least once a week. There was clearly already an incipient assemblage here that would make information flow from centre to village so long as one redefined 'access' to ICTs (not hands-on but mediated) and identified mediators who would produce that flow. The computer centre officer could redefine himself as an information officer whose role was to respond to requests by sourcing and disseminating information; the teacher could convey information requests and return to the village with information, provided it could be put in a proper material form. Ideally the solution would be a mobile and digital machine (today it would be a cheap tablet computer or two), but the practical solution then was simply a printer and photocopier so that material could be transported back to the school. The clearest indication of disconnect was simply that the computer centre printer had not yet been unpacked and that there was no access to photocopying. The communicative algorithm we worked out looked something like this:

Teacher + road/tro-tro + computer centre + ICT worker + website + DTP + photocopier + school = an ICT.

It is as routine and extendable as Sarah's, and like Sarah's – and unlike the computer centre's – it depended entirely on ignoring the boundaries and classifications of 'media'.

Conclusions

The stories I have told are clearly not simply about how to produce more or less reliable knowledge of new media in development (in Sri Lanka, Ghana or central London); they are about the relation of my research to various regulatory projects – whether global development or rural communication systems. If 'the media' is such an important normative term, what happens when I am asked to look at the impact of 'new media' in a southern place and I do not question the term 'media'? Retreating to the emptier categories of communicative assemblages and ecologies allows me to research how all the machinations around the idea of media (including my own and that of my funders) are part of the constitution of different systems for communicating. To be clear, neither term is meant to supply alternative theories or definitions of media, but merely to see how theories and definitions of the media operate.

But this strategy produces another problem which we will try to address in the next chapter: while this 'strategy of deflation' is very effective, and debunking, in returning the hard graft of communicating from the metanarratives of media to the mundane mechanics of putting resources together, it might be better at disabling the analysts than at capturing the way actors think and experience communications. It's great that I, as an analyst, have to see what communications people assemble rather than weigh in with my own preconceptions of 'media' and 'new media', but the people I am studying have extremely elaborate, sophisticated and often poetic (as opposed to 'material-semiotic') ways of thinking about and articulating what they are up to. Communications are structured and understood in terms of what might be labelled social forms or modalities or structures of feeling, and we'll need to turn to material culture studies to think about these.

3

Media Forms
and Practices

The previous chapter defined communicative assemblages largely in the manner of ANT: we directed attention to the ways in which communication might be routinely organized, whether or not the results are called 'media'. We therefore attended to the ways in which actors use notions like 'media' as part of the constitution of the field we are studying, leaving this term to the actors, and suggesting the use of alternative terms (such as communicative assemblage) that might contain both the actors' and the researchers' classifications. This move also results in what Latour (1986) calls a 'strategy of deflation', in that the researcher attends to the nuts and bolts of connection and association through which actors actually assemble their assemblages rather than conjuring them up through sociological abstractions such as 'media'.

However, neither this strategy of deflation nor this anti-realist or performative understanding of the assemblages formerly known as 'media' is enough to make sense of the ways people organize communications. As Latour (1986) himself argues, the mere means of 'inscription' to which we might reduce media are fairly meaningless unless they are connected to wider 'agonistics' within which types of representation and communication actually *matter*. Unfortunately, ANT has not proved as good at dealing with issues of this sort, and we will pursue them here more by way of material culture studies.

The specific issue that is at stake might best be glossed as an issue of *form* or *modality* (terms which I also see as close to Raymond Williams' [1977] notion of 'structure of feeling' in that they may inform any and all practices at a moment in time; another related term might be Ciborra's [2004] notion of 'mood'). Sarah's or the computer centre's assemblages, in the previous chapter, are and must be held together by the heterogeneous material connections through which they are reproduced, and ANT has been crucial in showing why a computer that is not attached to, say, the teacher's weekly trips to Korapo is a different machine from the one that is. But it is also more than those connections, a fact that we recognize simply by attending to the fact that the computer centre might be called a new medium and Sarah's assemblage won't be. At the same time, this is also more than, or different from, saying – as, for example, does Morley (2007: 297–8) – that media objects are symbolic in addition to being functional, as if these were separate aspects of the object, or marked its place in different social logics. Rather, to talk about media objects in terms of form or modality is to say that the media object is understood and enacted in terms of an aesthetic shape or pattern that connects it to other social phenomena in quite a different way than, say, Sarah connects roads and phones; it is closer to the way in which, in Barry (2001) or Riles (2000), the idea of a 'network' is an informational form or template that acts as both a categorization and an imperative, a map and a route across very disparate and otherwise unconnected types of social ordering. In this sense, I also mean almost the opposite of 'media practices' insofar as these are defined as all practices as they relate to media use; the point here is that forms or modalities traverse practices, and are not 'oriented to the media', but are partly constitutive of media and communications (just not through direct material connections of an ANT sort).

The idea of form or modality is important not because it suggests templates that might *explain* the replication of particular ways of doing things across different times and places (we need to resist explanations in terms of 'culture' in any form – see Shove 2005; Shove and Pantzar 2005), but because it points to people's capacity to see the same pattern in extremely different things and situations, to make analogical leaps between situations that are not literally, mechanically connected in an ANT sort of way. Indeed, form places us more on the terrain of Bourdieu: the habitus is not just a 'structured structure' that is determined by social relations; it is also a 'structuring structure' of transposable dispositions that can perform the same pattern of taste across diverse and unconnected fields, in relation to different materials, rules and interactors. What Bourdieu (1984) describes in terms of 'homology' is a considerable and consequential formal achievement. To be able, as in the Ghanaian case described below, to formally connect funerals, mobile phones and a history of donor dependency is both formidable and mundane; it is also fundamental to the construction of all three assemblages. And it returns us to the central insight of ethnographic holism, that by virtue of this capacity on the part of actors to connect disparate things, so too must the analyst make sense of things through leaps that connect entities that are not apparently attached to each other. Conversely, the kinds of communicative assemblages that are available to people might be decisive for the kinds of formal connections they can make.

This way of thinking is the stock in trade of material culture studies: we have often to understand the object under investigation in terms of onion-like layers of relationship and value which may seem, at first, remote or unconnected but which participants can actually and literally *see* in the transacted object, and relationships and values for which the transaction of that object may seem absolutely essential to participants (e.g., as formalized in ritual, but also less consciously in habits and routines). I cannot have a family, or be a father, without regularly enacting a certain type of family meal. Another way of putting this is to say that ANT misses or deals inconsistently with the idea of 'culture' (Entwistle and Slater 2012, 2013), as we shall discuss below.

We will start with an extended case study based on fieldwork in Accra, Ghana, between 2003 and 2005, in which two communicative assemblages were organized in terms of very different cultural forms or modalities. What was at stake between mobile phones and internet were different understandings of 'relationship': what kinds of thing relationships are, how they are sustained, what kind of obligations they entail, how they are to be calculated and acted upon. The media and media practices involved were understood in terms of different categories of relationships which they both expressed and enacted. The predominating uses of mobile phones and internet in our bit of Accra were not only different but diametrically opposed to each other. They are analysed here as being constructed according to contrasting modalities for negotiating social relationships: mobile phones were embedded in the practical work of managing the costs and benefits, obligations and reciprocities involved in existing relationships; internet was used in the pursuit of idealized new relationships with foreigners, attempting to capture them in a new web of obligations and reciprocities. Put more strongly, each modality imagines a very different ideal of what counts as a relationship or a connection and how these are to be effected through the material and symbolic resources at a person's disposal (including his or her communicative resources). These contrasting modalities are best understood not as instances of something digital but rather as responding to two different but long-standing and readily recognized modes of personal and social development in Ghana, two strategies for poverty reduction and social mobility: mobile phones extended the central Ghanaian concern with managing social networks, while the internet developed the project of attracting northern capital. In each case, the communicative assemblages went beyond the engineered interconnection of heterogeneous elements and had to be understood as material cultural objects that drew together disparate elements and relationships in a meaningful, formal way.

The implications for our trinity of media, development and globalization are considerable, as should be clear from the concluding section, in which we see that official ICT policy in Ghana was governed by a third modality – an 'instrumentalist' one – that did not connect or even recognize either of the other two modalities that actually informed the thriving communicative cultures we studied in our fieldwork. Just as with the material-semiotic disconnects that we looked at in the previous chapter, this disjuncture of forms meant that the various participants had entirely different understandings of fundamental terms such as media, internet, relationship, connection, and so on; and that the popular practices of digital culture in Ghana were not even visible to the official version of information society.

Media Modalities in Accra

During fieldwork in Ghana (2003–5), people in Accra, as almost everywhere, talked about the emergence of a singular 'information society', imagined in terms of new principles of social order, exchange and value. The social and political task at hand was to position Ghana's future in relation to that emerging information order, largely by making appropriate and effective use of the new media that ostensibly constituted its principle and its means of emergence. From this angle, all new media were to be understood and enacted as parts of a coherently emergent whole (and older media had either to be remediated into this new order or consigned to irrelevance). As we shall see in the last section of this chapter, this was an official as well as informal position in that enormous government effort over this two-year period (which was also the run-up to WSIS) was devoted to developing strategies for turning Ghana into a streamlined information society.

Empirically, however, the two main new media – internet and mobile phones – were in fact being used in entirely different, unconnected and in many respects opposed ways. In brief: mobile phones were largely used to manage and discharge obligations within existing relationships; internet, by contrast, was largely used for what we (i.e., the researchers involved) described as 'collecting foreigners' – attempting to turn virtual connections abroad into 'real' relationships. Moreover, as I'll argue in the last section of this chapter, *neither* media use corresponded to the way in which official discourses (governmental and ODA) envisaged the principles of the emerging information society.

I want to argue that these two different ways of using mobiles and internet were not simply different media uses (explicable in terms of different affordances of the two technologies) but rather involved different 'modalities' – structures of feeling or dispositions, or aesthetic forms, in which connection meant quite different things (ontologically and practically): for example, in the case of phones, the contact list objectified real and mutually acknowledged connections with enduring social obligations and opportunities; the internet contact list, by contrast, was literally virtual, a representation of accumulated social capital acted upon as if it were real. These modalities were evident not only across a variety of 'media' or communicative assemblages, across time, but also linked up disparate fields in a manner reminiscent of Bourdieu's (1984) analysis of homologies of taste (structures of dispositions that work analogically across apparently unrelated fields) or Riles' (2000: Chap. 1) use of Bateson and Strathern to analyse the 'network' as an aesthetics of informational form. In fact, the analytical language I will employ is derived from the latter authors. The two modalities or sensibilities distinguished here – embeddedness and escape – characterize two different formal organizations of 'connection'.

We will first map out the two modalities, paying particular attention to two themes that bring out the differences in this case study. Firstly, what is a relationship? Because a central feature of relationship in this story involves obligation (both creating and discharging obligations), a second theme stands out as crucially differentiating the two modalities: calculation. What are the costs and benefits of connecting?

The fieldwork took place over eighteen months in Mamobi, a poor community in Accra situated just north of the ring road that marks out its inner city. The site was largely populated over the post-war period by in-migrating northerner Ghanaians, as well as migrants from neighbouring West African countries. It consequently has a large (probably majority) Muslim population. This ethnic and migration profile, combined with high levels of poverty and a reputation for crime, gives Mamobi the local designation as a *zongo*, a Muslim slum. Male unemployment is high, with most employed men working as security guards or in the informal economy; women, as in most of Ghana, are almost universally small traders. Infrastructure is extremely poor, with regular water shortages in some areas, regular flooding during rainy seasons, and low levels of health and education provision. Most people lived in compound houses, comprising up to thirty-five individual two-room dwellings (known as 'chamber and hall') in each, lacking kitchens, running water or toilets (public toilets were used instead). One large sector of the fieldsite comprised habitations originally constructed as market storage structures, hence lacking windows. At the same time, partly because of its proximity to central areas of Accra, inhabitants had some access to wider urban experiences and facilities; moreover, media diffusion was impressive: although there were very few landline phones, both communication centres and mobile phone use were extensive, and there was widespread consumption of TV, radio, VCDs and videos, and of photography.

Mobile phones and 'embeddedness'

During the fieldwork period, Ghana exhibited the fastest growth in mobile phones anywhere in Africa. The mobile rapidly became central to everyday practices to the extent that, at least in urban Ghana, people assumed it to be the most effective form of communication in most contexts, and ownership had spread so fast that one could generally rely on making a connection with anyone, if not a direct connection, through mobiles. This diffusion took many forms. Network coverage expanded rapidly, and the several competing mobile networks were in a race to provide seamless national coverage. Individual ownership of personal phones reached the point whereby ownership could almost be assumed (though obviously skewed in terms of age and income, but less so than expected: people often made considerable sacrifices to sustain a phone, and for rather price rational reasons, as discussed below). At the same time, it was not uncommon to find people – e.g., a landlady in a housing compound – willing to let people use their phone, particularly to receive calls (making calls could be easily dealt with using the innumerable kiosks that sprang up on every urban corner), or for people to carry around several SIM cards they might plug into an available phone when needed. Not only had buying, trading and using phone units – bought via pre-paid phone cards – become an obsession, but the units themselves already functioned as an informal currency (e.g., a suitable gift to a girlfriend could be phone units, given by texting her the code on the back of the phone card). Phones were both a significant cost and yet ubiquitous and treated as essential; there was an obsession, reflected in everyday conversation, with purchasing enough units to sustain one's phone as a *functioning* object.

In fact, what seemed to be spreading like wildfire was not just phones or phoning but the circulation of phone *connections*. This was evidenced in that phenomenon which can be observed almost everywhere but in

Ghana was called 'flashing': you phone someone's mobile and cut the connection after a couple (or pre-coded number) of rings before they pick up; their contact list tells them who called and that you called. (A related ritual was for two people who had just met to exchange numbers by one of them calling the other's phone, and the receiver entering the resulting phone number in his or her list with the accompanying phrase: 'I've got you.') Flashing is paradoxical. On the one hand, interpreted contextually, a flash can convey a considerable amount of information: for example, receiving a flash from someone you were supposed to meet clearly means, 'I haven't forgotten about you, I'm just late,' and knowing where he or she is coming from, and how, may give all the data needed to estimate a realistic arrival time. On the other hand, flashing can be – even in the same instance – entirely abstract, formal and empty: the flash simply acknowledges and enacts a connection between sender and receiver, often in a ritual sense. It was not uncommon for young men to complain that their girlfriends demanded of them numerous flashes during the day as ritualized evidence of connection, care, concern or indeed good behaviour: 'I'm thinking of you' (and not of other things or people). Relationships involve obligations of connection, and the mobile phone was immediately popular as an efficient or even costless way of discharging those obligations: in the first case, it reduced the costs, including stress, anger and misunderstandings, of enacting connections (getting to the meeting); in the second, the flash both performs and signifies the fundamental fact that a relationship exists and its obligations are being acknowledged and indeed honoured.

In both respects, the phone is a practical solution to problems of obligation and connection, and in both interviews and everyday conversation, mobiles were discussed in an overwhelmingly pragmatic mode. My exemplary case was an ambitious young man who lived on his own in a room of a compound house in Mamobi. Every day started with a ritual chore of flashing the same five people: three nieces from his home village who were now attending a boarding secondary school in a different part of Accra; and two old school friends who were now pursuing rather successful careers, but were currently posted to northern parts of Ghana. Before the mobile, he lost entire days visiting his nieces to check on their welfare and discharge his obligations to his kinship network; it now took a couple of seconds and no monetary cost, and was no doubt preferable to the nieces as well. Similarly, flashing his old school friends was described in terms of the potential opportunities he would lose if he did not keep up these contacts. The same applied to both personal and business uses of the mobile (even though most people, particularly women, made efforts to distinguish the two on the basis of seriousness of purpose and legitimacy of costs): phones were understood and legitimated in terms of calculating the costs of coordinating movements, meetings and the reproduction of relationships.

'Calculation' is meant literally here: there was an extraordinarily detailed market knowledge of phones and there was price rationality to the extent that an almost economistic attitude was required in the eth- nographic research. People had an encyclopaedic knowledge of mobile phone price structures and tariffs and ways of shaving small savings out of the gaps between providers, times of day, special deals, and so on; and this detailed and constantly changing market information was a matter of incessant mundane conversation. Moreover, people did not just value this information as consumers: significant employment was created out of exceedingly small margins of arbitrage. Everyone always seemed to know and act upon the latest pricing information, and of course signi- fied his or her own market nous thereby. This degree of knowledgeability had a negative side, particularly for women. Given that everyone had a fine-grained grasp of what it took to keep a mobile phone in operation, a young woman with a mobile but without a job could attract rumour: it *must* be that a boyfriend is keeping her (and given that mobiles were indeed frequently given to women by boyfriends and 'sugardaddies' to keep tabs on them, the connection to sexual status was even more plau- sible). Conversely, however, this micro-economic knowledge was not simply instrumental or utility maximizing; it demonstrated social partici- pation, social skill and the honouring of connection and obligation to the best of one's ability. It would not be too strong to say that being a bad mobile phone consumer was close to being a bad Ghanaian, or a bad family member, in that one was not being intelligent and active in making connections to the best of one's ability.

Literature on Ghana (and not just anthropological: Appiah 2006) has generally emphasized the central importance of social connection, which is both crucial to gaining resources for support, for channelling and distributing resources, and also a drain on resources. The obligations of kinship and friendship, the draining reciprocities, are costs that are reck- oned openly and in detail. (I have to go back to my village, and it will cost me two days, the bus fare, a bundle of currency and the danger of unforeseen additional obligations arising from new circumstances back home. . . .) The point to emphasize is not whether or not phones actually make connection more efficient (or indeed more obligating), but rather the very fact that phones are understood in terms of the management of already existing and 'real' relationships and reciprocities. I am calling this an 'embedded' modality, in that the phone was associated with managing relationships that were understood to precede the means of communication, and in which the latter were embedded. This was in marked contrast to internet use.

The ways in which the complexity and reversibility of obligation and gain can be mediated through the phone were clear in how it was transacted between Ghanaians at home and abroad. Ghanaians who have managed to go abroad are assumed to be successful and are obliged to demonstrate their relative wealth with gifts which, at the same time, reaffirm their continued obligation to, connection with and membership in the family. As an informant wryly put it, sending a phone, or even a phone card, beats having to send home a fridge, as in the old days. At the same time, it is in everyone's interests that at least one family member at the Ghanaian end has a mobile and can therefore relay communications throughout the kinship network in both directions, which often involves a great deal of practical coordination. Not insignificant was the further, obsessive issue of keeping the phone in operation with a steady flow of units, which urgency could also justify demanding an open-ended flow of remittances from a relative abroad.

A practically and symbolically crucial example of these issues is the funeral, which is a central form of connection in Ghanaian life, involving assemblage of all the social networks of the deceased for several days of festivities. Ghanaian funerals are huge logistical and financial enterprises, often involving coordination of movements of people across several continents, and the planning and provisioning of an incredible range of food, freebies (e.g., souvenir T-shirts), music and spectacle, not to speak of the refrigeration of the body for months while this assembly is planned. When asked about their plans for future expansion of the mobile phone network, the main mobile provider in Ghana said that they would be 'following the funeral traffic', and this is as good a measure as any social network analysis could provide of the density of social connection around funerals and the practical and symbolic role of the phone in this concentration. In an added twist, we heard of family abroad having to suffer the additional obligation of supplying kin in Ghana with the mobile phones or units to coordinate the funeral organization through which they would incur further obligations: not just embedding but embroiling them. Indeed the phone – like all new media – is clearly experienced as a mixed blessing, one that mitigates some costs but also can make one available as a resource: having a mobile can be costly in all the many different ways that connection in general incurs.

This whole picture might be condensed into one image: a Ghanaian could be buried in a 'Nokia coffin' (Figure 3.1) that they could purchase from a carpenter's shop on the road between Accra and Tema. Phones and funerals are each practical means to accomplish the other, but they are also clearly equivalent and connected as part of the same modality of connectedness. Both phones and funerals (separately and together) are major enactments of connectedness, publicly representing, endorsing and

Figure 3.1 (Photo: Matti Kohonen)

reproducing the social networks of connection but simultaneously inseparable from the very practical forms through which that connectedness
is accomplished. Both funerals and phones make connections, represent
and proclaim connection, and reproduce specific maps and patterns of
connectedness such as kinship and old school friends.

Phones lined up alongside other communicative assemblages that had
the same form and aimed at the same functions. As we saw in the case
of Sarah in the previous chapter, there was the use of people as messengers, sometimes even as proxies (someone attending a wedding or
engagement in one's place, on behalf of the family, for example). And
older technologies such as video already had an established homologous
role: videos of engagements, weddings and funerals could be many hours
long, and professionally edited with lush soundtracks and special effects
at small photography and video businesses in Mamobi. The video could
be sent to friends and relatives abroad, who would then convene a party
in London or New York at which they would actually watch the entire
video (we were assured), thereby constituting the expatriate assemblage
as participation in the actual event itself back home in Ghana. At the

extreme, a young man working in Spain watched his own engagement party, held in Accra, on video, and this watching was considered performative of the engagement in an explicitly Austinian sense. (This is less surprising in that the Ghanaian engagement is more important than the wedding because it marks the contract between two families, whereas the wedding merely ratifies this with an arrangement between two individuals.) Yet again, embedded mediation is understood – as in the case of flashing – as reproducing a set of existing relationships while at the same time minimizing (in an economistic sense) the costs of the obligations they entail.

We can extend this embedded modality further and to another level which might be characterized as a kind of material culture of Ghanaian political economy. This is harder to capture but involves the ways in which Ghanaians routinely and mundanely, as well as sometimes explicitly and articulately, specified a certain view of development through the phone as a piece of material culture as well as in terms of its practical uses. For example, landline phones were still unreliable, if cheap, and hard to obtain (reputedly only installed during one's lifetime if one paid off the right people), and as a failed public service they seemed redolent of all the broken promises of socialism and the centralized state going back to Kwame Nkrumah in the 1950s and 1960s. The mobile, by contrast, was demonstrably succeeding by virtue of populist and popular entrepreneurship: it was embedded in the real actions of observable, immediate actors rather than in ideological dreams. Commercial mobile provision also lined up with the modality of embedded social connectedness. The daily visible heroes of this narrative were not just the galloping network providers but also the legions of people running kiosks, selling prepaid unit cards, unlocking phones, buying and selling pretty much anything mobile connected. A manager of the leading mobile provider estimated that the phone boom had already created in the region of 20,000 jobs. There was no way to verify this number, but, importantly, it felt entirely plausible: mobile phones alone had demonstrably created the kind of development activity (employment, technological access and use) that governmental and non-governmental bureaucracies had never achieved. To be clear, I do not mean this only in the sense that mobile phones somehow 'symbolized' or signified popular neo-liberalism and anti-statist sentiment. They did. But understanding that goes beyond seeing them as signs or as symbolic: the whole world of transacted phones constituted a material culture through which such values were mundanely performed as well as publicly demonstrated, through which they were aligned with organic and self-organized sociality (as exemplified in funerals), and from which they could be transposed to other sites and objects. The most obvious other exemplar at that time was radio, which was popular because it was commercial and therefore regarded as independent, as deeply and immediately responsive to audiences (largely exemplified in phone-in programmes and in the broadcast in local languages rather than the state-sanctioned English). And one of the most potent medial conjunctures was the use of SMS to send messages, opinions and votes to radio programmes (there was some use of this for TV as well): radio and mobile phones worked together both technically and ideologically as enactments of decentralized, non-state freedom, and this formal connection goes some way to account for both their popularity and their pervasiveness.

In this view of the world, things work and life progresses when practices are embedded in everyday life and relationships, and are based on self-activated initiative. And this configuration of populist, market-oriented and anti-statist values directly contrasted with the donor-dependency, top-down planning and attempt to attract northern goods that, we shall see, characterized internet use. This configuration of mobiles and populist neo-liberalism was, somewhat paradoxically, lined up with traditional life rather than the state, despite the fact (as we have seen) that people's understandings of the phone involved considerable ambivalence towards kinship and other traditional obligations whose costs the phones could both defray and perpetuate. The paradox might be exemplified in one stunning image painted by a local artist – Virgin Arts – in Mamobi. It happened to be painted in the local clubhouse of Dallas 'base'. (A 'base' was a group of young men, often extending over several decades and cohorts of members, which functioned as a combined gang, hang-out, football team and community activist centre; moreover, several base members scraped their livings out of phone-related opportunities such as buying and selling phones, phone cards and SIMs, or arranging repairs or unlocking.) The image, which (perhaps significantly) hung just below a list of all the mobile phone numbers of base members, depicted an American dollar bill with a picture of 'Osama B. Laden' where the head of Benjamin Franklin would normally be (Figure 3.2). It took some time to get beyond my (incorrect) interpretations to the artist's intended meaning: Virgin Arts was clear that the image did not say, for example, that Osama had, or had the potential to, undermine the US or its precious dollar, or that somehow American financial interests were involved in the aggression against Osama, or his aggression against them. In fact, the image was not at all about conflict and entirely about harmony. Virgin Arts told me: we love Osama and we love America, so I put them together in the same picture. But surely they don't much like each other? Osama is a good Muslim man who is trying to help his community just like us; America is a place of energy, success and progress. That is to say, for Virgin Arts, the overriding formal

Figure 3.2 (Photo: Don Slater)

concern was with autonomous activity embedded in everyday life, as the grounds of both obligation and opportunity. Much like mobile phones.

All in all, mobile phones lined up with perspectives on development and livelihood strategies that were based on a detailed and pragmatic reckoning of the costs and benefits of obligations and reciprocities, and the expenses and opportunities arising from relationship embedded in kin and community.

Internet and 'escape'

If the mobile phone was configured as part of the management of relationships that preceded it and whose reality was experienced as independent of their mediation, popular internet use was almost diametrically opposite: it largely comprised attempts to forge connections to foreign strangers and to transform them into, or make them behave as if they were, the kind of relationships in which mobiles were embedded. But the aim was also the precise opposite of embedding in community: it was escape from community and its obligations. If mobile phone use was intended to defray or neutralize the costs of obligation, internet use was intended to obliterate one's own obligations entirely while drawing strangers into new obligations to oneself.

The internet in urban Ghana saw massive growth over the same years as the phone. Given the cost of computers and the lack of landlines, this growth did not take the form of individualized domestic use, and there was not a great deal of workplace business or government access for most Mamobi residents. Rather, internet use took place in a plethora of very crowded and popular commercial internet cafés (ten were in existence on or near the main high street of Mamobi over the course of

research; up to six at any one point in time). These were purely commercial operations in that owners and managers (unlike in, for example,
the Trinidadian research I conducted with Daniel Miller) operated them
as purely money-making operations to whose content they were indif-
ferent: those we interviewed displayed little or no interest in developing
internet use, education or culture, or community capital, and had no
sense of a social role wider than selling a commodity. Occasionally one
of the paid staff demonstrated a concern with what people were or could
be doing, but the internet was largely mediated by peers (as in Bakardjieva's [2005] notion of 'warm experts' [see also Haddon 2011]). At the
extreme, the internet was so identified with moral danger (to do with
fraud more than the usual fear of pornography [Burrell 2012]) that the
headmistress of a local primary school publicly beat any child found in
a cybercafé, somewhat against the grain of the government's insistence
on the educational role of the internet in an information society.

The predominant use of internet was for what the researchers involved
came to describe as 'collecting foreigners', or 'collecting foreign capital':
the use of internet facilities – almost exclusively Instant Messenger and
chat rooms, plus some email – to connect with foreigners and engage
them in conversations. The aim was to secure a range of goods from
abroad that might include invitations to visit, help with visas, educational or business opportunities or information, marriage or friendship,
or simply a more extended list of foreign contacts. Almost no one we
interviewed in any café over eighteen months had ever knowingly visited
a website or used the internet to access information in the sense that,
say, government or NGOs might understand that concept. For example,
one very serious secondary school student had in fact visited a website
to find out about the then recent tsunami, but this was exceptional and
not repeated; she returned permanently to chat. It was also not, on the
whole, the kind of aimless hanging out or socially or sexually oriented
socializing one might expect of northern teenagers (see Slater [2000a] on
pornography trading, but also Miller and Slater [2000] on Trinidadian
online and offline 'liming'). It was more aimlessly instrumental, if you
will: other pleasures might be on offer (e.g., some chat partners might
be nicer or more socially forthcoming than others), but the instrumental
aim of accumulating diverse capitals was ever-present yet at the same
time amorphous. At one end of the spectrum, this activity might be
clearly business-like: Burrell (2012) found a seller of glass beads whose
years of dedication and tenacity in trying to sell his beads over the internet, entirely without success, became proverbial. At the other end, the
capital accrued could be more akin to symbolic capital (simply a longer
contact list, containing more people from more prestigious locations);
though even in this case the list had value at least partially because of

the hope or expectation that this capital could theoretically convert into another, more fungible form.

The amorphousness of the hoped-for capital connects to the amorphousness of the calculations involved in this communicative form. The initial shock as a fieldworker was to see how much time, money and effort people would invest, how far and long they would go despite no personal success and few stories of anyone else succeeding either. Such stories did circulate, but tended to be limited to people getting free stuff by signing up for special offers or to stories of successful frauds (Burrell 2012). On this slim basis young people would spend days in the cafés, their hourly spend on internet use competing directly with purchases of phone units to maintain 'real' relationships; moreover, children regularly spent all their 'chat money' – the allowance given by mothers to children to buy snacks and lunch at school – on a few hours' browsing, hence literally going hungry in order to go online. To the outsider, this mode of using the internet looked like a fantasy modality in contrast to the mundane practicality of phone use: investments, emotional and material, bore no relation to benefits, which were reckoned in an entirely different currency (dreams of transformation, escape, flight, riches). Both the practical and symbolic structure of practice exemplified what I have elsewhere called 'progressive embodiment' (Slater 2000a, 2002): starting from a virtual presence – a fly-by chat partner on MSN – one tried to make them and one's relationship with them ever more real, more embodied, often by trying to move the relationship onto a more embodied medium such as a phone call, letter or meeting. This seems the dialectical opposite to the mobile phone modality, in which people started from 'real' relationships and often tried to 'virtualize' them, in a sense, by transforming them into relatively formal and impersonal obligations (e.g., to reduce kinship obligations to routine flashing).

This kind of interpretation was not a hard-won analytical finding but rather an everyday understanding of this internet use. Some Ghanaian academics described the internet as a 'cargo cult' (Taussig 1980, 1993, 1997; Worsely 1957) in the sense of a magical way of dealing with the terms of trade between North and South: internet magically summons up and thereby potentially exerts control over the cornucopia of northern goods, diverting it southwards. Moreover, it was common for Ghanaian interviewees to explicitly situate what we called 'collecting foreigners' within a long history of North–South relations. For example, in interviews (particularly with more middle-class and older informants) people often associated this kind of internet use with memories of adolescent penpals, but also with the more extreme idea of *commswa*: this is a Twi word specifically denoting the practice of indiscriminately writing to every education institution one can get an address for in the hope of invitation, acceptance or scholarship. One interviewee recalled sending a letter to the publishing address in a Gideon bible. Internet and email merely accelerated and widened this field, but the form was easily recognizable to most Ghanaians and the homologies were readily acknowledged by them.

Making sense of these associations requires stepping back into a pervasive structure of feeling revolving around the idea of 'abroad', or *aburokyire/abrokyere* (literally 'land beyond the horizon' or 'far-away land'). The term is fluid, as is *obranyi*, which can mean white person, but also an Asian or Indian (who might approximate to a white person by virtue of physical features like straight hair or of social status such as being in an educated and managerial position), or it could relate to my research partner, Janet Kwami, who was black and Ghanaian and had at that time only been out of Ghana once but who was *obranyi* by virtue of being seen sitting comfortably conversing in fluent English with the foreign white guy. Both *abrokyere* and *obranyi* conveyed, amorphously, a wide range of connections to abroad but all of them revolved around the same themes: all good comes from abroad; and leaving Ghana to go north to the source of those goods is the only serious path to development or success.

It is not a giant step from this configuration around the internet to the political economy that opposes the populist neo-liberalism we found clustered around mobile phones. The issue here is not public versus private sector – the internet cafés, as we have seen, were just as commercial as the phone network providers; and although the internet had a closer connection to government policy, this did not feature in any interviews. (Although people expressed a generic sense that the internet was the future, there was little sign that they connected this to any of the government policies then being drafted.) Rather, whereas mobile phones, as we have seen, connected to a sense of agency that was both embedded in and constrained or compromised by the obligations of relationship, the internet (despite all the ostensibly entrepreneurial activity of going after contacts) was more like old-style foreign aid, development and donor dependency: the game was all about the thankless task of unlocking the wealth of the North, or striving to access it through migration.

Put this way, the two modalities – embeddedness and escape – therefore describe two opposed development strategies, or livelihood and poverty reduction strategies, that have featured in Ghanaian history over some time, at both personal and more collective levels: either to manage resources within existing social networks or to try to divert northern wealth southward. In this sense, mobile phones and internet were not new tools or technologies that needed to be assessed in terms of their potential role in development; they were essentially constituted *as* development or livelihood strategies in the very first place. *That* was the route through which they were intelligible and used from the start, and – rather more inventively than official development agencies, as we shall see below – at least Ghanaian popular culture came up with two visions – not just one – through the material culture of these different communicative machines.

Two fieldwork stories stand out in showing why 'escape' is an appropriate label for this modality. In group discussion, a set of late adolescent boys who had been friends since childhood were (like every other young person we talked to) entirely obsessed with leaving Ghana – how they would manage it, the problems of accomplishing it, the wonders and opportunities that would confront them abroad and the dead, futureless space they considered Ghana to be. They all agreed on one other thing: they would not tell anyone they were leaving until they were actually on the plane or had landed abroad, in a foreign city. If anyone knew beforehand, they would be likely, motivated by resentment and jealousy, to use evil wishes and witchcraft to prevent them from leaving, to cause bad luck that would render them unable to escape. Witchcraft and other transactions with the supernatural were themselves important communicative assemblages in Ghana, ones that trapped people in misfortune (usually by inflicting ill health); the internet could be set against this as an almost equally supernatural mode of escape from the ties that bind one in and to Ghana.

Hence the second story, which still strikes me as odd. During fieldwork at a cybercafé, a young male Mamobi internet user told Janet about his plans to study in the UK. He said he had found a degree course and applied for it online, and he proudly showed her the reply he had received. The letter clearly stated that he had been *rejected* because he did not meet the university's entry criteria. Yet he presented the letter to Janet, and to the friends around him, as an acceptance letter, and as if it were itself a ticket to London. He was literate; and he did not seem to be lying. One interpretation is that the symbolic charge of this embodiment of foreign connection – a letter from a UK university – was so magically redolent of escape that it neutralized the letter's literal content: the medium, the connection itself, actually was the message in this case. And that was the feeling that the internet seemed to promise to deliver continuously to young Ghanaians.

Media and Modalities

I have presented these modalities in terms of the media through which I first encountered them, but modality does not map onto media in a simple, let alone technologically determined, way. And that's the point. For one thing, I can give instances of the internet being used in embedded ways (dispersed families communicating mundanely through email) and mobiles being used for virtualization (as when contact lists represented aspirational social networks that were treated as if they were real). The two communicative modalities recognized and selected out specific affordances in each technology, but that is only one part of the story. More importantly, 'modality' points us to connections – often unexpected ones – between diverse communicative assemblages, and these connections are both metaphorical or classificatory (as when penpals, internet chat and international aid were universally reckoned to be equivalent in terms of a kind of relationship to the North) and practical (mobile phones and bus transport were complexly intertwined because the overarching concern was how to coordinate or engineer, efficiently, actual connections).

Clearly one could treat phones and internet as analytically similar by saying that they both exemplify the same Ghanaian obsession with social connectedness (compare the different understandings of connection or 'link up' in Jamaica in Horst and Miller 2005, 2006) and argue that the two different modalities are simply variants of the same underlying concern. Indeed, at a different scale of analysis this might be useful. What concerns us here, however, is that different modalities of connection did in fact assemble different communicative assemblages and different kinds of communication. Moreover, as we have noted, this had an ethnographic legitimacy in that the identification of different modalities, and mapping them across different communicative technologies, was more everyday common sense than deep research finding: relating internet use to penpals and cost–benefit analysis of relationships in terms of mobile phone costs were matters of everyday conversation. In a vivid example, the connection between northern technology and donor-dependency was made in a very popular song which declared that Kwame (Sunday's child, the lucky or blessed person) was of course born in the North where all the good technology comes from.

In other words, we need to keep explicit this sense of modalities as informational forms that traverse media and practices because these are classifications through which people in fact organize both their sense of 'connection', what connection means and is good for, and what the available means are of accomplishing desired types of connection. To replace or subsume these differences within an overarching view of media and connection – such as the official information society view of communicative modality that we will describe in the concluding section – would be a kind of analytical violence.

The problem, however, which we now need to address, is that ideas of form have been extremely difficult to deploy in studying communications or media, and have particularly been linked to 'technological determinism'. In a sense, *most* media theory has been formalist, just as it has been essentialist, in being concerned with identifying the intrinsic properties of new media objects and tracing how they impact on social 'contexts'. But we will start by looking at the (opposite) problems that ANT itself has with cultural forms and modalities.

Good form[1]

Communicative ecology and communicative assemblages were intended as ANT-style strategies for following the actors, and for not making any analytical moves (such as identifying 'media') beyond directly and literally demonstrable connections, relays, 'vehicles' or other machinery of association that the actors deploy (Latour 2005). In this sense, our escapist modality, for example, involves educational and livelihood strategies that need to be traced through the assemblage of things like passport offices, university admissions departments, online green card lotteries, and so on, looking at the recognizable practices and 'media uses' that are stabilized in and through them (what Latour [2005] describes as 'oligoptica').

The problem is that in our case study many of the connections are not literal but metaphorical or even poetic leaps from one context to another that is not materially connected to it: to go from penpals to chat rooms involves classifying selected formal properties of the two as 'alike', and without necessarily connecting them within anything like a network or in a manner that looks at all networky. Rather, there is the perception of an aesthetic form which, moreover, can be connected outwards even more metaphorically to things like a history of relationships with northern donors. Moreover, this overarching formal patterning or informational form is not simply emergent from specific, situational and local material arrangements but clearly moves across many different localities, is transituational, and is itself a way of making connections and organizing arrangements. Conversely, people constantly made sense of and acted within the more literal connections and assemblages by means of broader cosmologies (e.g., chat rooms made sense, and the internet could be perceived as useful, in terms of the kinds of relationships earlier performed through penpal letters).

Pushing this further, this sense of aesthetic or informational form looks rather like the kinds of overarching values that are usually talked about (in practical life and in academia) as culture, ideology or, indeed, values (Entwistle and Slater 2012, 2013). Different media are partly constituted in and through their status as material culture, as objects onto which one can project values and through which values can be enacted. Buses, mobile phones and funerals are all means to enact and at the same time symbolize what *Ghanaians* understand to be core Ghanaian values of embedded connection. Similarly Miller and Slater (2000) started from what we described as a perceived 'natural affinity' between Trinidadians and the internet, the basis of its immediate popularity, that involved projecting onto it and through it a range of 'Trinidadian values' (e.g., cosmopolitanism, joy in banter, 'liming' [hanging out]), Trinidadian experiences (disruption and distance through slavery and indentured labour) and Trinidadian projects (e.g., constructing themselves as global economic and cultural actors).

The two modalities we have been describing are in this sense not just assemblages but also objects of material culture, but this is only visible if one will allow the importance of overarching values as expressed and performed. This is problematic for ANT: Latour's strategy of deflation or debunking constantly rejects the idea of 'culture', dismissing its role in social research and analysis as a macro-structure or explanatory variable while ignoring the role it plays in actors' own efforts to make associations. While Latour would have us stick to the literalness of observable connection and not go beyond the actor's labour of association, we found in our case study that actors are themselves not so literal or crudely material: they are not just heterogeneous engineers but also poetic makers of metaphors, analogies and homologies – of connections that are sensible only in terms of logics of information and meaning that are not contained within literal materiality. Indeed, they clearly 'jump' networks and assemblages: the leap from penpals to cyberspace is not just a matter of making associations by other means, it is also a very specific cosmology of North–South relations, a transposable system of valorizing relationships, values, flows and of mapping the world (both representing and moving through it); or in Bourdieu's terms, homologous dispositions, structures of taste that can travel and can link different social spaces. And these values are deemed overarching (or, indeed, 'Ghanaian') and projected onto the material culture such that, for Ghanaians, the internet both reflects or instantiates these values and is moulded and takes its form from them.

The issues come out most clearly in Latour's *Reassembling the Social* (2005). The metaphor of the flattened topology that pervades ANT is designed to ensure that all connections are traced, and traced to tangible arrangements. As part of this, the macro and micro are refused as analytical frameworks to be deployed by theorists as 'contexts' that account for action within them. On this basis, 'culture', for example, appears in

ANT accounts (Callon 1998b) as an illicit analytical move in that it seems a way of wheeling onstage a kind of sociological *deus ex machina* in the form of an overarching context of values, meanings and motives that is meant to *explain* everyday actions and mentalities. The social theorist then has to impose an additional machinery of socialization, or internalization of norms, or functional adaptation or subjectification in order to connect actors to the macro structures and meanings that they have imposed on their world. To the contrary, as Latour notes, scaling is what *actors* do, and specifically what we researchers need to be studying: how *they* produce and enforce on each other different 'contexts'. Yet in his discussion of how to position the analyst so as to avoid the temptations of the macro and the 'Big Picture', something is lost. Latour distinguishes 'oligoptica' and 'panoramas'. Oligoptica are chains of connection that transport messages in clear and traceable routes whose fallibility and contingency are evident (the model being military chains of command). Panoramas, by contrast, look like 'ideologies': holistic views of 'the social', totalizations that clearly come from specific material arrangements yet claim to see and capture everything, to represent or stand in for the world. Panoramas are defined in Latour's argument (2005: 189) not so much in terms of what actors do with these grand visions but rather in terms of the kinds of epistemological delusions they point to: large-scale cultural schemas and narratives are treated as simply wrong from the standpoint of critical epistemology. What is missing, bizarrely, is exactly what we expect of an ANT account of panoramas – an account of their performativity, the role and logic by which they participate in the composition of common worlds. In this discussion, Latour acknowledges that his approach needs to recognize the existence of overarching narratives of 'the social'. And of course *We Have Never Been Modern* (Latour 1991) is all about massively overarching forms and styles of thought (the modernist constitution is a way of thinking about pervasive structures that permeate historical spaces). But in *Reassembling the Social* this formulation has become crudely reductive and has dropped all sense of 'cultural form' as effective within social organization: on the one hand, oligoptica reduce communication to chains of command which have to be specified in terms of specific and effective material links; on the other hand, panoramas are grand narratives, bad forms of thought which don't connect to actual practices, and should therefore 'vaccinate' us against totalizations (2005: 189). They have no role in theory except to demonstrate bad thought, and to prefigure a good society (composing the common world). This is bad vaccination: it would appear to make the analyst considerably more narrow and crude than the actor s/he is meant to follow. How can we follow Ghanaians who leap from funerals to phones to video marriages to the cost–benefit analysis of familiality unless we have a sense of assemblage as not just engineering but also poetry and metaphor, unless we can perform the same kind of aesthetic formalism that 'they' do as part of everyday life? And if we do not enter these formal games, don't we risk unconsciously asserting our own classifications again? (The use of mobile phones or internet is 'just' the assemblage of demonstrable practical linkages *because* we have cut the network not at a particular boundary but at a particular *scale* [Strathern 1996].)

Moreover, there is a serious asymmetry involved in the way 'culture' or form is treated in ANT. In the case of the social, the technical and the economic, ANT is concerned to return us, at the end of our analysis, to the world as it appears (not surprisingly for an approach that was considerably influenced by ethnomethodology). We deploy a strategy of deflation to trace the 'big stuff' like culture, capitalism or imperialism back to the material arrangements through which they are assembled by the tangible associations and movements of actors. If we start from the big stuff, and treat these terms as explanations of the assemblages ('culture explains different media'), we are guilty of short-circuiting research and of lazy thinking. However, if we do the hard work of tracing all these associations, of assembling the world empirically as the actors do practically, then we can return to the big stuff: we have managed to reassemble the social. The problem is that in ANT the social, technical and economic are deflated in order to reassemble them again in the form that is recognizable as the actor's lived reality; only in the case of 'culture' does a performed social form remain at the level of epistemological critique rather than demonstrable associations. Put in other words: given the extent to which actors configure their worlds through ordered patterns of things and meanings, through values that they can name and identify (and identify *with*), culture and cultural form need to play a different role than epistemological straw man or proxy for bad macro-sociology (Entwistle and Slater, 2013). We can agree that culture or form provide bad explanatory strategies to the extent that they are contexts projected onto the actors' world by theorists; but they are necessary analytical pieces of the puzzle to the extent that they represent a kind of association that is in fact deployed by actors, routinely, in the composition of their own world.

The most useful paradigm for admitting forms and modalities while retaining all the lessons learned from ANT would be Riles' analysis of *The Network Inside Out* (2000). Riles identifies 'networks' as 'a set of institutions, knowledge practices, and artifacts thereof that internally generate the effects of their own reality by reflecting on themselves' (2000: 4). She thereby acknowledges both the material-semiotic and performative character of these assemblages, but her account of what holds them together is rather different. Riles attends to the bureaucratic practices through which networks are performed not only in terms of material ('oligoptic') connections but also in terms of 'aesthetics': '[I]nformational practices might come into view as "designs" in their own right and also as maps across a territory, a path we might have taken or might take' (2000: 16). This approach claims lineage ultimately from Bateson: what is of concern is not events and objects but 'the *information* "carried" by events and objects'; the form of communication – 'pattern' – 'had become the very subject of analysis'; not 'social' linkages but the 'informational connections' made (2000: 62, original emphasis). In fact, in Riles' version of Bateson there is no opposition between connection, pattern and form: Bateson was concerned with information as 'an attention to the pattern which connects' (Riles 2000: 185 n. 4); aesthetics – the formal order or the 'persuasiveness of form' (Strathern in Riles 2000: 185 n. 4) – 'stresses identification with both the heterogeneity of actants and their systemic integration'.

Hence 'modalities': we need words not just for material-semiotic arrangements but also for different registers, classifications, cosmologies, and for different *logics* of connection, not just for the making of connection, words for 'the pattern which connects', and not just for the abstract fact of connection. Why is it different to discharge kinship obligations by flashing as opposed to emailing a thousand strangers to sell one's beads? The answer lies not just in how certain practices are assembled and stabilized but also in different histories and meanings of connection that can themselves be connected.

Bad form

ANT's problems in acknowledging cultural form or according it analytical status in its accounts stands in marked contrast to one of the longest-running themes in western discussions of communication, what I will call here 'media formalism'. This is the idea that the properties of the means of communication are the dominant or exclusive determinant of the content and consumption of communication, as in the slogan 'the medium is the message'. This problematic includes but is not confined to the issue of technological and material determinisms (e.g., as noted in Chapter 2, 'mediation' points to a Hegelian tradition concerned with social relations rather than materialities [Boyer 2006; Guillory 2010]). Moreover, formalism in this sense has been not only a theoretical position but also a modernist injunction, as exemplified in Greenbergian aesthetics: progressive modern arts are *about* their means of expression; painters should not attempt representation but rather make the formal medial qualities of painting into the exclusive content of that medium. It is in this sense that the founder of contemporary media formalism, Walter Benjamin, was also its most committed modernist (Frisby 1988; see also the excellent discussion of these issues in Lister, Dovey, Giddings et al. 2009: 62–3, and particularly of Greenberg's media purism versus theories of remediation): the central principle of emergent media, exemplified by film and photography, is that reproducibility which closes the distance between art and life, and whose true meaning is therefore a democratic deflation of cultish power. The heroes of this formalism are those like Rodchenko who consciously and with revolutionary commitment explored the technical possibilities for seeing things anew, for changing the techno-social organization of perception itself by means of the formal properties of new communicative devices.

The conventional next step in this discussion would be to wrestle with technological determinism, as did Adorno famously in his immediate responses to Benjamin, largely missing the point of the latter's desperation to build a *praxis* not (like Adorno) provide mere critique. However, we can be at least provisionally satisfied with an ANT or material cultural sidelining of this issue. The question of whether technology or social practice is primary only arises when they are treated as separate entities that then meet and contest. If we take the materiality and practicality of communicative arrangements as our starting point – the fact that both things and people are emergent materializations – then we can at least get on with researching what actually happens in specific and entirely contingent cases rather than seeking the essence of either media properties or human ones.

However, there is a second problem with media formalism that is certainly related to technological determinism but is in some ways more consequential: the connection between media formalism and *social* explanation. As we have just argued, ANT offers a cogent critique of form (social, technical, cultural, etc.) as explanatory context. Media formalisms exemplify this move not only in seeking the essential properties or affordances of media but also in trying to turn these into 'monological' causal explanations: specific media properties are treated as corresponding to the basic or first principles of particular societies. The real problem with media formalisms is a reductionism that seeks to find in a formal account of media a principle that explains or expresses or predicts history, that tells us what 'society' is or is becoming – the media theorist as soothsayer, visionary or, more often, Cassandra. In this sense, the problem with media formalisms is not that they are bad media theories but that they make bad social theories. The urgency of this problem should be very clear in a development context where the future of the world as an 'information society' is presented as inevitable and swift and this is largely derived from analysis of *forms* of communication and connection: if you do not immediately locate yourself within a global division of labour defined by nodal points within digital culture, you will drop out of history entirely. Governments and NGOs *want* to be able to give convincing formalist accounts, and enlist wide alliances to these narratives, in order to rationally organize control, planning, cost accounting, and so on. And it is from this vantage point of trying to extract first principles of social change from medial properties that both analysts and involved actors might try to represent Ghana in terms of a single, uniform 'information society' rather than as several complex and different (and contradictory, conflicting) configurations of meanings and practices, as it actually was.

It is hard not to see this issue as a latter-day rerun of Marx's unfortunately vivid slogan that 'The hand-mill gives you society with the feudal lord; the steam-mill society with the industrial capitalist' (Marx 1966: 103). In dealing with this version of Marx, we can easily be distracted by the issue of technological determinism. (Is he *really* saying that technological infrastructure entirely explains superstructure? Well, on the balance of his writings, probably no, not really.) The more fundamental issue is the social entity that Marx was proposing and trying to explain: a total mode of production that could be summed up in terms of fundamental structuring principles, including the underlying principle of its own dynamic contradictions. It is not a very long step from this to Castells (Chapter 4 and 5 of this volume), for whom the network form defines a new principle of social order and organization, entirely consistent with the idea of a new mode of production: the digital mill gives you the network society. Particularly after ANT and material culture studies, we are now better able to deal with the problems of technical determination versus social construction that arise from splitting the material and the cultural; however, the desire to see the resulting social arrangements in terms of a single coherent ordering principle and as a coherently ordered 'expressive totality' is more difficult to deal with.

The attempt to produce media theory as social theory by identifying medial principles underlying the social goes back a long way. After Benjamin, we would most likely visit Innis (2008; Innis and Watson 2007) and the 'bias' (space versus time) of communication media that provides the principles underlying different empires and civilizations. McLuhan (1974; McLuhan and Fiore 1967) gives a social psychological rendering of balance and bias, in which medial properties structure forms of social experience and participation such that characterizations of sociohistorical periods can reflect dominant medial principles (hot/cold, global village, etc.). A similar approach characterizes the rendering of the rise of literacies (Goody 1986; Ong 2002). A popular version has been the 'media ecology' (Strate 2004) of Postman (1987), in which medial properties are treated as a natural environment, as the expression of technical qualities of media. (And, incidentally, 'media ecology' is therefore the precise opposite of the idea of 'communicative ecology', which would focus on the emergent co-configuration of social and technical properties. For a confusion of the two uses of 'ecology', see Foth and Hearn 2007; Hearn and Foth 2007.)

To return to the Ghana case, we could talk about two kinds of formalism, or even bad and good formalisms. Both participants and analysts *are* formalists, and need to be. They see patterns everywhere: structures, forms, classification, cosmologies, shapes which they can transpose from site to site, situation to situation, from the shape of kinship to the terms of North–South trade to the proper way of organizing a wedding or funeral. When we look into the 'meaning' of, say, the internet in Accra as opposed to Bangalore or New York, we are asking about these forms and patterns, and about the unique patterns of patterns that define what we generally mean by 'a culture' (e.g., how does the embedded modality relate to the escapist one within the overall, 'holistic', dynamics of Ghanaian sociality?). This also means that – when we are moving from the idea of monologics or medial principles of a society to a more productive concern with the ensemble of communicative assemblages that make up an ecology – we are always moving into uncharted empirical territory: embeddedness and escape in Ghana are entwined in complex and unpredicted ways that themselves cannot be reduced to some first and founding principle (e.g., they are sometimes but not always binary opposites, sometimes but not always entirely unconnected).

The second kind of formalism is not material cultural but, rather, reductive: it wants to see form as expressing an essential principle, or as promoting one. Medial principles become the basis for analysing societies as what Althusser used to call 'expressive totalities', as the unfolding of a dominant social principle (or principle of social contradiction; see critiques of media formalism as essentialisms in Boyer 2006 and Turner 1992). One could argue, correctly I think, that Ghanaians operating in an embeddedness mode or an escapist one could also be formalist in this sense. For example, in normative discussions as to what is appropriate in mobile phone use, they would enunciate the most generalized values concerning reciprocity; phone use should and could exemplify more profound values and structures of feeling as to what is normatively appropriate. Conversely, by reducing kin obligations to the daily routine of flashing, the technology could be seen as a kind of stylization of normative appropriateness. Normative obligation is stripped back to its most schematically simplified formal properties: 'make contact' in order to signify responsibility. Again, this is the sort of thing we usually mean by 'culture': the patterns we detect and perform are experienced as the moral fabric of life itself.

From the researcher's point of view, there is every reason to start from the premise, as Thompson puts it very well, that 'use of communication media involves the creation of new forms of action and interaction in the social world, new kinds of social relationship and new ways of relating to others and to oneself' (1995: 4). But that should open up a complex and contingent field of action and research, rather than close down into a search for the first principles of an expressive totality. We have argued in the previous chapter that 'the media' is a black-boxed object that needs to be dissolved into the networks that sustain it. But that raises the very important further question of how we might recognize the emergence of diverse and contradictory objects in complexly overlapping networks. And that is a question not of 'What is the media?' but rather of 'What is an ecology?'

The Monologic of 'Information Society': A Utilitarian Modality

Approaches that either miss the poetics (ANT) or repress the diversity (media formalism) of communicative assemblages are therefore problematic. We need to look for principles but never for first principles. We can bring this argument back to the empirical case study in an important way: there was a *third* modality in operation in Ghana at the time of fieldwork, one that centred on discourses of 'information society'. However powerful and official this modality, we could say that it was just another modality, like embeddedness and escape, which simply construed the ideas of relationship and connection differently from the other two. We will characterize it as a 'utilitarian' modality, one which understood people as individuals with interests that they pursued through the use of tools such as media technologies that could provide useful information.

However, this modality was clearly of a different sort from the other two, discursive in a Foucauldian sense, in that by virtue of being *official*, it was inscribed in a power/knowledge chain of globally linked practices. This also meant that it had an enforced, disciplined and self-conscious coherence (up to a point) that was missing from the other two modalities. For example, the entire fieldwork period was traversed by two parallel projects. Firstly, there was a national governmental initiative that produced a mountain of white papers that aimed to constitute Ghana as an information society by the year 2023; this exercise involved writing policy and implementable planning documents covering every aspect of

Ghanaian life and governance (starting with the management of the President's office and internal government communications, and extending to detailed plans for health, education, law, etc.). These documents added up to the imposition of a consistent and singular language of informationalization on every aspect of Ghanaian life, a reconceptualization of social order and development in terms of the creation of informed market actors and citizens through the achievement of unimpeded flows of information by technical means; and of course this singular language was entirely warranted by monological development theories of the unfolding of an information society or network society.

The second project was WSIS, 2003–5, for which Ghana not only hosted crucial African pre-meetings, but also considered securing a leadership role crucial in maintaining its sense of itself as a successfully modernizing African nation. WSIS, like the Ghanaians' own white papers but at a 'global' scale, constantly reiterated the centrality of informationalization as the single principle of development and modernization; and both assumed this monologic as an inevitable future: the world simply *is* being reordered along informational lines, and Ghana had better restructure itself on this principle from the ground up if it is not to be left behind or become one of Castells' 'informational black holes'. In other words, the official modality or aesthetic form for understanding new media was not only powerful and managerial, but was also premised on a commitment to a monologic that was detected, or promoted, as emergent everywhere in social life.

In the next chapter we will look at this modality as a development narrative in greater detail. At this point I want to focus on the disjuncture between this modality and the others, and to show that it was analytically of a piece with the 'bad formalism' I outlined above. We have seen empirically that, at the time of fieldwork, our seriously poor and marginalized Accra *zongo* was participating in the most explosive increase in mobile phone use in Africa and in a significant popular culture of internet use. And yet this was entirely invisible to official ICT policy. Mobile phones, on the one hand, were clearly understood to be a significant part of informational futures, but, firstly, they were regarded as a private sector, commercial matter that was not to be governed by government informational policy, but merely deregulated; and, secondly, they were seen as matters of communication, not information. To the extent that they could be framed in terms of public distribution of information (e.g., SMS access to market prices, or remote medical diagnosis by MMS), then they might feature in the official purview, but these were pilot projects annexed to an internet-defined policy rather than the product of serious governmental attention to an exceptionally dramatic and complicated growth in this technology.

In official policy, internet use, on the other hand, could only mean information access, despite the fact that most people (not just in Mamobi but also officials in their private lives) recognized that email and chat communication were its most valued and popular uses. From this perspective, as far as officials and many development practitioners were concerned, there was virtually no or very little internet use in Ghana despite the fact that there it already clearly constituted a thriving popular culture: this simply did not count and was therefore officially invisible. And the feeling was mutual: none of the intensive internet users we interviewed or observed in Mamobi used the internet to access websites, search for information (in the official sense) or indeed understood their use of the technology in anything like these terms.

We have already seen this logic of disconnection and disjuncture at work in the empty computer centre at Korapo: internet use *means* an individual accessing a computer to pursue his or her informational needs in a utilitarian manner, and this view was secured through an incredible convergence of discourses (academic, governmental, NGO) as well as the high status of northern modalities of media use as performed by northern visitors but also as experienced or observed by Ghanaians through media or travel. More broadly, to the extent that media and development are understood in terms of specific objects and their unfolding logics, the locality into which these objects are dropped are regarded as *tabula rasa*, as empty up to now. Mamobi, to put it bluntly, despite being media-rich and media-dense, including in its popular use of mobile phones and internet, had no media use that *counted*.

The gold standard of relationship, in the modality of official ICT discourse, was not defined by either embeddedness or escape from enduring relationships. Relationship and connection were rather defined in a (neo?)liberal mode in terms of individuals who pursue their autonomously defined interests through social mechanisms such as markets, bureaucracies, politics and media, and for whom information should have clear utilitarian value on the basis of the theories through which these mechanisms were generally modelled. Such individuals may be more or less empowered in their pursuits by possession of various tools or resources, of which information has become the increasing focus of development discourse (as of virtually all discourses these days). Conversely, lack of individually accessed information indicates a vicious spiral of disempowerment and marginalization.

Hence this mode of communicative assembly was disconnected from the other two on several fundamental bases: it perceived different values and practices (information versus communication); it assumed different actors and relationships (autonomous individuals versus obligated kin); and it actually assembled different technologies (chat versus website;

mobile market prices versus communication along roads). More than this, however, it involved a different poetics, or, in Bourdieuian terms, a different structuring structure of dispositions and homologies across fields: it saw everywhere a new founding principle of social organization along which to remodel not just a few elements of life, as in the other two modalities, but absolutely every feature of Ghanaian existence. Ghana was to be remade as an information society, with an informationally defined position in a new global division of informational relationship.

Clearly, as we will argue in the next chapter, these claims about information society are not empirical descriptions that are or are not true. Nor are they required to be coherent or effective: when people talked about information society in Ghana, as elsewhere, it was very hard to see what actual principle, monological or not, was really at work; there were usually simply assertions followed by arbitrary and anecdotal examples that told stories about the importance of information. And there was very little evidence of actual assemblages in the case of the official as opposed to the unofficial modalities (that is to say, much was promised – e.g. in the mountain of Ghanaian white papers – and not much happened). The point is a material cultural one, about the way in which objects are acted upon, used and formed or configured as indexes of wider forces, developments, possibilities and principles that people are able to project onto them.

Conclusion

At one level, this chapter and the previous one have simply replayed an old motif in consumption studies, and a motif that I originally got into this research to explore: theories of 'the media', or of particular media, are fairly meaningless (or 'technologically determinist') if they posit media that are defined independently of the social worlds in which they are configured in actual use. However, simply to reduce this reconfiguration to mundane or 'material-semiotic' assemblages – as ANT tempts one to do – is to lose sight of precisely the radical leaps of meaning that make an assemblage more profoundly 'of a place', and which, in turn, make a place. There is no reason to get excited about the discovery of mere inexplicably contingent difference, that Sri Lankans use websites differently from Ghanaians, or Trinidadians from Californians; that would, or should, be obvious and unexceptional with even a little shift towards ethnography and a little shift away from institutional commitments to 'media'.

What is rather more useful is to understand how the forms of communicative assemblage fit into wider patterns of cultural practice and understanding, how different media or media uses are appropriate for certain kinds of relationships and not others, how technologies are configured in relation to longer histories and future horizons. It is at this point that the connections between media and development are a matter of more than the utility of information (though we will return to that issue). And it is at this point that connections between media and development can be thought about not as true or false claims about what different ICTs can do, but rather as complex theorizations of how the world is changing, how to plot a course through those changes, and what kinds of persons, social relationships and actions are emerging from these changes. In the next chapter we will look at these questions through the idea of ICTs as the material culture of development and 'network ethics'.

4

Making Up the Future
New Media as the Material Culture of Development

From the 1990s onwards, ICTs[1] became central to the ways in which most people, most places, imagined and acted upon 'the future', how they imagined change and 'development'. For many northerners, the ICT story extended much older narratives that started in the immediate post-war era such as the shift from a manufacturing to a service economy, the shift from Fordism to post-Fordism, the shift from modernism to post-modernism, and the increasing dematerialization or enculturation of economy. But the stories about informationalization, networks and ICTs clearly took on a central and organizing role in theorizing development that subsumed and superseded all of these: ICTs could be described as the 'material culture of development' in that understandings and calculations of the future were increasingly mediated through these prestigious objects and the social forms (information and networks) with which they were associated.

This statement – that the 'material culture of development' comprises objects through which people understand and act upon the future – rests upon a broadened notion of 'development'. The narrower conventional definition of 'development' refers to a specific way of organizing relations between North and South, particularly in the post-war era: countries outside the North are to be brought up to targeted standards

99

of welfare (e.g., Millennium Development Goals [MDGs]) and to be integrated into social and economic processes (such as democracy and markets) that will sustainably eradicate the more grotesque inequalities and unfreedoms. This sense of development involves institutions, practices and ever-shifting policies that define and measure standards of life, normative institutions and processes, the rights and responsibilities of donors and beneficiaries, and claimed causal relations between development interventions (aid, projects, policies) and developmental progress.

Indeed, any given period of 'development' has been dominated by particular models of social change and of development as a social process, and these connect it to a second, broader, meaning of 'development': models and theories of the underlying logic and direction of social change. The development industry has long been critiqued, correctly, for grounding itself in normative definitions of 'development' in this broader sense, in narratives of how the world should work or will work, narratives of the inevitable shape of the future. These have generally been unembarrassedly normative, whether we go back to earlier teleologies such as Rostow (1952) or to more recent ones such as neo-liberal structural adjustment. The story of the transition into information or network society is simply the latest account of 'development' as an inevitable restructuring of the social and economic, and of global geopolitical relations, this time around information-related principles such as access to networked means for producing, processing and circulating information.

Moreover, 'development', particularly in the second, broader sense of theorizing change, is a style of narration, even a genre, that has long been constitutive of the western modernist sense of temporality insofar as modernism has been bound up with trying to represent and make sense of experiences of temporal breaks and discontinuities, including identifying and periodizing these breaks in order to fit them into a meaningful narrative form (for the relation of media theory to such narratives, see Morley 2007). Social development is a sequence of ages or periods, each based on a fundamental principle (often a technological or communicative one) that maps out an unfolding dialectical logic of development (Kumar 1978 is still an excellent survey of this trope). Although the teleological character of this logic has been subjected to the most critique (e.g., Lyotard and master narratives), its reductionist style is equally important: like the bad media formalisms discussed in the previous chapter, what is most striking is the desire to reduce social transformation to a single unfolding principle which is then treated as the generator and structure of the future, and which – in the narrower world of the development industry – can be treated as the key to development, to policies that are in tune with the direction of history. Moreover, the development industry has often organized itself and its 'beneficiaries' around technology-based stories in which privileged technologies map out the normative logic of our journey into the future. Large-scale public works projects! Green revolution! Structural adjustment! Information society! ICTs became salient in a material culture sense as the latest privileged and paradigmatic objects through which people could imagine the logic of the future and seek to secure a place in it.

The problem is not with narratives of development as such. Everyone – individually and in various groupings such as families and communities and aid agencies – is in the business of trying to understand social change under ineluctably uncertain conditions (we can never know what happens next until it has) in order to act in ways that will be 'good' (normatively appropriate or instrumentally effective). We can in fact define 'development' – in a truly banal and empty way – as an existential condition, and a central political point of this chapter is the demand to treat *everyone* as a development theorist in this sense, as equally floundering around in the confusion of living through history. It may well be that some social worlds involve only minimal articulations of temporality (as opposed to 'our' modernist obsession with it), but I don't think we know of any cultures without an origin myth and hence an account of their own developmental logic, a historical account that informs what they should do *next*. And there is an interesting negative version of this incessant narration: it is common, indeed almost taken for granted, in informal conversations between development workers to tell the story of the development industry as a history of disappointments and failures (much like older activists and Marxist theorists for whom history is the persistent failure of the revolution to arrive): each failed development theory or strategy means finding out yet again that they had not discovered the key to history but merely another well-intentioned practice; on to the next one and better luck this time.

This chapter, then, focuses specifically on the developmental narratives that people have been telling and performing through the material culture of new media or ICTs. Even more specifically, we will look at two dimensions or questions of 'development' as I've defined it:

- What are the pragmatics of imagining different developmental futures in terms of ICTs and information? How do people calculate futures and ways of getting to the futures they desire through ICTs?
- What are the 'ethics' of ICTs and development? What kinds of personal and social transformation are imagined, and for whom? How do people understand *agency* and *sociality* in terms of stories of ICT-driven change?

The asymmetry in 'development' is two-fold. Firstly, stories of network or information society are clearly northern theories that are presented as social facts into which southern people have to fit themselves. But, secondly, they are stories that are asymmetrically applied, or in which asymmetrical roles are assigned: within ICT and development stories there is what we will describe as an 'international division of ethics'. Whereas northern narratives imagine – through the material culture of ICTs – fundamental transformation in people's subjectivity and sociality, in who they are and how they connect, southern ICT 'beneficiaries' are normally rendered as 'tool users', people who are not expected to change in any fundamental way but simply to use ICTs instrumentally, as tools that might 'empower' them to more effectively be what they already are and have always been.

Two Development Theorists

America! America!

Here's a story about development theorists in the flow of action. A researcher on a project in Tamil Nadu, part of the UNESCO-funded programme ICTs for Poverty Reduction (ictPR), wrote up in her field notes an encounter that struck her, and everyone else, as profound. The project was based in a Chennai veterinary college with a long experience of educational extension work; they wanted to build on their models of connecting into communities by locating ICT facilities in houses belonging to well-established women's self-help groups (SHGs). Each SHG could use the facilities to develop their own projects, though with a strong steer towards 'income-generating activities' such as developing their small businesses selling artificial flowers or spices. They could also extend ICT access and training through SHG networks in their area (e.g., most SHGs were organized into regional federations), usually by offering computer literacy classes that could fund their own activities. This model clearly aimed both at instrumental use of ICTs, with a strong vocational and business focus; and at participation and 'ownership', such that the SHGs could become mediators of ICTs to their communities. Six SHGs were involved, two in each of three locations that were increasingly rural and remote from Chennai.

The incident in question occurred at one of the two villages most remote from Chennai, where a woman who was closely involved in the participating SHG had just arrived for coolie labour in a field. As she arrived, the other women called her 'America! America!' Just how derisive or sympathetic or humorous this teasing was intended to be was

unclear, or more likely ambivalent, double-edged, but the chain of associations it invoked was obvious to everyone, including the researcher:
the woman was in material, social and symbolic touch with, and had
some degree of ownership and control over, a prestigious but indetermi-
nate object, condensed as 'the computer' – an object that was clearly the
key to the next 'future' that was being propounded to the women
through word of mouth (particularly via relatives in the city), advertising,
films and schools. And like all futures since colonial days, this future
emanated from America. The women seemed used to the idea of having
to position themselves within successive narratives of social change,
whether as a future they aspired to join, or as the next in a long line of
futures to exclude them, that was not 'for them'. So the woman was
connected to America/the future by the computer; but not really: the
presumptuousness of this claimed connection – between a coolie labourer
and America via a computer in the SHG house – was the basis of
the teasing.

Both 'America's' connection to ICTs, and the incident itself, struck
everyone as 'symbolic', in the sense that the computer had been reduced
to a sign which evokes a system of meanings, or of represented relationships, that float free of material usages. Indeed, the women doing the
shouting did so partly because of their very separation from the object,
which they had not touched and possibly had not even seen yet; they
were being placed in a 'purely symbolic' relationship to it. Put slightly
differently, there is no question that, without embodied knowledge of
such an exemplary object, its most salient properties would be magical
in character – a power to transform the woman's ('America's') social
status which the women in the field ascribed to new media access as
such, rather than to any specific affordances, practices or usage.

But to leave the story at this point, and to accept that ICTs were
'symbolic' in this situation, would be to beg the central question of how
the object came to mean in this way in the first place, and how its 'symbolic' significance was separated from its 'instrumental' usage (Morley
2007: 293–303). What story about development was being told through
ICTs, and on the basis of which theories and knowledges?

In material cultural terms, ICTs are transacted objects, and their social
status cannot be detached from the relationships and processes through
which they circulate and which are partly reproduced through their
circulation. The women in the field ridiculed a direct connection between
the SHG woman and America via the ICT object, but they were very
aware of the chains of transaction on which that connection depended:
the ICTs had arrived in the village by way of UNESCO, working with a
string of long-networked NGOs, and the 'last mile' of actors (relatives,
media, schools, private computer schools) that were pushing an ICT

future, and that were all linked through a well-known veterinary exten-sion education institute. The women could trace the paths of incoming objects and resources and understand them in terms of the linkages they reflected. The programme had, moreover, anchored this chain specifically in the house of one SHG amongst many, which therefore appeared as gatekeeper and owner of this captured prestigious capital. In contrast to the 'symbolic', quasi-magical story about transformation ('America!'), people were acutely aware of this very material story of how local power and status are realigned through struggles to control incoming resources, especially prestigious ones: how did that SHG get access, and how will that change relations of power and status in the locality?

There was a kind of conversation that occurred repeatedly in field-work, but most explicitly in Sri Lanka. At the end of the fieldwork, in response to almost my last formal question, I asked the director of KCRIP: what – at the end of the day – was the main benefit of ICTs for his project or his community? His answer was that it had brought me and my fellow researchers and other UNESCO people to Kothmale, it had allowed KCRIP staff to attend conferences in countries they had never before visited and learn things they could not otherwise have accessed. Ritual and polite elements of this response aside, the answer went on and on, tracing transactions and connections, without making any reference to the affordances or technical properties or uses of either radio or internet. But the man was not talking about symbolic circula-tion, or ICTs as signs; rather it was a pure material culture story, a tracing of the kinds of relationships and connections that could be sustained through the transaction of this very particular kind of object.

Hence, one meaning of the 'America' call is simple and certainly not symbolic: possession of the computer connected this woman through new skills, associations and transactions to a more general new moder-nity that is associated with the US, and all her workmates understood this and – crucially – acted upon it by teasing her. This was a develop-ment narrative or development theory that required very little knowledge of the specific principles or properties enunciated through computers (such as 'information society'), but did involve a more generalized nar-rative – much like the Ghanaian ones in Chapter 3 – in which the North is the paradigmatic development path, and is continuously passing on opportunities and obligations: in the past we were left behind by literacy, now we will be left behind by computer literacy.

The little 'America' vignette presents an extreme story of development in that people were trying to make sense of social change and the future under conditions of very little knowledge, few theoretical resources and a kind of exclusion such that the computer was pretty much devoid of function or content: it was purely 'symbolic' because it had no other content beyond connecting a local woman to 'America' as the vague origin of the logics of change that these women fully expected would soon overwhelm their world. ICTs therefore had little meaning other than changing 'America's' social status in a somewhat magical way. The women knew that another revaluation of their (and everyone's) skills, plans and status was on its way, foisting on them the obligation to figure out yet again how the world will work and how one will survive or, with luck, prosper under new and unknown conditions and processes. 'America' identified a new blank space that would have to be filled in: everyone would need to be able to *theorize* it in order to act rationally in relation to 'it'. And 'America' likely provided a perfectly adequate development theory for these actors.

Maneeksha

'America' was an extreme case, so let's supplement it with a more quali-fied case, from the same ictPR project in Chennai, involving a much more informed and sophisticated development theorist: Maneeksha. Maneek-sha was an illiterate single mother whose husband had left her shortly after the birth of their now 10-year-old daughter; she was therefore both extremely poor and of the lowest social status, employed in coolie labour on the road or in the field. Already a long-time member of the SHG that had possession of the TANUVAS equipment in her area, Maneeksha theorized ICTs and development in several opposed directions. Firstly, as with so many parents encountered in fieldwork, Maneeksha under-stood ICTs as emblematic of a future that was not for her but for her daughter. The inevitability of that ICT-driven future (whatever that meant) was hammered home to her from all sides (not least via her daughter), including word of mouth from contacts in various cities, glimpses of circulating media such as film and TV, advertisements for computer literacy courses that were appearing on every wall, school and now UNESCO and her own SHG. Maneeksha simply *knew* that her ICT involvement was the best thing she could do for her daughter. The imme-diate impact of this was to add a heavy burden on Maneeksha as a development theorist and practitioner (which was integral to her sense of herself as a responsible mother) to theorize new social processes and act upon them, at great cost, on her daughter's behalf.

Maneeksha was already devoting heroic, eye-watering proportions of her minute income to keep her daughter in a decent school and to buy some private tuition (Rs30 a month on private tuition for her daughter, plus the cost of transport and school meals), and she went to great lengths to involve herself and her daughter in the UNESCO ICT centre as soon as the possibility arose. In talking about her hopes for her daughter she said:

> M: I would like her to become an office worker. But I don't know. She is studying well. I don't want her to work in the hot sun. She should work in a cool place. Working in the hot sun and getting low pay is horrible.
>
> R: How are you going to educate your daughter?
>
> M: I can educate my daughter up to SSLC [Secondary School Leaving Certificate] in Varakalpattu. After that I have to send her to Cuddalore or Nellikuppam. Government is giving free bus pass. I have to spend little more. I will educate her. It is the only aim of my life.

As a development theorist, Maneeksha was conceptualizing a leap from field work to information society by way of the category that she understood most clearly: white-collar office work that is secure (rather than daily and unreliable) and that is indoor rather than outdoor. Her understanding of the connections between ICTs, education and future employment was based on little direct experience of any of them. She had never seen the inside of an office until recently, when as part of her SHG duties she had entered a bank, hence she knew little of office work other than, as she says, it's out of the sun. Gaining ICT skills for her daughter is a necessary but completely vague step into a world of work that defines her familial aspirations yet of which she has little experience or understanding. What does provide a framework for her theorizations is (her daughter's) *education*, 'the only aim of my life'. Maneeksha thereby made sense of ICTs and development by connecting them to a very long-term development and livelihood strategy that reaches back to colonial days: familial advancement means accruing educational credentials, as well as certain currently valued and iconic skills, in order to secure white-collar employment in an office, which not only has status and remuneration, but also the kind of security associated with civil service-style jobs for life. Development means climbing painfully upwards through a tree of examinations, as high as you can. In the recent past, Maneeksha would have been investing – to an equally painful level of sacrifice – in English classes and secretarial courses; now it was computer literacy.

In regard to her daughter, Maneeksha's concepts were formalist or credentialist: she was not concerned with her daughter's substantive knowledge, creativity, agency, enjoyment or anything other than accumulating pieces of paper that would prove her qualifications to future schools or employers. However, Maneeksha's own relationship to ICTs was entirely the opposite: she demonstrated, and took pride in, an exceptional affinity, enthusiasm and skill with ICTs that was coupled with a visual flair in which she clearly revelled. One day she led me around the village telling me what and whom to photograph, and why, like an experienced art director; she then disappeared with my camera to take her own pictures for several hours. She loved MS Paint; and though illiterate, she not only loved to see her name on the monitor but also to navigate word-based menus with rapidly increasing facility. This sense of the joy of mastering technologies (and the most prestigious ones at that) extended to answering the telephone and operating printers: they all equally presented both prestigious and simply fascinating technological processes for her to be absorbed in. It was *fun* to do technology with her. But, in contrast to her instrumental and formal framing of her daughter's involvement, Maneeksha's was entirely substantive in the sense that she did not expect any progress for herself, she did not expect this ICT engagement to move her from field to office: the pleasures of these processes were ends in themselves. However, she was very articulately clear about the ways in which her experiences of ICTs were transformative in wider senses, and this certainly had implications for her own sense of status and worth and possible opportunities for more tangible advance (e.g., by teaching computer literacy or being responsible for specific machines). If ICTs contributed to Maneeksha's 'empowerment' (as development discourse puts it), it was not by making her more efficient at achieving exogenous goals but by helping her to encounter a newly imagined sense of herself: the core of her experience concerned her development as a person rather than her material development as a 'beneficiary', a mind-set she reserved for thinking about her daughter.

Maneeksha's story had a bad ending, only partially redeemed. Her adeptness with the technology proved threatening to higher-status SHG members. One day, the computer trainer – the higher education-trained daughter of the powerful woman who led both the SHG and the federation of which it was a part – was unable to get their printer working. Maneeksha – who had only seen it in operation once before – showed her how to do it (the trainer had been feeding paper in the wrong way). Events led rapidly downhill from this moment of techno-democracy, in which know-how overrode status and credentials. Maneeksha came under all manner of accusations of being overbearing and controlling, and eventually of financial mismanagement. She and her daughter were banned from both the ICT centre and the SHG for many months. Her daughter was finally allowed back to attend computer literacy classes. Personal development and social development met and conflicted in a disastrous way and the costs and contradictions of 'empowerment' were made manifest. Insofar as Maneeksha believed ICTs to be 'the future', they were also clearly a new burden placed upon her as a responsible parent by the latest wave of modernity: she suffered increased poverty, huge anxiety and – in the end – a doubled social exclusion in the effort to secure a future for her daughter in an emerging world that she could not enter or understand, let alone predict. In this sense, all the rhetoric of ICT revolution and newness made ICTs appear enormously old – tiresomely, boringly, depressingly old: they were experienced (by the women in the America story as much as by Maneeksha) as the latest burden imposed on poor people, yet another impossible demand to keep up with progress or be left behind. By the same token, they were experienced as the latest promise held out to them. In any village – as in any development agency – you will find ICT believers and ICT cynics, and you will find a majority of people who are stuck in ambivalence, hedging their bets against the future by learning to use this stuff but without expecting a brave new world.

The main point, however, is that whatever her complex views of ICTs as burdens and as possibilities, Maneeksha was producing development theories and strategies, analyses that tried to connect ICTs and 'development' as a basis for her plans and actions. And of course in Maneeksha's story there was a perfect symmetry between an illiterate single mother and UNESCO – they were equally confused development theorists. Both 'knew', narratively, that ICTs were the future, and that this entailed urgent action, and yet neither could specify precisely how ICTs and development futures were connected. And of course I only met Maneeksha precisely because a communications officer in UNESCO's Delhi office believed that basic research was required in order for him to answer the very same questions that Maneeksha was trying to cope with, and funded me and others to work on the problem. Moreover, the very meaning of the object ('an ICT') was at least partly constituted in our transacting it.

For Maneeksha, unlike the women in the field, 'America' was already partly filled in, but with very contradictory possibilities and commitments. And indeed with unresolvable contradictions: ICTs were not a solution to development problems; rather, they posed new problems of development to various participants. In Maneeksha's case these consisted of both the burden of making sense of the new and the burden of dealing with the power of the old, which defeated her.

Instrumentality and ethics

One last point to make about these stories: there are two dimensions involved in thinking development through the material culture of ICTs – an instrumental dimension and an ethical one. In Maneeksha's case these are even split into two different narratives in a way that we will discuss in some detail below: she thought about her daughter in instrumental terms, in which ICTs were tools to improve her life chances; she thought about herself in terms of fundamental transformations both of herself as a social agent and of the social relations in which she moved. A central aspect of Maneeksha's story is that as a development theorist, she produced complex and multivocal discourses, articulating multiple ways of thinking and enacting the future, in relation to the different processes and relationships she understood herself to be dealing with (e.g., familial projects, community cooperation and competition, official and formal discourses shared with public bodies like UNESCO).

However, we can also think about these two dimensions as analytically distinct aspects of any single development story. Maneeksha's thinking and planning about herself and about her daughter each included both dimensions. Firstly, she – like anyone – needed to produce empirically grounded social analysis: maps and models of interrelationships between social agents and social events, descriptions of these interrelationships that had explanatory or predictive plausibility such that they provided her with reasons for acting in particular ways ('Getting my daughter a computer literacy qualification is a good investment because of the connections between credentials, new technology skills and employment'). Development theory – whether hers or mine or UNESCO's – is social theory. (We will look at the nature of theories and knowledges in development, and struggles for 'interpretive power', further in Chapter 6.) This analysis was connected to limited but clearly specifiable knowledge (things that UNESCO said, visits to the bank, stories told by relatives returning from cities). This social analysis is fundamentally strategic and calculative: how could Maneeksha decide what to do both for herself and her daughter, except by elaborating partial and provisional theories about such things as the future of work, the changing shapes of power and status, and so on? Theories are best guesses about the future, just enough to be getting on with in the practical world, and – again – this went for UNESCO as much as Maneeksha: as we will discuss further in Chapter 6, the entire ictPR programme was constituted in terms of doubts and confusion as to what the relation between ICTs and development could or should be, in terms of the perceived necessity for basic research and exploratory learning.

Secondly, however, Maneeksha was equally necessarily concerned with the 'ethical' dimensions of development: with forms of personhood and agency, with forms of appropriate action, and with defining the substantive values that should govern conduct and sociality. The distinction between 'ICTs for herself' and 'ICTs for her daughter' was the most fundamental ethical divide, whereby different developmental trajectories were mapped out on the basis of what kind of person development was *for*, and what kinds of persons should emerge from development. The central question of ethics is how social actors can arrive at understandings and choices about how to behave properly in concrete circumstances – how they can reflect on the rightness and goodness of their actions, relationships, character, and so on; how they are 'to develop' (their selves, families, generations, communities, nations) in relation to a normative but very uncertain story about where the world is going. This sense of ethics obviously sounds strong echoes of Foucault, and particularly of governmentality theorists (Barry, Osborne and Rose 1996; Miller and Rose 2008; Rose 1991, 1998, 1999). What kinds of person – subjectivity, agency, relation to the self – are imagined and enacted through the distributed discourses of ICTs and the practices they inform? And how do discourses specific to ICT and development align with wider prevailing discourses, particularly neo-liberal ones, as to the proper conduct of conduct? However, against Foucault, we can also draw on the less discursively fixated definitions of ethics that have been introduced by several recent anthropological approaches. For example, Lakoff and Collier, drawing critically on MacIntyre, suggest an anthropology of ethics guided by the study of 'regimes of living': '[C]onfigurations of normative, technical, and political elements that are brought into alignment in problematic or uncertain situations. A given regime provides one possible means . . . for organizing, reasoning about, and living ethically – that is, with respect to a specific understanding of the good' (Lakoff and Collier 2004: 427). This formulation brings out the character of ethics as practical reasoning. Though oriented to behaving rightly or well in relation to overarching values, ethics is not about the application of moral universals to the particular and unique. Rather, ethics is a style of thinking about the 'best' way through the thickets of the unique present, and therefore technical and institutional specifics are as much a part of ethical practice as are grander moral values. Ethics in this sense is nearly coterminous with 'culture' (see Laidlaw 2002). That is to say, to assemble the actual structure of practical wisdom for particular people in a particular instance, we need to assemble what amounts to their cosmology as it is lived out through particular practices, relationships and institutionalizations: beliefs about who they are, about what is human, about the proper way in which beliefs themselves can be secured, and so on. This does indeed cover roughly the terrain of Foucauldian ethics of the self as self-formation, but in terms of lay belief and practice, rather than the genealogy or epistemic structure of wider discursive formations (here see Laidlaw's [2002] arguments about ethics and freedom, *contra* Foucault). In studying this sense of ethics, we are asked to unearth the entire conceptualization and practice of 'normative sociality' (see Miller and Slater 2000) as they might be understood and institutionally ordered through new communicative assemblages like mobile phones or internet. Moreover, as discussed in Chapter 2, if (following both ANT and material culture studies) we treat agency as relational, to be understood in and through connections that make up the fabric of lived relationships, then ethics need to be specified in terms of the particular communicative assemblages through which people make connections.

Northern Narratives and 'Network Ethics'

We can now turn from development 'beneficiaries' as development theorists and train the same analytical lens on northern development theorists: what instrumental and ethical stories about the future of the world have been conjured up through the material culture of ICTs? The most striking feature of northern understandings of ICTs is that they have been amongst the most extreme narratives of human and social transformation to be found outside of apocalyptic quasi-religious narratives and science fiction (and of course the first generation of cybercultural writing often involved an outright refusal to distinguish social theory and science fiction [Featherstone and Burrows 1995; Shields 1996; Springer 1996]). Moreover, although the two configurations we are about to examine – cyberculture and new economy discourses – are not only extreme but historical, it is clear that the material culture of ICTs is always available to project transformative and futurological visions onto: even after the extensive mainstreaming of ICTs in the North or the pricking of the bubbles of hype through dot.com and financial crashes, new waves of equivalent visions keep arriving. Discussions of social networking, mobile internet and digital political mobilization (as in the Arab Spring) are stories of the digital transformation of self and sociality entirely equivalent to the ones we are about to discuss. (We can also add new waves of avant-garde political and social theory, some of it extended from the earlier generation [Manovich 2001, 2002, 2003; Terranova 2004], some uses of software studies, media materiality approaches and some uses of Kittler in a clearly post-human direction.)

The purpose of discussing cyberculture and new economy in this context is obviously not to offer a comprehensive history, let alone to support or refute any particular claims about ICTs made by these narratives. The aims are, firstly, to place within the same frame both northern and southern attempts to deal with development in terms of ICTs as material culture: the question is simply, what hopes and fears about the future have been enacted in and through these technologies? And, secondly, in the next section, I want to argue that the (extremely) transformative visions of the North are not generally extended to the South, and they thereby participate in constructing an international division of ethics within development and ICTs for development.

Cyberculture

Castells (2001) rightly identifies a range of counter-cultural and avant-gardist movements, pre-1990s and sometimes stretching back to the 1960s, as central to the genealogy of the idea of network society. This lineage is particularly explicit in the idea of cyberculture, in which networked technologies were experienced as vehicles for a fundamental transformation of the human and the achievement of a post-humanity (a term that could be used metaphorically or literally). The most persistent tropes running through cyberculture were virtuality, disembodiment and disembedding, all of which emphasized the textuality, information-alization or digitalization of material or corporeal social existence. Or, more simply, 'you are what you type'. Virtuality gives a transformed social status to shared representations and representational spaces such that they can be treated 'as if' they were real; and this establishes a social space for elaborating identities and social relationships independently of the constraints of bodies, places, communities and other real-world or 'RL' (real-life) limitations. ICTs might constitute safe spaces for realistic exploration of identity and community, as the most exciting sandbox for personal and social experimentation since the Wild West itself (explored from very early in the game by Turkle [1995], but also Rheingold [1993] and Negroponte [1996]; see also Barlow 1996); they might ground a real transhumanity that deconstructs gender, race and all other social divisions; they might stand as a material critique of belief in the authenticity of identities and normative sociality, a practical enactment, and even proof of poststructuralist and postmodernist assaults on essentialism; and they might – in dystopian mode – signal the descent of the social into a Baudrillardian vortex of merely simulated sociality that no longer refers to any real world. Much of this continued – though in less avant-gardist language – into the age of social networking, Second Life, iPhone and software studies.

The extent to which all these discourses are indeed development theories elaborated through ICTs as material culture – i.e., a kind of reading of the tea leaves of technology to glimpse the social future that was either desired or feared – comes out clearly in a juxtaposition from early in cyberculture. Mark Poster (1995a, 1995b, 1995c, 1995d, 2001) wrote an exciting and visionary series of works which sought to articulate the new sense of politics and community that he believed to be imminent in cyberspace. Poster's arguments embrace the image of the internet as intrinsically free (as in John Gilmore's famous claim, 'The Net interprets censorship as damage and routes around it' [Elmer-Dewitt 1993), and the basis of that freedom is unlimited interactivity: there is an unlimited access to unconstrained relationships and dialogue that is radically democratizing. With a postmodern slant, Poster argues that positions for speaking and acting are thereby radically decentred. Whereas conservatives fear that virtuality will bring about the decline of 'real' community, Poster believes that the internet allows us to recognize the virtuality of real communities, and thereby be liberated into social creativity rather than being constrained by the false facticity of social relations: 'Just as virtual communities are understood as having the attributes of "real" communities, so "real" communities can be seen to depend on the imaginary' (1995c: 90) – above all, on communications. The 'imaginary' and non-material quality of new media marks a collective experience of *pure connection*, which is also a turn to truth and to political creativity.

For Poster, this offers a strategy to transcend a now exhausted modernity. For Kevin Robins (1995, 1997; Robins and Webster 1986, 1999), in a series of publications that were roughly contemporary to Poster's, this strategy is merely a fantasy escape from modern dilapidation, a desire to simulate a now-lost sociality: 'There is on-line communion, but there are no residents of hyperspace. . . . What we have is the preservation through simulation of the old forms of solidarity and community. In the end, not an alternative society, but an alternative to society' (Robins 1995: 150). The cybercultural claims about 'deliverance from material and bodily constraints' express a desire to escape the founding modern division between mind and body, and a desire to give up on the modern dream of unified identities.

What clearly connects the two authors and arguments is best understood in terms of material culture: a projection onto and through the new media of their hopes and fears about the fate of sociality and politics at (what they both agree to be) the exhausted grand finale of the modernist project, an obsession they shared with most engaged social thinkers at that moment. Tellingly, both of them based their positions entirely on readings of cybercultural theorists and their programmatic pronouncements rather than on empirical studies of actual new media users (Robins did this later); hence these are both commentaries on the commentaries of the avant-garde theorists. What they reveal is not the impact or use of new media but rather the dramas that were being projected onto them, the social concerns that were being articulated through them and narrativized in ICTs as a material culture through which to express and act upon ethical concerns. It was significant that studies of the more extreme cybercultural practices online already showed a far more complex and ambivalent stance on the part of participants – for example, those in highly sexualized sites were often obsessed with performing normative and even hyper-conventional sexualities (Bassett 1997; Slater 2000a); and the nature of 'real' community and politics did not really emerge so obviously from the technical space itself (Dibbell 1994; and this is even more evident now, e.g. Boellstorff 2010). Moreover the very distinction between online and offline, on which both the utopian and dystopian renderings of this material culture depended, was not absolute but had itself to be treated as a variable social accomplishment (Slater 2004): participants sometimes made it a sharp distinction, sometimes they didn't make it at all, but in every case it was a complex social assemblage (Hine 2000, 2005). Moreover, the evolution of such distinctions, therefore of the ways in which the material culture of ICTs might be read and performed, was clearly a historical matter: as ICTs seemed to be mainstreamed and rendered mundane, the academic debates became concerned less with the fate of modernity than with the structures of everyday life (Bakardjieva 2005; Green and Haddon 2009; Haddon 2004, 2011; Wellman and Haythornthwaite 2002)

New economy and network society

Hence, northern cybercultural stories about connection – utopian or dystopian – could be regarded as a very localized identity crisis. But narratives of economy and of capitalism itself during the same period were characterized by equally or even more extreme narratives of transformation. These came in two main flavours, new economy and network society.

New economy narratives shared significant themes (and personnel) with cyberculture, particularly through publications such as *Wired*. (Poster [2001] himself later announced the internet-based emergence of 'liquid capitalism'; the pun in the title, *What's the Matter with the Internet?*, stated the theme clearly.) Epochal shifts in the nature of capitalism had long been announced, certainly from the 1950s, as transitions to service economy, post-Fordist economy, informational economy, and even to a network form of inter-capitalist linkage (Piore and Sabel 1984; Thompson 1986). All of these debates were either given a new lease of life or incorporated within debates about the specific impacts of ICTs on developmental futures. Seen from this angle, new economy narratives – like cybercultural ones – therefore also linked ICTs to a concern with crisis and exhaustion at the heart of the modern, to a need for renewal and a fear that the new developmental strategies on offer might be snake oil.

Identifications of a new economy linked to new media primarily fed on the idea of a dematerialized world in which goods were increasingly produced through informational and digital processes (including R&D), increasingly took dematerialized form (e.g., as brands, design, styles, and as dematerialized cultural goods in the move, say, from music albums to digital files), and whose value was to be understood in terms not of priced components but of intellectual property and cultural salience. Memes would replace commodities as assets. Simultaneously, a dematerialized circulation of goods is also one that is disintermediated, weightless, frictionless: things move faster and further, and at less cost, and forms of regulation (states, market regulations, labour and consumer protection, perhaps property itself) appear – like censorship – to be forms of noise that the internet would re-route itself to avoid. A slogan that nicely encapsulates the movement and its intrinsic link to new media was offered by Waters: 'material exchanges localize; political exchanges internationalize; and symbolic exchanges globalize' (1995: 9). The same technical means and metaphors would inevitably also signal new forms of subjectivity, social agency and social organization, crystallized in the idea of 'networks'. On the one hand, these new ontologies and forms of transaction called into being new kinds of economic subjects (e.g., the 'fast subjects' that Thrift [1997, 1998, 2000, 2005] saw in management training, publications and policies). On the other hand, they entailed new networked forms of organization that were defined by flattened hierarchies, project-defined and delimited partnerships rather than stable organizational structures, distributed agency, learning, innovation and creativity as the imperatives of their operation. An exemplary contemporary statement of this sense of radical transformation of capitalism and capitalist subjects, articulated from within the avant-garde wing of capitalism (*Wired* magazine) was Kevin Kelly's *New Rules for the New Economy: 10 Radical Strategies for a Connected World* (1999), which theorized strategies for development with slogans such as:

- **Feed the Web first:** 'as networks entangle all commerce, a firm's primary focus shifts from maximizing the firm's value to maximising the network's value. Unless the net survives, the firm perishes.'
- **From places to spaces:** 'as physical proximity (place) is replaced by multiple interactions with anything, anytime, anywhere (space), the opportunities for intermediaries, middlemen, and mid-size niches expand greatly' (Kelly 1999: 161).

But of course it was Castells who formulated these developments in terms of the emergence of a 'network society', a new 'mode of development' in which technical, organizational and managerial arrangements are organized around a new technical paradigm (the 'informational paradigm') which is the fundamental and structuring principle of social order in the developmental future. What underpins this new order is the network form. Although the network form predates new economy (Castells persistently gestures against charges of technological determinism), it has become dominant through recent socio-technical changes: '[T]his new economy is *global* in the precise sense that its core, strategic activities have the capacity to work as a unit on a planetary scale in real time or chosen time' (Castells 2000: 10). And for Castells, this is a good thing: however much empirical and political analysis needs to be devoted to the inequalities, uneven distribution and uneven development, the digital exclusions and informational black holes which are part of the inevitable structural contradictions within this new mode of production, network society is a progressive development. The world – agents and their social ordering – is changing out of all recognition and in promising ways.

'Network ethics' and the value of connection

Cyberculture, new economy and network society concepts can all be regarded as versions of 'networks ethics', ethics being defined as above in terms of normative versions of agency and sociality. They all attempt to produce such normative visions by working through the material culture of ICT to discern what kinds of agency and sociality are emergent from these new forms of connection; conversely, they are meditations on the value of connection from the standpoint of subjectivity and social relations. It is worth pausing to situate these discourses in a much longer history of such meditations: it is at least possible that they got some of their force and plausibility as development narratives precisely because elaborating development narratives in terms of communicative assemblages is very far from new in western thought. This connects ICT and development to very long-term themes in material culture and consumption studies (Campbell 1989; Slater 1997a). Network ethics can be traced back to the origins of modern liberalism, specifically to Adam Smith and David Hume (and, even earlier, to Lord Shaftesbury [Campbell 1989]): all these figures contribute to an Enlightenment argument that the evolution of moral sensibility and of 'refinement' (the development of taste, culture and 'sensibility') depends on an expanded realm of commerce and 'social intercourse', on the value of increasingly dense and diverse connection. This idea starts as a moral philosophy, later becomes a critical epistemology (Hegel), revolutionary practice (Marx) and finally social theory (Simmel or Durkheim), but throughout it is a development narrative based on the conviction that humankind will progress by virtue of the proliferation of *connections*.

What is most significant for the present discussion is that such arguments valued connection as such and did not separate out communication, let alone media. Rather, Smith and Hume place moral experiences rather than communicative acts at the centre of the picture: increased connection develops people by forcing them to reinterpret themselves continuously from the standpoint of the other, and an increasing number of 'others', through the gazes of an ever-expanding universe of heterogeneous others encountered through modern experiences of discovery and colonization, trade, division of labour and urbanization. Communication often supplies the privileged template (the sainted coffee house, the art of conversation, salons, encyclopaedias, tourism, forms of display, letters and correspondence societies), but Smith and Hume have equally in mind increased trade, exploration and colonization, as well the division of labour: the 'economic' link that connects Indian cotton to London merchants or the movement of ships to Australia is just as much 'social intercourse' as is a well-turned phrase; and conversely conversation is also called 'commerce'. Whereas later liberalism and utilitarianism turned back into the fetish of mundane difference (each monadic individual possesses his or her own diverse preferences which are mechanically reconciled through markets or elections), its founders often sound closer to the contemporary: it is the connections which make us rather than we who make connections, and the more connections we make, the more developed, free and individual we can be. By contrast with liberal utilitarianism, this theme is clearly continued and developed in non-liberal figures like Marx and Simmel, for whom modern capitalism constitutes an explosion of (respectively) use values or objective culture – the production of an unprecedented new sensorium – which dialectically produces humans as creatures who are 'rich in needs' (Marx) or 'refined' through an expanded (if fraught) subjective culture (Simmel). But we could also cite Latour yet again: whereas we used to believe that the more social connections there were, the less individual agency we have, social theory and practice increasingly operate with a 'productive' version of agency, often associated with Foucault, in which agency and power are not mutually limiting forces in a zero-sum game but rather co-constituting. As Latour puts it, the only way to liberate a puppet is not to cut the threads but to multiply good connections. 'The more attachments it has the more it exists' (2005: 217). It's hard to imagine Adam Smith disagreeing.

This kind of argument also seems important from another angle, one much more specific to development practice. Starting from this tradition of thought (embracing Smith, ANT and material culture studies), we would elaborate a far more complex version of both materiality and deprivation, and of the relation between these and ICTs (or any means of connection). As we have seen, the emphasis in these approaches is not on things as such, and therefore not on the enumeration of objects and possessions, money wealth or indices of accumulation, as if these could be proxies for the lifestyles that are accessible to particular people. Rather, the *relations* between entities, the density of connection and transaction, the number of full-blooded *mediators* (Latour) or objectifications (Miller 1987, 1998, 2001, 2012) are what are important. Quantification does indeed count for something in this tradition (Smith, Hegel, Marx and Simmel are all concerned with the expanding range of modern experience as an indicator of moral as well as material progress; Latour calls for ever more connection; Miller regards increased consumption as essential to the reflexive development of subjectivity). Poverty – lack of things and means – is not merely a result of arrested development; it is *in itself* an arrested process of development. This is not to say that 'poor people' have no culture or debased cultures. Precisely the opposite: the implication of ANT and material culture (and Marxism) is that 'real poverty' is the condition in which people do not have the material and symbolic resources for self-development, are not sufficiently connected. This leads us to a positive and expansive understanding of development – it is not about setting and satisfying quantitative minima or baselines of need, but about the far more complicated and maximal demand that social arrangements should support the open-ended, unfolding and self-directed process of development. This takes us close to Sen, in which the benchmark – which is defined differently in different places – is the capability to participate in those social processes which are locally deemed to be essential to being human and developing as a human (to be continued, and critiqued, in Chapter 6).

Tools and Transformations: The International Division of Ethics

Northern narratives of development that are elaborated through the material culture of ICTs are narratives of often extreme transformation in which both people and sociality are fundamentally altered; moreover, these narratives connect to much longer traditions of thinking about the relation between subjects and objects, people and their development through an expanded universe of entities to which they are connected. This is a dialectical view of the world in that entities emerge from their relationality, interactions or co-configurations. We could of course look at Maneeksha's development theories in a similar light, which is why it seemed important to examine her thinking as both instrumental and ethical, as not only about how to do things more efficiently (a concern that was uppermost in her own mind when it came to securing her daughter's future) but also what kind of person in which kind of relationships she might become through the very manner of her doing things.

It is precisely this kind of epistemological symmetry which is lacking in thinking through development as practised. Whereas northern subjects are seen as transforming through new mediations, southern beneficiaries of development are regarded more in the mode of tool users, and ICTs are regarded as tools rather than as material culture: development bureaucracies in general act solely on the instrumental relation to technology in which a person or community is expected to use new tools to achieve pre-given ends (or even basic needs generically defined in terms of hunger or health) without any expectation that they could, will or might want to be changed by the very experience of engaging with new material culture.

That is to say, the aesthetic form of ICTs in development is generally *not* the network but rather the tool; hence, the ethical framing of development worker and beneficiary is quite different, with the development worker belonging to a world-historical transformation from which the beneficiary is conceptually excluded. If there is a digital divide that should concern us, this is it: the supposed universality of new economy ethics posits an inclusiveness but – at least in this case – actually produces a very profound otherness. While promising to extend the material gains of new economy to the third world, it consigns that world to a quite separate ethical universe. And what applies at a project level also applies at the level of political economy: we have silicon valleys for the North, call centres and data entry factories for the South.

There can be no better example of this exclusionary thinking than Castells' bizarre distinction between the Net and the Self (Castells 1996a,1996b). In Castells' formulation, the Net denotes the new social structure of functional interconnection in which the North finds its new self.

> People increasingly organize their meaning not around what they do but on the basis of what they are, or believe they are. Meanwhile, on the other hand, global networks of instrumental exchanges selectively switch on and off individuals, groups, regions, and even countries . . . in a relentless flow of strategic decisions. There follows a fundamental split between abstract, universal instrumentalism, and historically rooted, particularistic identities. *Our societies are increasingly structured around a bipolar opposition between the Net and the self.* (Castells 1996b: 3)[2]

This seems to offer the very opposite to a relational view of agency as emergent from and understood through specific socio-technical assemblages. Rather it seems to map the classical sociological split between agency and structure, or the Habermasian distinction between system and lifeworld, onto North–South relations: 'the Net' is a reified logic of organization (global networks of instrumental exchanges) and 'the Self' is a residual sphere of meaning, identity and agency that is largely reactive – one asserts agency in opposition to 'the Net' not through it; or one resists the Net through the Self. And this assertion or resistance through the Self is oddly characterized as 'cultural' rather than structural or systemic; the Self is an affirmation of identity and a search for 'meaning and spirituality' that is largely identified with fundamentalism, nationalism, ethnicity and new social movements. There is a rather traditional notion of identity (and of culture) at play here: localized and bounded, hence eroded by the globalizing capacities of the network.

On the one hand, this division does not even apply to the North, as we have just seen (and as Castells [2001] himself argues). ICTs and the systems of 'the Net' are understood by northern analysts and participants neither as purely instrumental systems nor as opposed to 'the Self' and identity, but rather they already have a long track record as entities through which new forms of both system and self have been imagined and acted upon: our stories about cyberculture and new economy (and Castells' own 'network society' narrative) would make little sense otherwise. That is to say, 'the Net' has been elaborated as material culture not as instrumental tool or system. On the other hand, when Castells' distinction is mapped onto North–South relations, it places the modern North well within its normal conceptual coordinates: it is powerful, oppressive and scary, but it is also progressive and futuristic; whereas the (cultural) South is residual and regressive, however heroic (though only in its resistance), and it exhibits agency only in its attempts to retain its 'authenticity'. This positions 'the South' in a double-edged relationship to 'global networks of instrumental exchange': on the one hand they are – or should persist as – 'cultural' (heritage, indigeneity) in the face of instrumental global systems; on the other hand, their 'development' is seen in terms of instrumental integration into these systems (information access, off-shoring, computer literacy, etc.). It's a bit paradoxical: either the North is pure instrumentality and the South is all culture, resisting instrumentality; or the North has developed a new culture (network organization, creativity, anti-hierarchy) and the South appears as purely functional tool users seeking a place in the new division of labour, and not as transforming agents.

The option that Castells does not hold out to anyone in this Net/Self distinction is precisely the one that we have been trying to pursue throughout: southerners may be keen to re-imagine agency through new technologies and even to do so in utopian ways that bear comparison with northern imaginations. Yet there is little hint throughout Castells' work that southern people – like northern ones – might find their identity in and through new forms of mediation, that their actual use of mobile phones or internet might be part of a coherent self-formation rather than a subsumption within a northern network form.

'Empowerment'

A research workshop during the ictPR programme generated a heated, but very typical, debate about 'proper' use of ICTs in the projects: the favourite ICT activities of project 'beneficiaries' in South Asia was invariably games and entertainment (music, films) and – where internet connections were then available – 'communications', meaning chat, as opposed to 'information' (all of which we also saw in Ghana in the previous chapter). The default options for legitimating game playing in projects were either instrumental (e.g., playing games develops computer skills such as facility with the mouse and confidence in using computers, which can support further, 'more important' uses) or ethical (users' preferences and desires should be at least part of the equation). Disapproval of game playing was equally divided between the instrumental/economic (this is a scarce resource such that any improper use detracts from achieving serious aims) and the ethical (but really regulatory – the responsibility of project and staff is to knowledgeably promote development in ways mapped out by the project proposal; good and accountable governance must outweigh user preferences). Two additional issues informed both sides: 'taste' – there was something distasteful, even to those who were OK with playing games, about frivolous, personal and pop cultural use of this prestigious technology; and 'reputability' – whatever the researcher's view of playing games, the reputation and future of the project – with respect to stakeholders, funders, local constituencies, and so on – would very likely depend on other people's views of its perceived seriousness and its insulation from frivolous, taboo or illegal uses that might spark moral panic.

And then, predictably, one workshop day, a participating researcher was discovered playing solitaire on a computer during the tea break, with no evidence of irony, at least until the contradictions were pointed out by the others to great hilarity. For total comic effect, the researcher had of course been one of those who had most strongly disapproved of playing games. Immediately, all the questions raised during the discussion looked beside the point: the serious issues were not to do with determining what ICTs were really good for but rather how the ICTs were used to construct and position different participants as subjects or objects within development processes. The solitaire-playing researcher – who was university-educated and a stakeholder in her project, but was at the same time very local to that project – clearly distinguished a public position in which ICTs were tools to be used for exogenously defined ends (empowerment, poverty reduction, livelihood strategies) from her personal relation to ICTs, to which she immediately reverted when off-duty, or indeed off-stage (and which she could legitimately assume was understood and shared amongst the other participants by virtue of their similar social position and cultural capital). Put crudely, but not inaccurately, ICTs are tools for beneficiaries (and must be seen to be tools), whereas for the development workers ICTs are the medium or the infrastructure of their world, a *modus vivendi* and the ground on which they act and relate. Part of the researcher *not* seeing herself (as opposed to beneficiaries of her project) as someone to be developed or empowered was being able to see ICTs as complexly interwoven within her life, including feeling able to manage this interweaving in an ethically responsible manner: as a professional working under the terms of a 'network society', she felt herself able to balance solitaire playing with writing reports, managing email, using social media for networking, and so on, all on the same machine and indeed within one uniform technological flow. Had this event been observed today, with the ubiquity of Facebook and Twitter, these assumptions would likely have been even stronger (and she would not have been playing solitaire during the break but – like most of my students up North – would have been multitasking me and parallel streams of Facebook discussion and activity throughout the workshop).

The researcher unproblematically identified herself with what I have described as 'network ethics' that – beyond specific instrumental or transformative uses of ICTs – presume certain kinds of subjects in certain kinds of relations both to connection and to the available contemporary means of making connections. Neither she, nor anyone else in her particular project, subscribed to a cybercultural, new economy or even particularly Castellian version of this ethics for themselves let alone for poor beneficiaries in the projects. Nonetheless this event was built on new notions of career, agency and connection that she did not feel called upon to share outside of the northern networks in which they had been elaborated.

The development industry is in many respects very 'networky', very new economy: development workers at all levels carry out increasingly portfolio careers (McRobbie 1998; Sennett 2000) in which they might frequently move from contract labour on a specific project, to operating as a consultant, to employment within a large hierarchical organization like UNESCO; they coordinate and organize through networks that are instantiated and reproduced through heterogeneous communicative connections that involve a lot of email and mobile phones, conference circuits, and personal contacts with overlapping professional, political and friendship networks; and much of their work is defined in network terms (and as tasked with the production of networks) such as assembling partnerships and stakeholder groupings. This is the world described by Riles (2000), in which the entire meaning and rationality of being a development worker is defined by the injunction to 'Network!', to configure everything in terms of the aesthetic form of the network, and to treat everything as an instantiation of the network form. And the network form is to govern all forms of association, to the extent that modernization is increasingly synonymous with people's ability to perform network forms, whether in economic participation in global markets or NGO participation in the world of global governance. That is also to say that development itself – the transition of the backward regions into the normative future – is now measured by their 'networkiness'. Hence, network ethics need to be learned and performed by local development workers, and, indeed, to distinguish oneself (in a Bourdeuian sense) as part of the development apparatus from the poor beneficiaries of development means demonstrating oneself to be a networker and to be 'on the network'. And everyone uses the word 'networking' in both senses of digital interconnection and face-to-face schmoozing with exchange of business cards.

In sum: I think we can move easily from the matter of a right to play games on computers (and to feel that this is a part of one's natural relation to these machines, one's habitus) to the kind of world described by Riles in terms of 'Network!' as both an aesthetic form and a performative injunction (you must see and represent all connection in a networky way and you must treat that map as a template or plan for all organizing). What this simple story begins to introduce are the asymmetries in ethics: a distinction between different kinds of subjects for different kinds of development. New economy and network society embody ethical imaginations, visions of good agency and sociality. Their universalistic pretensions also necessarily involve the projection of this ethical vision: in my research, every time a development agency attempts to transfer ICTs – the obvious tools of the future – to southern peoples, it must also negotiate the extension of its ethical imagination to very different kinds of people. Can they, should they, conceptualize Delhi slum dwellers or Ghanaian palm oil smallholders as Nigel Thrift-style 'fast subjects', or *Wired*-style networkers, or as portfolio careerists, and so on? If they do,

is that a new form of imperialism? If they don't, is that a new division
into two humanities, a new international division of ethical personhood
and sociality?

'The ephemeral, the fugitive, the contingent'[3] in Delhi: Seelampur and other surprises

The challenge, then, is to see ICT for development in terms of a full-
blown network ethics, in which ICTs are fully a material culture through
which people (North and South) can imagine, articulate and enact social
change. Can we, in an almost Adornian move, capture for everyone's
development the utopian kernel that northerners have glimpsed in ICTs?
Could we even render this in the mode of Freire (2005 [1970]), as a
pedagogy whose developmental aim is to make not better tool users but
rather more reflexive social subjects, able to engage with and transform
their own historical direction? And is it possible that, under contemporary social conditions, this may well come down to the right to play
solitaire? In this section, I would like to think this possibility – and the
international division of ethics it critiques – in terms of the mechanics
of assemblage of several projects within the UNESCO ictPR programme
in South Asia (from which the Chennai stories at the start of this chapter
also came).

The solitaire-playing researcher was part of a programme, ictPR, that
was as a whole conceived in an extremely networky or new economy
way (the research organization will be described in detail in Chapter 6):
for example, it was conceived as innovative in its research organization
(even branding its methodology as 'Ethnographic Action Research') and
it was defined as a 'learning process'; the project was seen in terms of
linked nodes rather than line management, with network linkages effected
by a combination of ICTs and meetings between projects and researchers,
and one of its major outputs was a network of projects and researchers
that persisted after the programme ended; each project was structured
through stakeholder networks; and participants saw the programme in
terms of increasingly complex but cohesive connections with unpredictable outcomes, and (at least ultimately) as a licence to be creative and
exploratory.

Yet, against this backdrop, many individual projects were originally
conceived in quite narrowly instrumental, tool-using terms. The Seelampur project was an ICT project for young women situated in a very old
Muslim section of north-eastern Delhi, and specifically, and innovatively,
located in a *madrasa*, a religious education establishment for boys. The

project was initially conceived in an entirely anti-networky way, largely as vocational training. There was a long tradition of women's skills in dress-making and embroidery in the locale, and the aim of the project was initially simply to use computers and the internet as teaching aids, to help in design, to develop business skills and for supporting business-related functions such as marketing and bookkeeping. A second focus of the project was to use computer education to help young women to return to full-time education, both by giving them new skills and quali-fications, and by interesting them in education as a means of social advancement.

From the very first day of the project, the young women's actual use of the project and the media was gratifyingly contrary. Very briefly: firstly, the new media facilities were largely important in legitimizing access to a protected space in which the women could talk and socialize freely, have fun, develop relationships. Their media practices were incor-porated within a wider structuring of the project space into discussion areas, message boards and display spaces. Rather symbolically, the dress-making classes were soon held in the corridor outside the centre, whereas inside the computer centre very little happened that was textile-related. Secondly, their actual new media use ignored vocational skills and focused exclusively on creativity – drawing, singing, storytelling. Thirdly, their aesthetic practices drew on local traditional forms as one resource amongst many that embraced cartoons, magazines, films and mythologies across the Hindu–Muslim divide. Fourthly, there were strong indications that they resisted being ghettoized as traditional craft producers, and saw both their media use and occupational possibilities in more 'modern' terms: for example, their digital design practices were conceptualized more like graphic design or interior decoration than as craft. Even more extremely, one of the most enterprising young women actually started a business, but it was a computer business – she attempted to replicate the computer centre itself in her family's home village (unsuccessfully, it turned out, after which she turned to market-ing textiles).

Crucially, the ways in which the girls related to ICT as material culture revolved as much around the social and physical spaces it was part of constituting as around specific instrumental or 'empowering' tool-like uses. The project room itself was regarded and used as a place of social-ity, play and freedom, to the extent that the girls left their hijabs at the door and once inside felt able to say or do what they wanted. In discuss-ing the benefits of the centre, the girls unanimously and consistently emphasized sociability and free 'commerce': they often said that this was the first time they had had friends outside the family, or that they could discuss matters that were important to them. The girls, for example, took great joy in teasing me as well as the very upper-crust retired Indian army brigadier who was one of the project sponsors – two senior men whom they could not talk to outside these walls, let alone joke with informally. This was an interesting inversion of a remark by the *Maulana* (the major religious figure in charge of all religious education in the area, and hence of the *madrasa* in which the project was based): you foreigners, he said, think we oppress the women of our community, but they are entirely free to do what they like within the four walls of their room. In this case the room was a protected space, but one that was both socially shared and subsumed under the values that came with the project and its ICTs: the same kind of liberal, innovative, sociable, networky values that defined new media in the North. The most important spaces in the centre for much of the day were not the counter-tops with computers but rather the walls of the room, which became rapidly expanding bulletin boards, the banner that was regularly draped across the room with the name of the topic they were discussing each week, and the central floor area, which was generally where the chairs were pointing, in a discussion circle, rather than facing the computers along the counter-top. The connections through which these values and enactments of free sociability were attached to 'ICTs' are hard, maybe impossible, to summarize, partly because they had to do with form and modality as much as specific mechanical attachments, forms that shaped the space as much as they shaped practices or meanings. The computers clearly symbolized freedoms and associations because they came wrapped in that package, not least through UNESCO's framing of those machines in this specific programme; but equally it was in that social space that the girls could find and act on very contradictory possibilities in these machines. But without a doubt what the girls valued most in and through this material culture was *connection*, and connection meant more than anything, to the extent that any particular activity seemed to be more a vehicle, or even alibi, for sociality rather than sociality being a means to carry out any particular activity.

This kind of thing happened throughout the programme and made for 'development' as a series of surprises and disruptions to the programme: specifically, we had to attend to the overall *space* constituted around the ICTs (literally as well as metaphorically) much more than to the specific uses or even their affordances in any meaningful sense of that word. Two parallel examples:

In Sitikunde, located in a traditional largely Muslim rural area in Bangladesh, there was an even more extreme spatial separation of instrumental and ethical engagements with the computer: partly through a combination of a boring computer literacy teacher and the narrow approach of the main stakeholder, the young people using the centre were excited but frustrated. The classes were not engaging in either style or content, but nonetheless gave them two shockingly powerful experiences: firstly (as almost everywhere), basic drawing with MS Paint gave them a taste, or reminder, of the sensation of creativity in the sense of play unstructured by educational angst; secondly, boys and girls found themselves sitting together, talking freely, informally and in the cooperative pursuit of an engaging task (painting, not literacy). They took these experiences next door to an empty room adjoining the computer room, originally intended as a library for computer manuals (i.e., an extension of the more instrumental uses of the machine), which they turned into a youth club in which boys and girls from the classes could sit together to do nothing that was explicitly connected to ICTs – play music, sing, gossip, *socialize* – except that it too was all a reinvention and reorganization of the values of connection. Unsurprisingly, this meeting place became the object of moral panic and had a precarious existence; however, there was clear evidence that elements or offshoots from it rapidly extended into other youth practices in the community, with some impact on gender relations.

In Darjeeling, the project involved four computer centres strung out along the Himalayan railway leading up to Darjeeling itself, symbolically paralleling the old railway with a new information conduit. This somewhat romantic imagery played very little role in practice; there were in fact simply four centres which each developed contrasting styles, practices and organizational cultures. At one of the centres, with a significant and enthusiastic youth involvement, it became clear that although there was much enthusiasm for doing stuff on ICTs (painting was as popular here as anywhere), what engaged people in a more immediate but also more political way was the very idea of information, and above all of *free* information (in the sense of being costless, of being freely accessible regardless of caste, class, gender or age, of information circulating freely). The right to information: the centre was an enactment and representation of the principle that you did not have to pay someone to find out the name of a decent doctor or what government grants were available; you did not even have to find a more educated mediator to do it for you. This idea evolved in many different ways: demonstrations of information access by the workers; the enactment of the free circulation of information through the mundane sociability of people hanging out in this space; statements by staff, UNESCO and others; the computer and the internet as an already recognizable icon of information access. But above all, all this was crystallized in 'the wall': the core of the centre (which the staff finally renamed from a 'computer centre' to an 'information centre') was a wall on which people could post job ads, lists of doctors, lawyers and other expertise, notices of educational opportunities and so on.

People knew these bits of information to have been sourced from anywhere, including ICTs, but equally word of mouth or the press: it really
didn't matter. The wall made visible and meaningful a communicative
assemblage that embodied free information through unhindered connection and sociability.

A story from a neighbouring project in Darjeeling gets at the same
point from another angle: a man said that he had never been able to
watch a television before the free space of the centre was opened, for the
simple reason that the only TVs in the area were in the houses of upper-
caste people which he was not allowed to enter as a member of a lower
caste; where sociability would mean ritual defilement in one context, it
was a regulating principle in the project. It would be hard to find a clearer
example of the revaluation of connection, but one less easy to pin down
to either the instrumental or symbolic affordances of an ICT.

At Seelampur (and to a more restricted degree in Sitikunde and Darjeeling, because the researchers and project staff were not supported in
the same way by stakeholders), the project workers were exceptionally
responsive to these developments, and effectively tore up their project
proposal and strategy and rethought it from scratch, choosing to take
their lead from the participants – a possibility that was open to them
because of the structure of this particular UNESCO programme. Similar
situations arose across the entire UNESCO programme, though the
response of project workers and of stakeholder NGOs was variable and
complex. What I can certainly generalize across the programme was that
all project staff had to contend with the fact that their beneficiaries were
generally using the new media more like *they* were and much less as they
were meant to.

It should be noted that the Seelampur project was a place of conflict
and disagreement like any other project, and particularly in one respect
that we have already discussed in relation to Maneeksha: worry over
the conflicting demands of instrumentality and ethics, formal/creden-
tialled development and 'transformative' development, or two different
versions of empowerment. Some of the more anticipated lines of tension
did not materialize (e.g., gender or family conflicts); the main tension –
which was expressed largely but not exclusively in disapproval from
the girls' mothers – was about whether they were wasting their time
on frivolous activities that would not get them anywhere; more specifically, whether the centre was of any use if it did not provide structured computer skills teaching leading to exams, qualifications and
credentials. The girls, who were in no doubt about the multiple
values of what they were doing, nonetheless also felt conflicted about
this, and eventually the staff did introduce conventional classes and
qualifications.

Conclusion

Development, whose ostensible aim is equalization and inclusion, is precisely where you would expect to find asymmetry, division and distance, as well as some of the more circuitous ways of trying to reconcile these polarities. Our concern with new media provides a different vantage on this situation: if we can get some distance on the instrumental questions (do new media aid development or not, and technically how could they help it more or hinder it less), we can look at the ways in which 'everyone' is necessarily involved in re-theorizing social change through this particular form of material culture, and that this material culture raises the most profound questions about the nature of connection, and therefore about the kinds of social agency and social relations that could make up our worlds. The most politically urgent issue that this raises concerns not so much access to new digital resources but rather the ability to raise and pursue these questions and therefore everyone's right to be recognized as a development theorist and strategist whose views of social change should be treated seriously and rendered potentially consequential.

5

Scaling Practices and Devices
Globalizing Globalization

Globalization is the final term in our title to be reworked from resource to topic, to be returned from framework to fieldwork. Like many such terms, globalization has largely transcended its period of vogue and controversy and passed into common parlance. It is therefore worth starting the discussion with a story from earlier days, when the linkages between new media, development and globalization were still fresh. As often happens, this event occurred on nearly the last day of fieldwork, in Trinidad (Miller and Slater 2000). Miller and I had built up a consistent picture of new media in Trinidad in which people, regardless of ethnicity, age or gender, were confidently taking on the internet as if it was a natural part of their lives, and its naturalness appeared to be based partly on an affinity with its cosmopolitan reach. Trinidadians, we came to argue, had long understood themselves to be global actors either by force of modern diremptions (slavery and indentured labour) or by their own energies (they felt equal to acting on many global stages). That is to say, Trinidadians all had a view on 'the global', and they very articulately as well as practically used the internet to represent and enact their relation to very wide spatial scales. For example, we were able to explore the religious understandings of the internet (both Catholic and Pentecostal) as both representation of and means to achieve God's community on earth; young people in cybercafés treated distant online contacts as entirely equivalent to those physically co-present, to the extent that we could not tell from interviews whether a 'fiancé' who was mentioned was 'real' or 'virtual'. Most dramatically, our fieldwork coincided with Trinidad hosting the Miss Universe contest. Trinidadians were passionately concerned to demonstrate not only that they could throw a world-class party and public event, but that they could do so online, mounting a then state-of-the-art, world-class website, and could use this to leverage long-term connections to blue-chip software companies, including Oracle and Microsoft. Trinidadian businesspeople explicitly claimed that this achievement would not only secure their leadership role in the Caribbean but also catapult them into global markets.

These are all examples of what we will call 'scaling practices', the construction and mapping of connections at different distances, in which the metrology is objectified in the practice itself: people understood the internet in terms of the kinds of scales they believed it capable of producing. Hence the Miss Universe site demonstrated to Trinidadians the many ways in which the internet might raise the island from a local Caribbean place to a global player on international stages. We can therefore also talk about the internet as a 'scaling device' – people made and imagined connections both in the practical use of its affordances and in the kind of spatialized world they could imagine in and through it. This idea of scaling practices also connects to the idea of 'locality' as constructed at the intersection of particular relations (Massey 1992, 1995, 1996; Moores 2003, 2005, 2012; Savage, Bagnall and Longhurst 2005): Trinidadians defined themselves as 'a locality' by locating themselves in the devices and practices through which they made and measured connections at a range of distances. This was as true of the internet as of many other scaling devices and practices, such as migration, to which the internet was of course closely connected (Madianou and Miller 2012; Miller 2011).

This was the context for the event I want to discuss, an invitation-only breakfast seminar for the cream of the Trinidadian business community in June 1999, at which the main speakers were Canadian representatives of IBM and KPMG. The message they delivered was that the internet and the information-based new economy would be the last train to global modernity, productivity and profit. This train, they said, has already left the station, but if the Trinidadian elite run very quickly they might just jump on the caboose. The Trini response was both feverish and self-castigating: the participants already entirely accepted that the global internet was the inevitable future; the seminar simply stunned them with the amount of ground they had already lost, yet again, in securing their proper place on the global stage; they felt (and were told) that this was their 'last chance'. Globalization is the technologically propelled next wave of history from which you will be excluded if you don't move fast; and in fact you may already have missed it, you may already have been finally and irrevocably left behind by the future (Slater 2008). This was a disturbing message for people who saw themselves as intrinsically global actors.

This breakfast seminar effectively globalized globalization: Trinidadian practices and devices for constructing scales and locating themselves within them, for placing themselves and making places, were replaced by the imposition of a universal process – globalization – in relation to which 'Trinidad' was a local instantiation. This opposition between the globalization of 'globalization' by KPMG and IBM and the everyday scaling practices of Trinidadians was not only stark but it was also articulated in the form of panic. Trinidad could merely fall into one of any number of local types (resistant, residual, progressive, authentic, marginal and excluded, Castellian black hole or pre-modern selfhood), all defined in relation to a new paradigm of interconnection that was entirely abstract but at the same time universal, inevitable and a quasi-natural force or law. Indeed, 'globalization' as presented that morning was not simply something that was happening but rather took on the status of a Kantian *a priori* that precedes the phenomenal world (Savage, Bagnall and Longhurst 2005). 'Globalization' was an empty and abstract measurement of 'connection', much as one would see from social network mappings of internet interconnections; a structuring dimension like space and time. To be clear, KPMG and IBM were also performing scaling practices, but this is not how they appeared: they spoke for a future time and an impersonal, containing space in relation to which everyone – themselves, Trinidadians, businesspeople anywhere – were mere particulars. And in at least one obvious sense 'mere particulars' is precisely what they were transformed into. The same scaling and geo-positioning were endlessly repeated, such that the governmental elite in Ghana, as we have seen, could spend several years writing up white papers on the country's transformation into an instantiation of information society. To quote a key policy document, *'There is no doubt* that the world economy is experiencing the impact of rapid globalization and the emerging information age – which is bringing about a new global economic order to be dominated by information and knowledge-based economies (IKEs)' (Dzidonu 2003: 62). With similar certainty, the WSIS concluding declaration could position the entire world with the words, 'The emergence of the global Information Society to which we all contribute provides increasing opportunities for all our peoples and for an inclusive global community that were unimaginable only a few years ago' (WSIS 2005). Apparently we 'all' now live in an exceedingly abstract space.

Globalization as Development Narrative and Scalar Narrative

Increasingly over the past twenty years, development and new media have been naturally connected through the idea of globalization: the three terms are so fused that each automatically implies and includes the other two. In these accounts, new media exemplify, or cause, new forms and orderings of connectedness that compress time and space such that, as Giddens (1981, 1999, 2001) argued, events in one place have immediate impact elsewhere, or, as Castells (1999, 2000) maintained, the normal (and optimal) form of social coordination has become networks characterized by the coordination of spatially dispersed action in real time. Globalization was generally understood as technologically driven by ICTs and information flows. Despite ritual denials of technological determinism (e.g., Castells 1996a: 15–16), globalization appeared as a reduction of all exchange (political, economic, cultural, social) to access to circuits of information which could be represented by, or simply equated with, the internet. We now live in a technically interconnected world; the only question is who is left out of the networks (digital divides and informational black holes).

Globalization could be described as a 'scalar narrative' (Gonzalez 2006), or perhaps as itself containing numerous possible scalar narratives in the sense that there are many varying mappings of increased global interconnectedness: accounts of how the world will work that make connections between events in time or space (Cameron and Palan 2004a, 2004b). The idea of scalar narrative, defined by Gonzalez (as 'those stories that actors tell about the changes in the scalar localization of socio-political processes' (2006: 839), is useful, and we will particularly focus on how globalization narratives produce new maps of the world. However, it is important that the idea of globalization is not solely about spatial distribution; it is also a development narrative. Globalization is a theory of social transformation, a story about the future of the world and its transformational logics, a way of making sense of change and rationally coordinating action along the lines we laid out in the previous chapter. Conversely, development narratives have always also been about spatial distributions and connections, even when this dimension has been limited to the unequal distributions of the capital necessary for whatever development logic is currently regarded as normative.

This point is underlined by the fact that, to some extent, 'globalization' was invoked to replace or supersede 'development', if we define the latter in terms of the post-war, postcolonial project of global modernization (Lewis and Mosse 2006). As foreign direct investment, capital flows, transnational corporations, private remittances and other transnational arrangements have increasingly dwarfed international aid, 'globalization' appeared to render 'development' marginalized, or needing to migrate into new forms appropriate to the new scalar narratives (as we have seen in Chapter 4, the network ethic, but also global governance and international NGOs). Moreover, 'globalization' has appeared to replace 'development' as a kind of non-ideological substitute for structural adjustment and neo-liberalism: no longer would North–South relations be organized through donors but rather through autochthonous, technologically enabled networks of deregulated interconnections, governed by new institutional structures defined at a supra-state level. That is to say, even within the development industry, the very ideas of modernization, social justice and rights moved onto the terrain of globalization. Whether globalization was simply neo-liberalism by another name (as evidenced in the World Trade Organization) or whether it afforded the possibility of 'globalization from below' or 'emancipatory cosmopolitanism' (Pieterse 2006), the project formerly known as 'development' would henceforth work through a different logic and different actors and networks. Moreover, as a development narrative, the idea of ICT-driven globalization had an urgency that was not only unprecedented but extreme, invoking an 'imperative to connect' enforced through policy and funding patterns (Green, Harvey and Knox 2005). Unlike previous developmental waves, ICT-driven globalization appeared impersonal and inevitable: 1960s/1970s modernization spoke in the name of a teleology of progress but was clearly contextualized within unequal North–South power; 1990s structural adjustment was clearly ideological; but ICT-driven globalization appeared as a force of nature to which both North and South were subordinate.

Media, technology and globalization

The contextualizing of development within globalization, and the general production and globalization of 'the global' as a universal position from which to see all localities (and within which all localities must position themselves), depend on claims about mediation and communication: if new economy is the future, then the future is informational and entirely dependent on digital media that are inherently globalizing. But looking in more detail at how globalization claims rest on claims about communication gives us a greater vantage on the process of globalizing globalization: as in Trinidad, we are looking at the difference between media as scaling devices through which people make connection, and media as a universal measure of connection in relation to which 'localities' are evaluated and must position themselves.

We can do this firstly by looking at academic discourses on globalization, a move that is warranted by the simple fact that these academic discourses are often directly cited and used within development, and therefore appear in this account as performative parts of the field as opposed to theories to be critiqued here. Gonzalez (2006), for example, provides an interesting account of how academics are cited in development planning to source and to authorize particular scalar narratives. Similarly, Green, Harvey and Knox offer a detailed story of the 'imperative to connect' as a directive implemented through the EU in several digital Manchester projects: '[I]t was regularly asserted that all this effort was simply a reflection of an inexorable transformation of the world into a "network society" (Castells 1996[c]); the transformation was already under way, irrespective of the activities of the European public sector,' and Castells was regularly cited by participants to confirm this 'inexorable transformation' and 'as proof of the urgency of implementing and completing the development projects in which people were engaged' (Green, Harvey and Knox 2005: 807).

We can start with David Held's definitions (Held, McGrew, Goldblatt and Perraton 1999): globalization is a way of looking at social change though the transformation of interconnection in terms of density, extension, velocity, impact. The very possibility of this kind of linkage, in this argument, clearly depends on electronic transmission of information: time-space compression or distantiation. By the same token, it is hard not to attribute a causal role to new media technologies, or to slip from necessary to sufficient cause: all globalization theorists have to take a position on technological determinism (i.e., they need to ritually disavow it) for the usual reasons diagnosed by Latour et al. (having separated out technology and society, connection is either technical or social, when of course it is always already both). Held relies largely on Thompson, whose formulation, as we have seen, includes a strong sense of mediation that is not entirely at odds with ANT: the way in which we connect changes the ways in which we relate, which is surely unarguable.

More problematical, however, is the central axis in this globalization concept: the idea of 'connection'. It is not simply that the term is never defined and covers pretty much any linkage between any social things such that any contact might count as connection: at this level of generality one would not expect a tight definition. Rather, there is an immediate leap to entirely contingent lists of types of connection – political, economic, social, cultural – that are identified as important from within a theory of globalization but for other social theoretical reasons: the grand narrative of social theory itself. In this way, 'connection' comes to represent an abstract measure that can be applied to anything: any particular can be an instance of 'connection', much as any 'locality' can be an instance of 'the global'. On this basis globalization can clearly travel.

We have already seen a similar logic at work in Castells' opposition of Net versus Self (which also looks suspiciously like system versus life-world): the global is an abstract and formal vector defined in terms of an empty but universal category – connection – whereas 'the local' comes to be defined in terms of the substantive, of content, of particularity (this also feels rather like exchange value versus use value). In a very sharp paper, Shaun Moores (2003) teases out the way in which Castells' notion of the structural logic of the 'space of flows' becomes increasingly abstract while the notion of place becomes correspondingly overly concrete. Whereas Castells at first seems to argue that 'place' becomes absorbed in the network and therefore has to be understood relationally, and in relation to flows, he then asserts that '[a] place is a locale whose form, function and meaning are self-contained within the boundaries of physical contiguity' (Castells 1996c: 423, in Moores 2003: 3–4). Once again new media flows produce an abstract global space in relation to which locality persists as a romanticized essence, to be protected and persevered, and which relies on a simplistic notion of (physical) contiguity and co-presence that denies the relational and scaled character of anything and everything that might count as 'a location'.

Globalization narratives, then, have been grounded in claims about the media in the material culture sense that new media provide a way of thinking and enacting a particular concept of 'connection'. It is an abstract and empty notion of connection, and therefore a framing one in that it can subsume any form of link and evaluate it in terms of norms of progressive, developmental linkage – the network. Green, Harvey and Knox nicely capture the way in which the new 'imperative to connect' plays upon abstraction. It is precisely because the new media appear 'space-defying' that they might be useful in 'political place-making projects': politically orchestrated reconfigurations of spatial relations in practice could be treated as 'simply a reflection of an inexorable transformation of the world into a "network society"' (Green, Harvey and Knox 2005: 806).

In some respects, this account is unexceptional (and therefore travels well to almost anywhere) because it is virtually a truism. It would be absurd to deny that – all other things being equal (and there are of course rather a lot of other things out there) – new media enable faster, wider, deeper, more immediate connections, as well as endless meta-discourse on connection. I've certainly not yet had a field experience in which people did not reflect on technology and connection. For example, when asked what email is, school children in Sri Lanka generally explained that it was extremely fast or instantaneous mail. But to reduce all connection to this kind of abstract connection (rather like reducing the material specificity of 'use value' to the common denominator of 'utility') is to miss out the essential issue of how people deploy media to make particular kinds of connections at particular kinds of distances and classify them into different kinds of scales. That is quite a different kind of enterprise from the globalization discourse, or scalar narrative, which constitutes the global as a place or vantage point from which to observe localities. And this is not ameliorated by complexifying local–global dynamics or rejecting old homogenization theses. There is an imposition of scale, global versus local, which structures media use at the same time as claiming to be structured by it. In this sense, we can treat the very notion of 'the global' as a heuristic that invokes scales in order to produce locality as a space of divergence, difference, the particular and the multicultural (Savage, Bagnall and Longhurst 2005; Strathern 1995a, 1995b; Wastell 2001; Wilk 1994a, 1994b, 1995, 2006).

Scaling, Scaling Practices and Scaling Devices

The academic discussions of globalization and their performative adoption in development contexts appear to be clear examples of Latour's claim that social scientists 'use scale as one of the many variables they need to set up before doing the study, whereas scale is what actors achieve by scaling, spacing, and contextualizing each other through the transportation in some specific vehicles of some specific traces' (2005: 183–4). Actors invest hugely in the framing of connections, which is essential to their world-making activities; the logics and practices integral to the ways in which they make associations must be allowed expression in our analyses and not simply be placed within or replaced by the analyst's absolute scale. Rather, Latour argues, we need to be able to flow, empirically, from one frame to the next, and – we would add – to bring our own analytical frames into heuristic conversation with all the others in the field.

The obvious response is the conventional ANT one to which we have regularly resorted: retreat to an infra-language that allows the actors to speak their own spatial constructions without privileging any particular spatial classification and allowing it to contain or frame all the others. Indeed, this move is even more important in the case of 'globalization' in that the language of local and global connects directly to the languages of universal and particular, formal and substantive, deep structural and contingent that lie at the heart of modernity's 'God's-eye' construction of knowledge: 'the global' is a view from modernity's 'nowhere'.

The infra-language deployed here has been used by Latour, and will be presented largely in his terms: the new language is one of scale, scaling, scaling practices and scaling devices (though the term has also been current in geography and is also particularly associated with Strathern's work on comparative anthropology). In Latour, 'the global' is identified with the modernist stance, exemplified in idealized views of science, that takes a God's-eye position, a view from above, the perspective of a disembodied Cartesian brain in a vat, entirely separated from the externalized world of objects. Latour's deflationary strategy is one in which '[t]he global is accompanied back to the rooms in which it is produced' and returned to the 'life supports' and 'ecosystems' which sustain it (2009: 140). This is not a reductive move in the sense that nothing is lost because 'the global' has never been a habitable space, a space that anyone could actually occupy. It is, rather, the modernist non-space: 'There is no access to the global for the simple reason that you always move from one place to the next through narrow corridors without ever being outside' (2009: 141).

> Is space [something] inside which reside objects and subjects? Or is space one of the many connections made by objects and subjects? In the first tradition, if you empty the space of all entities there is something left: space. In the second, since entities engender their space (or rather their spaces) as they trudge along, if you take the entities out, nothing is left, especially space. (2009: 142)

Hence, 'The global is part of local histories' (2009: 142). Latour in fact retains the language of local and global in order to play around with it: much of *Reassembling the Social* (2005), for example, is structured around this opposition as it provides a point of entry into the contrast between modernist and flattened topographies: to the extent that we retain any notion of 'global', it should presumably open up critical investigation of how we construct and deploy the widest and most generalized views of the world, the ones which the moderns take to naturally but which are in fact uninhabitable spaces. 'We have never been global' in the sense that 'the global' is not the different level, place or God's-eye view that it takes itself to be, and not a kind of non-spatial space that contains everything ('the universe'); it is rather 'a form of circulation' within mundane networks, and 'not what could contain them' (Latour 2009: 141). 'The global' marks out this space of the generalized in Latour; we could equally say that the term 'global' marks out his engagement with modernist positions on space and universality (including the current obsession with globalization), whereas anthropologically we need to be even more general, in a Strathernian manner, and keep entirely open the question of scaling and the classifications of scale, as well as the clash of scales that is incipient in and constitutive of every ethnographic encounter (Strathern 2004 [1991]).

By the same token, 'locality' or place is not an origin or authenticity, or only when it has been effectively black-boxed: 'An "interaction" is a site so nicely framed by localizers behaving as intermediaries that it can be viewed, without too much trouble, as "taking place locally"' (Latour 2005: 202). From this perspective, locality or place is an intersection, an identifiable, stabilized, named crossroads where often very far-flung trails connect (Moores 2003). As Latour puts it, most elements of local interactions are already given from somewhere and to find the local we have to trace 'the meandering path through which most of the ingredients of action reach any given interaction' (2005: 193).

The categories of local and global, then, help us get a grip on a modernist game, the construction of an abstract and topological ordering of the world, the construction of a position or standpoint on that world, and the construction of a system of measurement in which every particular place is rendered identical in the sense that all places are 'particulars' in relation to the universal or global. But the overarching, or infralinguistic, term that contains all this is 'scaling': we can think about the ways in which people identify, classify, construct and act upon connections at different degrees of proximity and distance, but without making any *a priori* assumptions about the shape of the connections or how they are represented. We certainly should not assume that the terms local and global, let alone globalization, even feature in any particular person's spatial classifications and scalings; or, as in the case below, we might find that participants have multiple locals and no real global. What we mainly need to focus on are scaling practices and scaling devices, the means by which people assemble and act upon scales. As in the case of Asturias in the next section, we would want to look at several features of scaling practices: the actual connections that people make and stabilize and the means they use to do this; what counts as a connection and what doesn't; what connections are valued and why; how connections and the distribution of connections are represented (the maps people make); the devices that are deployed in the making of connections (including communicative objects and assemblages); and the narratives, explanatory models, strategies, projects and principles that people formulate to conceptualize connection.

Asturias: Scaling Cultural Flows in Northern Spain[1]

We can look at a very concrete fieldwork experience of these rather abstract issues and explore how one might move from 'globalizing globalization' to thinking about 'scaling' and scaling practices. This was a research project that, usefully, comes from the North – Spain – rather than from a classically underdeveloped southern place. The story was nonetheless framed as a development story by the northern actors involved: it was a story about the regional regeneration through cultural policy of a long-declining industrial working-class province – Asturias – that was to be revived by catapulting itself out of the industrial age and into the new economy of creative industries. An exceptionally diverse set of actors were signed up, enthusiastically, to the building of a mammoth cultural centre, the Oscar Niemeyer Cultural Centre (CCON), that would tap into global cultural flows and divert them to the rust-belt town of Aviles, initially in the form of tourists (who might, for example, get package tours that would also include the neighbouring Bilbao Guggenheim), but also in the form of under-specified knock-on effects, such as the retention of local human resources (youth who would otherwise migrate), the synergetic stimulus to local creative and cultural activity and a generally profitable rebranding of the place with international recognition. Symbolically, the cultural centre was to be built on reclaimed and detoxified industrial waste-land, formerly part of the steel industry that had dominated the economy until its decline – land which lay across the river upon which the bourgeois inner city had turned its back long ago. Whereas only recently the old medieval core of Aviles had been pedestrianized and turned in on itself as a picturesque tourist destination, the city was now to turn around and open up sight-lines to the global cultural industries springing up on the other bank.

This development strategy depended on the constant demonstration, the materializing, the reiterated citation, if you will, of 'global culture' and Asturias' real or potential place in it. The entire project originated with some young and rising, elite-educated young diplomats in the office of the Prince of Asturias Trust, an organization that conferred an annual Prince of Asturias prize (which was often referred to as the Spanish Nobel Prize) for cultural achievement, generally to iconic household names of global culture such as Woody Allen, Stephen Hawking, Bob Dylan and Norman Mailer. The young men wanted to move beyond merely giving out a prize and started to leverage this global connectedness into a project that would capture and channel more global cultural capital to regenerate the region, with which the Prince of Asturias had long been associated. The project started with plans for an enormous cultural white box donated by a previous Asturias prize-winner, Oscar Niemeyer, who – it was wryly noted – had long expertise in depositing modernizing buildings in the middle of nowhere (he was the architect of Brasilia). The whole project depended on both invoking global culture (scaling practices) and positioning Asturias within it through a building (scaling device) and the networks constructed around it. And in this context, the researchers (Ariztia-Larrain and myself) as well as the London School of Economics (LSE) were enlisted. CCON planned to convoke an annual meeting of the 'C8' – the Cultural 8, along the lines of the G8 – of leading players in global culture, such as the Lincoln Center, the Pompidou Centre, the Barbican and . . . CCON. And the LSE, which was not only itself a global intellectual brand, but was also particularly closely associated with the theorizing of globalization, particularly through its former director, Anthony Giddens, and David Held.

Hence, to use Latour's phrase, (global) scale was very clearly not a realist force, context or structure but was rather 'what actors achieve by scaling, spacing, and contextualizing each other'. The 'global' was persistently invoked and staged as the vehicle and legitimation of the project, but also as something constructed through the project itself: the meeting of the 'C8' *was* globalization. And CCON's entire aim was to position itself within this scaling, though this was ambiguous – or 'fudged', as we described it – in that all these enrolled and invoked actors had quite different concepts of both culture and global culture, and different models (development theories) as to how 'global cultural flows' connected up to each other and to other (economic, political) processes. Yet the continuation of the project depended on maintaining agreement about these things even though very little actually existed. CCON, partly owing to its roots in the Asturias prize, and partly to distinguish itself from a crowded field of other centres (above all the Bilbao Guggenheim), positioned itself at the 'cool' end of global culture: it would have a commitment to the highest cultural 'standards', to a sense of global culture as a culture of global (i.e., world-class) quality, recognition and significance, but its paradigmatic offering was seen in terms of art film (both showings and an archive) rather than, say, fine art. The feather in its cap was Woody Allen's new-found love of the region. At the same time, this version of scaling and positioning sat in uneasy – 'fudged' – relation to competing ones that needed to be enlisted: the president, the mayor, the cultural managers, the local arts activists. The president of Asturias, for example, had an entirely different model of cultural flow: tourists would be enticed to Asturias by CCON, and once there would be diverted into experiencing its local national culture – Asturian cuisine, music, landscape and national forests, history, and so on. By contrast, the president's minister of culture, an economist, imagined cultural flow entirely in terms of ticket sales. Everyone was enthusiastically signed up to the project, but often on the basis of entirely different or even conflicting cultural maps of the world.

At which point we come to the research itself. It needs to be said that at first CCON was unclear as to whether it wanted actual research that could be used or whether it merely wanted the symbolic presence of the LSE (as global brand and as theorist of globalization). Our mere presence was another citation of the reality of globalization and global culture. We pressed for the opportunity to do substantive research and the negotiated result was another expression of the same strategy that CCON was pursuing throughout: we were asked to do a study of youth culture and new media which would provide a basis for thinking about youth participation in CCON. The research was initially conceived in local–global terms in which CCON represented or spoke for 'the global' and youth were 'the local', conceptualized as a place into which CCON would need to be embedded (not just economically but also culturally, socially, experientially) in order to become part of the place. Conversely, this embedding depended on the participation of the local, including youth, in the various cultural offerings of the centre and hence their participation in 'the global'. In other words the very framing of the research – in terms of local–global culture – already enrolled everyone in the globalization of globalization in general and of CCON as a specific project of globalization.

However, the situation could be put rather differently, and this governed the actual research: CCON – both the project and the projected building – could be understood as a 'scaling device', as an assemblage that actors could use to do all that 'scaling, spacing, and contextualizing [of] each other'. What kind of device was it? What kinds of scales did it project? What kinds of scales as well as dialogues and reflections upon scale could it allow between its various participants, including the 'local' youth it constructed through its very operation? By the same token, what were the scaling practices of the young people we researched and in whom CCON wanted to find a local anchor; and what devices did they use in their scaling? Let me first give a summary description of research findings, and then we can tease these out analytically into four themes through which we can relate this research story to others, including some of the ICT4D stories already discussed.

The ways in which the young people we researched scaled practices and relationships, and the ways they classified them, did not map onto the local–global classifications of CCON, or its characterizations of either of these terms, and they could not be contained within any simple local–global dichotomy, although of course the young people we talked with could all use these categories according to their conventional and official meanings. 'Locality', for example, as the place in which one lived or acted, was understood in various senses, and articulated through various devices. Three 'localities' loomed large in interviews and walkabouts. Firstly, Aviles was clearly a particular city, with an official identity which could be represented in terms of things like tourist maps and

CCON as a regional development project, about which 16 year olds could be extremely informed and articulate. Secondly, 'the local' was *smaller* than Aviles, in that for teenagers it consisted of particular places and routes, specific streets and venues, that were temporally assembled into 'an evening', a party, an errand, a social life. Thirdly, locality was *larger* than Aviles, for two reasons. On the one hand, most young people considered Aviles too small to sustain a social life, so it had to be assembled across the wider conurbation, Oviedo–Asturias–Gijon, as a result of which the significant scaling devices were in fact bus schedules, SMS and Fotolog (a Spanish-language-based alternative to Facebook or Myspace). On the other hand, seasonality normally included spending summers with family, generally grandparents, in rural Asturias, which thereby defined a 'locality' (particularly in contrast to the alternative of holidaying in a cooler part of Spain or Europe). In addition, a fourth sense of locality could be gleaned in young people's new media use, which was overwhelmingly 'local' in the sense of being used to mediate practical and social connections with people they would, or could, meet otherwise, face-to-face. The normal pattern of new media use was anchored in Fotolog, where the links and contact we traced were overwhelmingly Asturian, then Spanish- or Spanish-language-based, and rarely led to centres of 'global popular culture' (US or UK) and seemed rather to be embedded in relationships that were as likely to be equally pursued in the street, school and club. This was integrated into phone and messenger/chat use, in which new media were really about carrying on conversations that may have started on the street with boyfriends or girlfriends, arranging meetings or getting help with homework.

Following the Fotolog contacts of our interviewees indicated that there was almost no connection to any of the 'global' places that would make up CCON's cultural map. Intriguingly, even some hiphop-related websites were as likely to lead to Spanish (Barcelona- and Madrid-based) and Latin American sites as to the expected US or UK ones. Young people were intensely aware of other people's maps: they had a clear idea of what might count as global culture, and could discuss the production values of, say, Hollywood film in comparison to Spanish film. But this was only one kind of cultural conversation, and, moreover, young people's scaling at levels above the various 'locals' was based on quite different criteria than CCON's. Two kinds of large scale emerged from the research, both of which look more like regional or meso-categorizations than global ones. Firstly, young people mainly talked about the non-local in terms of interesting places one might go on holiday or on school trips or exchanges or when one was old enough to travel without one's family. Secondly, rather than valorizing places in terms of their position in global cultural flows, young people talked about 'cool places', and cool places were defined in terms of music as paradigmatic of real cultural experience. Cool places were those reckoned to have a cosmopolitan diversity of music, and most of it in the form of live gigs. What made a cool scene cool wasn't so much where the music came from (i.e., the fact that you could get easier access to the latest hiphop in Madrid than in Aviles), but rather the surrounding quantity, diversity, liveness and dynamism. And by this definition, young people were as likely to talk about Madrid and Barcelona as London or New York.

This clearly sent a message to CCON: young people were saying, fairly consistently across the research, we can see the merits of this regional development strategy and support it, but we have no interest in its cultural content unless it conforms to our paradigmatic case of culture, 'the gig'. Global connection has no value for us if it does not have the qualities that we look for in connections and associations. That is to say, the mapping of scale in the end came down to a definition of 'culture' – the live gig – which they clearly did not share with or recognize in the CCON project. Right at the start, this distinction emerged in conversations about skateboarding: any young person looking at the plans for CCON with its enormous concrete spaces immediately knew that they were looking at plans for the best skateboard venue in Spain, if not the world; the question was whether it would be allowed to realize this potential, and that would depend entirely on how people understood the relation of skateboarding to the kind of global culture that CCON wanted to be associated with. (During the research involvement, the feeling was ambivalent: it could go either way in that the desire to position CCON nearer to popular culture, as in film, did not rule out skateboarding in principle.)

Finally, the valorization of live gigs also brought the scalar issue round full circle to a cultural stance that Ariztia-Larrain and I described as 'cool globalization': despite the diversity of scales and young people's multilingual fluency in articulating diverse scales in diverse interactions (of which more below), what mattered to them was not scale, but the qualities they sought in cultural connection. And it was in this way that new media made sense. One day the old square of Aviles was filled with teenage skateboarders videoing each other. Obviously they were going to put the videos up on YouTube, and mainly to be seen by 'local' friends, including the other boys who were now physically present in the square too, and also videoing; but they knew the same videos could be seen by anyone anywhere in the world – doesn't matter, 'it's cool'. This seemed no different from the CCON people, who felt they could tap into global cultural on a mundane and routine basis (not least through their ability to link themselves by email to the flows of cultural capital they were trying to make real and at the same time capture). The ability to make certain kinds of participation mundane, domestic, in a sense to abolish scale entirely, was not a property of the media but constituted a different kind of scaling practice, the envisaging of certain kinds of relationships and connections, this time ironically shared by the supposedly 'local' youth and the 'global' cultural actors of CCON.

Scaling and Development

The Asturias story points up the complexity of scaling practices and the conflicting (or fudged) profusion of different scales applied by actors to themselves and others. This is all potentially homogenized by the abstract metrics of 'globalization', which seems to see only quantities or densities of connection rather than the wild diversity of ways in which actors understand and act upon connections. Both the ways in which actors do this and the extent to which this is recognized, valued and voiced are central to the kinds of 'development' that might be imagined or enacted, and the place of new media within this. Essentially, can we ground development thinking and acting in the ways in which particular people use new media as material culture to think and act upon connection? And can we do that with the expectation that, as in the case of Asturias, even the same actors will have multiple and even contradictory scales and scaling practices? Bringing the Asturias story together with stories of scaling practices and devices from other fieldwork suggests to me four major dimensions along which one might open up the study of connection in this way; the list is not meant to be comprehensive but simply to indicate the kinds of issues that should be visible.

1   Geo-positioning and the qualities of connection

We can start from where the Asturias story ended: scale cannot be simply about intensity, extensity, velocity and impact (Held), in that scaling is about making and classifying connection, and connections have qualities and values ascribed to them. They must have certain qualities even to be counted as connections by particular actors in the first place. Even Smith and Hume, as overexcited in the eighteenth century as Castells is today about the opportunities offered by global commerce and 'intercourse', had in mind specific kinds of encounter (those that encouraged moral sense) and not contact as such.

In the Asturian case, young people articulated different kinds of connections, all of which could be evaluated in relation to a normative standard of connection and culture that they found in 'the gig', and which they defined in terms of qualities of 'being there', in an exciting place, where things were happening and where there was a confluence of cultural flows. They were entirely able to articulate the official CCON view of development and the kinds of connections it entailed, as we will discuss in a moment, but they located themselves in terms of the qualities that for them identified cultural connection. They recognized CCON's global culture as an entirely legitimate and promising strategy; it just had nothing to do with them because it had nothing to do with the qualities of connection that they valued. That obviously gives an entirely different relationship to 'development' for youth than for the CCON planners, for whom globalization promised access to their cultural pot of gold (global networks, world-class culture, household names).

Constructing convergences between communicative assemblages, development theories and scales requires that we look at what counts as a valued connection, for whom and why; and how those qualities of connection position people in temporal and spatial narratives. We can relate this Asturian story to several we have already told, plus a few more: Sri Lankan youth at KCRIP, as we noted in Chapter 2, often produced websites that prominently featured local shrines, temples and natural beauty spots, and I associated this – like radio – with values concerning the moral centrality of villages. As in Kumar's story, 'globalization' (a word he used) promised a kind of connection that reasserted that moral centrality by affording possibilities of drawing everyone (including migrant Sri Lankans abroad and foreigners) into that moral centre. Trinidadian youth also featured icons of Trinidadian identity in their websites to an astonishing extent (e.g., national flag and national anthem), but with an almost opposite purpose to the Sri Lankans: like most Trinidadians we worked with, the assumption was that they were intrinsically cosmopolitan actors who could successfully take on the world, and the websites were more like proud announcements that they had finally arrived on the global stage from which they had previously been excluded. Where Sri Lankans often acted on the assumption that they could only be real when they were home and the internet could connect them to home, Trinidadians seemed to embrace the internet as a medium through which they could be Trini wherever they were in the world, and being properly Trini often involved being somewhere else in the world. The most explicit manifestation of this stance was one that long preceded new media but was certainly central to how young Trinidadians understood new media: music. Trini views of globalization or geo-positioning were exemplified in the growth of soca music, which encountered and absorbed pretty much any world music on its own terms – aside from the 100-plus steel drum orchestras playing Beethoven's

9th in carnival processions, there seemed to be fusions of soca with every known music in the world, producing, for example, rapsoca and technosoca.

By contrast, while both Sri Lanka and Trinidad saw new forms of medial connection as extending (what were understood by them to be) ethnically specific values, and they valued the new forms of connection in terms of those values, we have seen a very different sense of connection in Ghana (see Chapter 3), one in which all scaling involved very ambivalent calculations of cost and benefit. Mobile phones were connected to scales measured in terms of embedded obligations, above all to kinship networks; the internet was connected to a transnational scale envisaged in terms of escape from a devalued South to a North that was the source and location of all development.

What is so obviously striking in all this difference is that in every case young 'local' people are as necessarily globalization theorists as they are development theorists: scaling, mapping and positioning is simply a condition of action and relationship, and this requires locating oneself in spaces that one at the same time engenders as one trundles along. Everyone can and does do cool globalization in the sense of having to think connection at any conceivable level of distance or proximity.

2 Multilinguality

During the Asturian fieldwork, Ariztia-Larrain went on a walkabout around Aviles with some young people he had recently interviewed. One of them, Pedro, was demonstrating 'his' Aviles, the city as he practised it, including places where he met up with friends, the paths they would follow over an evening, the Asturian folk pub and the heavy metal pub across the street from it that made up his 'locality'. In the middle of this walk, they ran into Pedro's father, who was very concerned that Pedro had shown their esteemed visitor the official Aviles, the Aviles of churches and medieval squares and buildings that one shows off in tourist brochures and to which one takes visitors. And of course Pedro *had* already pointed out all those landmarks. By the same token, Pedro – like all the young people interviewed – was able to articulate (critically discuss) CCON's development plans and the cultural maps on which it was based, even though the cultural content didn't inspire much personal enthusiasm or identification. Pedro, again like most young people, was pretty supportive of the plans on economic and regional development grounds, but didn't feel they would have much to do with his cultural life.

Pedro was properly multilingual in his scaling narratives, able to identify and position himself not simply within one particular map but in relation to the diversity of maps that he might encounter. Not only could he use and explain the tourist map, his own personal map and CCON's map, but he could make his own sense of a world in which all these maps coexisted. This is an impressive and at the same time mundane achievement that rests on the fact that the making, classifying and evaluation of different kinds and qualities of connection is part of everyday social action, and in the same way that we described 'everyone' as a development theorist: we have to model the world in order to act in it. What this certainly does not allow us as theorists is the possibility of treating anyone's scales and maps as simple, univocal, predictable or deducible from official maps and discourses.

3 Scaling classifies the classifier: scaling as a relationship

There is another dimension to Pedro's story: he could not only position himself in different spatial scales of connection, but he could also see how others, like CCON or his father, positioned him (indeed he was rather offended that his father could think that he *wouldn't* have shown his honoured visitor the proper touristic Aviles, that he was that type of lad). Indeed his very multilinguality seems to already presuppose an awareness that people spatialize themselves and others, and that others spatialize us.

Hence the paraphrasing of Bourdieu: scales classify, and scaling classifies the classifier. Insofar as scaling categorizations can be seen as 'structuring structures' (dispositions through which we order the world and come to act in recognizable though not particularly predictable ways towards it), we can also see where others are coming from. The young Turks of CCON positioned Asturian youth as 'locals' in an officially bifurcated model of local–global relations; this positioned and distinguished them, by contrast, as members of a certain kind of elite that had ready access to widely distributed ('global') connections that could contain and view Asturian youth from above, indeed from the empty God's-eye view by which we defined 'globalization' in the previous section. And it is not hard to see the relation between youth and CCON in crudely Bourdieuian terms. CCON consisted of largely Madrid- and Barcelona-based young men from elite schools and universities, fast-tracked through the foreign service and blue-chip multinationals, and now settled in an elite royal institution close to national power. This 'global' was very local and could be instantly recognized as such by any teenager we interviewed.

A vivid example: a young Trinidadian told us – in outrage – that during an internet conversation with a random Californian teenager, in the midst of the usual 'getting to know you' banter (then known as 'a/s/l' – age/sex/location), the American didn't ask 'Where is Trinidad?' but rather '*What* is Trinidad?' The Trini youth was particularly furious that while he knew where the American kid's town was, the American kid not only couldn't place Trinidad in the world but didn't even properly recognize that it was a *place*. The inequality was positively existential, and crystallized both a geo-politics and a symbolic violence. The Trini youth felt that US kids used the internet in a state of general ignorance and apathy that made the rest of the world, including him, unreal; other people were not spatialized and therefore had no place, and the internet did not relate to any map at all. By contrast, he, like most Trinidadians, was preoccupied not just with scaling, with the social relations of placing and being placed, but with geography in its most conventional secondary school sense. Miller and I watched the Miss Universe contest broadcast on television in a squatters' settlement on electricity stolen from a neigh-bouring grid. The early teenage daughter of the household not only knew where every country was and recited this as its contestant came onstage, but also knew the governmental system of each, which she explained to us, country by country. This geographical orientation was itself com-plexly over-determined: for example, it owed as much to the girl's tre-mendous respect for and embrace of traditional British colonial schooling as it did to complex migrations and migratory aspirations that ran through her family, as through any other Trini family; and it clearly articulated both a Trinidadian sense of herself as incipiently cosmo-politan and an ambivalent Trinidadian relationship to a history of Ame-rican power and privilege which rendered such knowledge relatively unimportant.

In any interaction, but particularly with new strangers, I not only position the Other (Where are they from? How did they get here, and under what conditions am I encountering them? How expansive is their field of connection, and how far beyond my own understanding/experi-ence/access?), but at the same time I also need to know *their* scaling framework – how are *they* positioning me (Do I appear provincial or cosmopolitan? Do they have any idea whom I know or where I went to school, where I've worked?). Latour notes, with reference to Boltanski and Thévenot, that actors expend a lot of energy in 'modifying the rela-tive scale of all the other participants', and in justifying their behaviour 'they may suddenly mobilize the whole of humanity, France, capitalism, and reason, while, a minute later, they might settle for a local compro-mise. Faced with such sudden shifts in scale, the only possible solution for the analyst is to take the shifting itself as her data and to see through which practical means "absolute measure" is made to spread' (Latour 2005: 185). There are obviously particularly important 'others' with scaling practices that position me (governments, schools, corporations, brands and other marketing objects whose languages I need to understand in order to see how I am being positioned and how to comply or resist). But the ways in which we scale and are scaled, and are aware of this and factor it into understanding and performing relationships and actions, permeates all aspects of life.

4   Social forms and modalities

It is important to reiterate in relation to scaling the point made in relation to media in Chapter 3 and the material culture of development in Chapter 4: scaling, too, is not just a matter of assemblages, of devices and practices, or even of narratives circulated through 'oligoptica'. For example, all the instances of geo-positioning discussed above involve transposable patterns or aesthetic forms that are homologously applied across situations. In fact simply describing the geo-positioning of Trini or Sri Lankan or Ghanaian youth necessarily involves moving across media, music, migration, and across historical time. Similarly, there is another sense in which technologies such as ICTs need to be addressed as the material culture of development (and neither as tools nor symbols). In Chapter 3, for example, we saw that internet and mobile phones could be seen as articulating different political options and geo-political mappings of North–South relations. The internet connected with a history of capturing northern 'capital', of every Bourdieuian stripe, in ways that could be linked, sometimes counter-intuitively, to a history of top-down and donor-dependent development. It can also be noted that most of the entrepreneurial options being explored for the internet in Ghana evidenced the same kind of international divisions of capital flow, albeit more 'realistically': the top option, given that the country had ostensibly fluent English, high literacy and reasonable educational capital, was unsurprisingly to develop call centres for northern firms. By contrast, mobile phones, despite being closely connected in their practical use to discharging familial and social network obligations that might be regarded as 'traditional' (with funerals as the prime example), were at the same time associated with non-state self-development, enterprise and a kind of populist neo-liberalism that disliked statist, including interstate and ODA, prescriptions for development. Not uncommonly, as we shall see, this translated into a complex narrative in which the opposition between dynamic mobile operators and the oppressive and failed national telecoms company also articulated political choices around postcolonial allegiances, the role of the state and Ghana's relation to the rest of the world: in the case of both media, individually as well as in their opposition, people were addressing options by which to practically position themselves in relation to both local political options and global realignments.

Daniel Miller and I wrote up an equivalent layering of articulations in Trinidad, and these, too, revolved around liberalization of telecommunications: the national telecoms provider, TTTS (a partnership between the government and Cable and Wireless), appeared to be cutting Trinidad off from the North, from freedom and development, from its cosmopolitan destiny, by exercising an inefficient monopoly, and the government, by refusing to clearly deregulate the ISP business, was ensuring that (legal) internet access would become expensive, uncompetitive and difficult to obtain. As with mobile providers in Ghana, internet providers in Trinidad were simultaneously aligned with technological modernization, developmental futures, anti-state freedom of a populist liberal sort and a postcolonial shift of the axis of connection away from an old colonial hangover (the British-identified Cable and Wireless) and a European model of telecoms as a monopolistic public service utility. The internet was used in public debates as leverage to reconfigure telecoms to shift the very idea of Trinidadian development onto a North American and neo-liberal axis. The most interesting aspect of all these associations was that people regularly articulated the entire story as one in which the telecoms company was blocking or turning off 'the pipeline'. This connected the internet story to Trinidad's industrial past, in which its modernization and special status in the region have depended on its position as an oil-processing and shipping point from the 1930s onwards. The oil pipeline has been key to understanding, narrating and enacting Trinidad's relation to the world and to 'development' for decades; to talk about the internet as a pipeline (often literally, as in the undersea cable; or more metaphorically, as the socio-technical chain being blocked by TTTS) was to organize a whole history of connections between technology and development, and to map out political options and challenges.

Trinidadians were characteristically concerned with barriers to their entry into global fields of economic and cultural competition, a desire to be where things are happening that was often frustrated by political and institutional disconnects. Sri Lankans also evidenced a pipeline-like way of looking at technology and development, but to an almost entirely opposite end. Sri Lanka has long been interpreted as a 'hydraulic civilization', an idea that originated with Wittfogel (1956) to look at the relation between technology and the organization of political, territorial and bureaucratic power; it therefore bears a strong relation to Barry's (2001, 2006) notion of a 'technological zone'. Sri Lanka was a quintessential example of this analysis in that its history comprises a couple of millennia of very large-scale construction of enormous man-made reservoirs and highly complex, technically sophisticated and geographically pervasive systems for distributing water. Such public works involved the institutionalization of control and power in complex and dispersed bureaucratic assemblages. They also in a sense made power visible in the material culture of technology itself; everyone in Sri Lanka could regard themselves, and be regarded, as positioned either upstream or downstream of the central material of technical and political regulation, in a dependent or controlling position, depending from which direction they were regarding the flow. The overriding issues formulated in and through this material culture involved questions and conflicts about the terms and conditions under which resources did or did not 'flow' into different points along the channels. We have already discussed the idea of Sri Lanka as a nation of villages, and this can be further placed within this hydraulic theme. The flow of communications, transport, radio and internet was seen in similar terms and through this informational form: for example, answers to virtually any question about KCR involved extraordinarily long narratives that detailed plots, machinations, long genealogies of interests, actions and feuds. These had the feel of chronicles rather than histories, descriptions of long chains of events up and down the conduits through which resources flowed, all designed to explain linkages and blockages that might eventuate in the arrival of particular resources in this village.

A final example of analysing ICTs as material culture at the level of collective histories and national projects is afforded by Uruguay. As discussed further in Chapter 6, Uruguay was the first country fully to implement a One Laptop per Child (OLPC) programme, handing out an XO (the OLPC machine) to every child and teacher in the country, additionally building both technical (e.g., wireless) and organizational (teaching support, repair centres) infrastructures. In this case, as argued by Beitler (2013), the programme was specifically organized in and through a set of values that had long played a part in the narration of nation: Uruguay, the story went, had been the most socially inclusive and egalitarian society in Latin America, and therefore also the most stable and prosperous. These values were anchored in and symbolized by its education system. There had been a significant fall from this state of grace over recent years, largely through economic crisis at the turn of the millennium; the OLPC programme was a way to resurrect these values and reconnect with that history: it was an inclusive, egalitarian, educational programme. Beitler's ethnography shows both the relaying of that narrative through the implementation of the programme, and the contradictions around it both in implementation and in use. What is never in doubt is that the XO acts as a material culture through whose transaction the long-term stories of Uruguayan development are revalorized and remediated.

Development as a Scaling Device?

The development industry publicly spoke in the name of globalization, and this was invoked as an imperative and as a logic, though often ambiguously, particularly in the run-up to WSIS. Development was certainly an agent in globalizing globalization – much like the KPMG and IBM speakers in Trinidad with whom we kicked off this chapter – in installing the idea discursively and practically as the assumed backdrop for all future development, in the same way as and in connection with new media and the information or network society. In the academic literature, the following kind of statement (chosen virtually at random) has been commonplace: 'A variety of factors point to the long-term importance of "being connected." One can argue about the costs and benefits of globalization, but not its inevitability' (Colle and Roman 2003: 76).

At the same time, development also constituted a scaling device in another sense that we have already discussed at various points but will only be articulated fully in the next chapter. Development agencies, international NGOs, and even the more localized and national NGOs and governmental organizations that are networked into transnational development policies, programmes and institutions are all contradictorily poised between, on the one hand, intervening in the absolutely specific circumstances of particular places and, on the other hand, operating across regions, continents or even globally, with a strong pressure to generalize across circumstances and to manage and measure different interventions according to standardized metrics. In some respects they appear as machines – 'scaling devices' – for generating the kind of God's-eye view, the no place, that Latour identified with 'the global' as a modern standpoint.

Development as a scaling device that produces 'the global' can arise from its managerial and bureaucratic forms: development agencies are like empires that need to manage processes across vast landscapes of difference; forms of generalization such as best practices, indicators, standardized methodologies and measurement tools, and so on, are *de rigueur* in order even to appear to rule rationally; and these need to be implemented – made visible, disciplinary and performative – through forms and formal procedures. As we shall see in the next chapter, this is the case even when this process is articulated in terms of difference, bottom-up planning and participation. Moreover, development institutionalizes a role of bureaucratic theorist or generalizer, who must pragmatically but conceptually link spaces, in consonance with complex regulations and relationships. There must be rational bases (theories, models, generalizations) for policies that operate across vast social landscapes, and in the name of global developments like new media, the information society and globalization itself. All these tools operate as something like the extension of a 'technological zone' in Barry's (2001, 2006) sense, except they are less to do with literal standards and interoperability and more to do with homogeneity of indicators and best practices as assumptions of eventual uniformity (cf. Green, Harvey and Knox 2005 on the political use of 'globalizing' technologies in local place-making).

Conclusion

If you are solely concerned with globalization or with how ICTs bring about globalization, then these questions don't particularly arise: you repress (in theory and – if you are doing development – in practice) the ways in which actors use ICTs to construct and represent their spatial relation to the world, and their sense of how things connect up. To talk about people in development – whether donors, academics or 'beneficiaries' – as engaged in geo-positioning themselves and others through scaling practices and devices is simply an extension of thinking of all people necessarily and equally as development theorists (and of course as heterogeneous engineers of communicative assemblages): understanding and acting within uncertain conditions, temporal and spatial. No one is 'local', if only because no one exists in one single 'context', and no one fails to interact with actants from what they perceive to be other contexts (strangers, officials, visitors, people with different social status from their own 'locality'). All the usual provisos are in place: people have different analytical and informational resources, different status and power, their scaling practices have different range and impact, but analytically we are all in the same situation – our specific ways of scaling and being scaled are part of the making of connection.

6

Conclusion: Politics of Research

Forms of Knowledge, Participation and Generalization

> Knowledge is like light. Weightless and intangible, it can easily travel the world, enlightening the lives of people everywhere. Yet billions of people still live in the darkness of poverty – unnecessarily.
>
> World Bank 1998: 1

> To achieve this praxis [action-based critical reflection] . . . it is necessary to trust in the oppressed and in their ability to reason. Whoever lacks this trust will fail to initiate (or will abandon) dialogue, reflection, and communication, and will fall into using slogans, communiqués, monologues, and instructions. Superficial conversions to the cause of liberation carry this danger.
>
> Freire 2005 [1970]: 66

Research – in the sense of strategies and practices for producing knowledge – has been a central concern throughout this book: the aim has been to view the three terms in the title from other places so that they are not taken for granted as analytical framings within which we should do research. Moreover, I've tried to present this case from the standpoint of specific examples of ICT research. This approach warrants, or even requires, a chapter about knowledge itself: how do our three terms enter into the practical production of knowledge, and how are these terms themselves reproduced through specific forms of knowledge production? Furthermore, there is an obvious twist here: the idea of 'knowledge' is itself a term on a par with the other three – it is an informational form, possibly the most structuring of them all, and perhaps the one that needs the most thorough anthropologizing. To what extent are new media, development and globalization themselves organized and performed in terms of specific understandings of what counts as knowledge, what knowledge should look like and how it should be formed and structured, what knowledge should and should not do, and how it is properly to be produced, circulated and processed?

In fact, these kinds of questions are not at all new to development, and not just asked by its critics: they have also been worked over within the development industry itself from at least the 1990s onwards, such that questions of knowledge have long been integral to even the most conventional areas of development bureaucracy (Jazeel and McFarlane 2010; McFarlane 2006a, 2006b, 2011). Moreover, this concern with questions of knowledge precedes, or is at least contemporary with, discourses about new media, new economy and information society, having followed a closely related but still distinguishable path through concepts of knowledge society, empowerment and participation. Indeed, this development focus on knowledge – which produced seriously consequential sea changes in the conduct of development (e.g., the rise of participatory research, the conversion of the World Bank into a 'knowledge bank') – was partly in response to post-development critiques that challenged it in great measure in the Foucauldian terms of knowledge/power regimes. In other words, it is not simply that knowledge became important for development as a result of claims about an emergent global information society; it is equally the case that, conversely, a focus on knowledge in and for development was part of the context in which 'new media', 'development' and 'globalization' were produced and performed over the past two decades.

Do we, then, need an infra-language to deal with knowledge and research? It would be a bit presumptuous to propose a new word for 'knowledge', but I do want to address the same kinds of questions that I have raised in relation to the other three concepts: in practical terms, how can one open up the idea of 'knowledge' to challenge, to being regarded as an enunciation by participants rather than a disembodied framing device? This is an immediate practical and political issue when, for example, project funding, project briefs, monitoring, staff careers, beneficiaries' involvement and technology use all depend on formulations of knowledge, and stipulations as to its bureaucratically enforceable correct forms, right down to specific tabular structures (e.g., 'log-frame analyses' as a condition of funding [Aune 2000; Dale 2003; Dar and Cooke 2008; Green 2003; Mueller-Hirth 2012; Power, Maury and Maury 2002]).

As in previous chapters, I want to use one particular case study to talk about different ways of formulating knowledge within development and some of the problems of shifting the manner in which we claim to know about the three terms in our title. The underlying question will be the conditions under which people can open up assumptions to view and to challenge, and under what conditions people can act on such openings. The basic form of this question is Habermasian, though that theoretical language will not be developed here: Habermas identifies 'discourse ethics' with the potentials for rationality that are opened up if and when (and it is a very big 'if', as Habermas repeatedly states) people opt for deliberation rather than violence or force (Habermas, Cronin and De Greiff 1998). They are able, in that case, to draw on presuppositions of communicative action that involve relations of reciprocal recognition ('equal respect and solidaristic responsibility' [Habermas, Cronin and De Greiff 1998: 39]), and to evolve procedures for argumentation whereby all claims are open to challenge by any participant. If notions of media or development or globalization frame North–South relations yet are difficult to challenge discursively, in Habermas' sense, as socially located claims or assumptions, then any agreed empirical or normative view of the world will be forced or strategic rather than rational and arising from argument. In our present discussion the question is how can we ensure that the assumptions underlying research design and knowledge production are discursively open and challengeable.

Though the question is Habermasian, the discussion will be unsurprisingly ANT-ish and material cultural, focused on how specific knowledge arrangements are assembled and sustained, and on the forms or modalities through which they are organized: that is to say, it will look at research assemblages as material constructions rather than epistemological structures. I will do this by describing one of the ICT4D programmes that has featured several times in this book – ictPR. Two central themes emerge from this empirical case and are expanded in the following two sections. Firstly, knowledge in development has been framed for at least fifteen years in terms of 'participatory' research and development. If top-down planning is believed to have failed, then development depends on the mobilization of the beneficiaries themselves, who can sustain development initiatives through their knowledgeable engagement. However, participation is a contradictory notion that mirrors the asymmetrical application of 'network ethics', discussed in Chapter 4: participation can be understood in purely instrumental terms as tools for more efficient development management, as way of circulating or 'depositing' (Freire

2005 [1970]) information; or participation can be understood as the basis for learning, innovation and reinvention of self and sociality. Secondly, while participatory research has been integrally connected to a revaluation of the empirical (a focus on describing located and contingent social processes), there is in development theory and practice a tremendous pressure to be theoretical, to generalize, a pressure to produce explanations and models. This drive to the generalized and the theoretical is over-determined but surely has to do, on the one hand, with managing and cost-accounting development projects within the bureaucratic administration of development; and, on the other, with the forms or modalities of thought that are legitimated through academic institutions and careers. The conjuncture of development bureaucracy and academic interests is not generally edifying, and is to the detriment of treating ICT and development as a learning process in the Freirian sense, a process whose outcome is not 'truth' or operational rationality but social transformation (Freire 2005 [1970]; McFarlane 2006a).

ictPR and EAR

UNESCO's ictPR (ICTs for Poverty Reduction) programme was funded for two years (the normal UNESCO funding period) under a 'cross-cutting theme' initiative concerned with poverty reduction. It was conceptualized from the start as a learning process, a conscious attempt to assemble, or carve out, a space for knowledge production that would explore the potential connections between ICTs and poverty reduction by establishing nine innovative ICT projects, each of which focused on different possibilities for ICT in development (the main programme documents on which this section is based are Slater and Tacchi 2004; Slater, Tacchi and Hearn 2003). The innovations might be technical, organizational or social (or several in combination), and there was a concern to look at how new and old media might be used in combination (see Box 6.1). The open-endedness of the programme perhaps reflected a particular historical moment (2000–3): it came out of doubt and disillusionment with ICT for development, particularly on the part of the Delhi office for communication and information in which the programme was based. The hype around new media and ICT use was already producing its counter-reaction, in the sense that no one knew what to claim, while at the same time the realignment of development around the idea of information society seemed already to have gathered irreversible momentum, all currently building up to WSIS, a process that began before ictPR ended. There was an underlying sense that, yes, ICTs were changing everyone's lives, but with very little sense of how and to what

Box 6.1 Innovation and research sites (Slater and Tacchi 2004)

Darjeeling Himalayan Internet Railway (Darjeeling, West Bengal, India) established four community ICT centres at stations along the Darjeeling Himalayan Railway (DHR). The network aimed to offer secure, central and easy computer and internet access for poor people living in communities close to the railway.

Empowering Resource-Poor Women to Use ICT (Chennai, Kancheepuram and Cuddalore, Tamil Nadu, India) has put computers with internet connectivity into the homes of women's self-help group (SHG) members. The project selected a mix of rural, urban and semi-urban areas in order to look at how women in these different communities can use ICTs in familiar spaces to meet their needs. Particular attention is given to income-generating activities and the need for product development and marketing.

ICT Learning Centre for Women (Seelampur, New Delhi, India) is an open learning centre for girls and women located at an inner-city *madrassa* (Islamic school) in a high-density, low-income area of New Delhi. A range of interactive multimedia content has been developed and used to support vocational and life-skills training and to build awareness of health issues and livelihood opportunities. A website was established in early 2004 to facilitate marketing of products produced by women and girls in the centre.

Jakar Community Multimedia Centre (Jakar, Bhutan) is part of a remote Bhutan Broadcasting Service production station in Jakar. Local TV and radio production feeds into the national broadcast system, allowing for increased level of content from isolated rural areas. High-speed connectivity offers the local population access to new online services, like e-mail and e-post, and new resources.

Nabanna: Networking Rural Women and Knowledge (Baduria, North 24 Parganas District, West Bengal, India) uses grassroots processes to build information-sharing networks among low-income, rural women. Networking is done face-to-face and through web- and print-based mechanisms, linking women and their groups from different parts of the municipality. The network has dealt with a range of information topics, with a current in-depth focus on health.

Namma Dhwani Local ICT Network (Budikote, Kolar District, Karnataka, India) combines a radio studio, an audio cable network that delivers radio to local households, and a telecentre with computers and other multimedia tools. It is run by and centred on a network of women's self-help groups (SHGs) and linked to a local development resource centre. Daily community radio programming addresses local information and communication needs, drawing on productions by local volunteers as well as a variety of multimedia resources, like websites and CD-ROMs.

Tansen Community Media Centre (Tansen, Palpa District, Nepal) works with local youth from poor families and traditionally marginalized caste groups, training them in audio-visual production and computers and internet skills. The centre is made up of a digital production studio and a computer/

internet access centre and is linked to a local cable TV network. Youth participants' audio and audio-visual programming is aired on local media.

Uva Community Multimedia Network (Uva Province, Sri Lanka) uses a combination of radio and new technologies as a way to facilitate responsive development and governance on a province-wide basis. A series of community multimedia centres, combining FM radio and telecentre facilities, have been established alongside a series of grassroots 'knowledge societies'.

Youth-Led Digital Opportunities (Sitakund, Chittagong District, Bangladesh) established a rural ICT centre linked to a grassroots youth development network that works to address root causes of poverty and key areas of social and economic development. It promotes the empowerment of marginalized youth through ICT skills training and access to computer, internet and other multimedia facilities.

end, and of what was the best way to use them in development practice. This perceived need to explore basic relationships perhaps made the project organizers more receptive to the idea of ethnographic research, in addition to which the entire programme was governed by a sense of urgency about open-ended, exploratory and loose research and practice: that is, action research of an ethnographic sort. Ian Pringle, the project coordinator, in introducing the entire programme to the newly selected participants at the very beginning, put it extremely well: 'If ICTs are the answer, what was the question?'

ictPR therefore found itself addressing (at least implicitly) a number of fundamental questions about knowledge as a potentially open-ended and evolving entity, and how knowledge might be part of project development and practice. Firstly, the programme itself, as described below, was conceived as something like a communicative assemblage, a structure for making information flow across disparate locations in creative ways. Secondly, central to the whole experience were disputes as to what informational forms were to count as knowledge, why and to what purpose? And what forms of knowledge could best be connected to development practice, and vice versa? Thirdly, the programme related to a much wider agenda of 'participation' and 'participatory research' (of which I was only vaguely aware at the time, being a newcomer to the field of development): how did the idea of participation structure the form of research and the circulation of knowledge? Fourthly, and finally, a decisive issue turned out to be the tension between theory and generalizable findings, on the one hand, and commitment to empirical uniqueness and specificity, on the other: this was a pragmatic and political question concerning the various aesthetic forms of knowledge and research that could be mobilized and how they fitted into the various interests and intentions of the actors involved.

The research component of ictPR was formulated under the banner of 'Ethnographic Action Research', an approach to research in ICT for development that was devised by Jo Tacchi and myself in 2002, and took the form of a name (and even its own acronym – EAR), a training manual (Slater, Tacchi and Hearn 2003), workshops for development researchers and implementation within the ictPR programme, with very strong support from our UNESCO head office in Delhi. EAR came out of the same thinking as 'communicative ecology' in that it sought to reposition the relation between research and development practice as far away as possible from 'monitoring and evaluation' and from identifying and measuring 'impacts'. It can be summarized in three main dimensions, all of which strongly connected to the idea of 'learning'.

Firstly, EAR aimed to conceptualize research in ethnographic terms rather than as instrumental impact studies: researchers would be trained in exploratory research design, innovating both research questions and methods that would grow out of the specific social worlds they were studying. In the ictPR programme, this meant investigating both communications and poverty as they are uniquely assembled in different places and processes. This approach built on ethnography in starting from a fundamental commitment to 'emic' knowledges and classifications that extended from questions of 'What is communication?' or 'What are media?', as explored in Chapters 2 and 3, to the question of 'What is poverty?' – how is it understood, experienced, performed and reproduced *here*? Far from being able to draw lines (whether straight, mediated or meandering) between 'media' and 'poverty', both were assumed to be uncharted territory to be explored, and also to be treated as co-configuring (rather than largely regarding media as a tool to reduce poverty, or poverty as a condition that reduced media access).

Arising from the same commitment to building concepts from lived practice, EAR also adhered to a version of ethnography as methodologically open-ended, innovative and responsive, and concerned to elicit the unintended, unpredictable and surprising. Rather than measure against an immovable baseline or starting premise, ethnography expects to grow and develop as it responds to its empirical engagement. Ethnography learns rather than measures. It therefore seemed a research model in tune with framing ICT projects as learning, evolving and responding to their users. Hence, the EAR training manual and workshops aimed to provide a toolkit of qualitative methods, as well as a contextualizing of survey methods within ethnography, but these were explicitly presented not as technical solutions but as ways of making sense of social processes, of generating questions, and of providing bases for innovating new methods and adapting old ones in response to empirical engagements. That is to say, ethnography was presented as properly made up as you go along, in response to concrete occurrences; training could not provide formulae to be applied but only experiences, examples and approaches to be appropriately adapted.

Secondly, conceptualized as an open-ended learning experience, ictPR was concerned from the start with the relationship between knowledge and practice, and this took explicit institutional forms. UNESCO committed itself to employing one full-time local researcher in each project, and 'EAR' was initially designed to train local researchers as ethnographers. 'Local' is an obviously problematic term, but in the context of ictPR it meant university graduates (from diverse disciplines) with strong local ties, including fluency in the local language(s), who would also commit to living in the area in which they were researching. EAR was originally thought of as 'quick and dirty' training for 'quick and dirty' ethnography. As opposed to the purism of anthropological training and the length of its ethnographic commitments, EAR started from the frankly pragmatic position that whatever ethnographic involvement one could sustain, however messy or truncated, was better than any alternative.

The full-time researchers were to be core members of the project team, living in the project area, working in the project (and usually as a development worker, not just as a researcher) and fully integrated into the management structure of the project. Knowledge was not to be understood as outside project development, or as something done before or after project development (as in baseline surveys and monitoring and evaluation). Rather, research was to be an integral part of project development. Moreover, this approach meant that research and project development could be seen as mutually responsive: research throws up priorities and problems, demands and aspirations that need to be addressed practically; project work throws up questions or problems that need to be investigated immediately and directly, not through standardized baseline or end-of-project evaluations.

The most fundamental concern of EAR was to make research integral to institutional learning processes; this therefore included considerable discussion about how to ensure that researchers and their results were integrated within the everyday work of project development (going to meetings, including research issues within all policy discussions, ensuring that researchers were also project workers, engaged in daily operations, etc.). But there was also a strong focus on development projects, practices and participants as *producers* of knowledge, not just users or consumers. EAR conceptualized knowledge primarily not in terms of 'local' knowledges to be elicited and articulated but rather in terms of knowledges that arise from processes – knowledges are produced as consequences of doing or using development projects. People have experiences, over time, which they articulate, discuss and analyse, and they 'become experienced' in this sense of increasingly knowledgeable, skilful and reflective. People produce stories and anecdotes, embedded languages and idioms, metaphors and paradigms – they evolve, and dispute, cultural apparatuses as part of the very process of participating and carrying out practices. Projects also comprise processes which continually leave behind material traces or trails that can be followed as research material (Latour 2010; Marres 2012): browser histories; suggestion and complaints forms; sign-up sheets and user surveys; post-it notes and messages on walls and boards; rumours, gossip and arguments.

This signals a central premise of EAR: to understand development projects as learning processes in that they generated much of the knowledge they needed to make sense of themselves. What seemed most methodologically urgent was not new research techniques, or knowledge generated from different ('objective', 'external') vantage points, but rather a framework or approach that could revalue, formalize or structure and help reflect upon the knowledges that development projects already continually produce in the form of traces and inscriptions, 'experiences' and stories, embodied and routinized operational knowledges, and so on. Put simply, ICT and development projects – like any institutions – are always already knowledge-producing machines, but the knowledge produced is generally set aside (as personal, subjective or anecdotal as opposed to the 'real' knowledges produced by real research methods). To a large extent, we felt, if EAR researchers could simply identify, articulate and acknowledge what participants already knew as 'knowledge', and then integrate that knowledge into project development as a legitimate basis for action and decision, then research might be more effective and participatory, or at least it might do less damage than other research approaches, which frequently devalue participant knowledges, or exile them to the tacit and informal hinterlands of organizational life.

Thirdly, issues of analysis and generalization arose strikingly in the implementation of EAR within ictPR. We wanted to avoid the imposition of standardized categories and indicators: on the one hand, we did not administer any common survey or even interview questions across the eight projects that were researched; on the other hand, we also tried to ensure that any of the terms – such as 'ICTs' or 'poverty' – was open to analytical challenge and to variable interpretation. But this extremist position obviously threatened the programme with incoherence: in what sense could there be an overall programme at all, let alone research outputs that could offer substantive 'findings' other than to point out that things are different in different places (and it requires some kind of common frame even to identify banal difference)? The strategy that we adopted was a thematic one: much as in coding qualitative data, the idea was to identify themes that would make sense in each project, and raise interesting questions both for each project and across the programme. The themes that we arrived at – media content and use, poverty, learning and education, empowerment, social networks and embedding in communities – also structured research to some extent: being able to commonly discuss, say, the theme of empowerment, we could generate questions that seemed important for all the projects to investigate further, but in their own terms. For example, one such question concerned the ways in which 'empowerment' is experienced not only as positive but also as frightening, painful or even dangerous; this question could be used to generate or analyse a considerable amount of heterogeneous material. In sum: we understood the connections between projects not in terms of generalizations or metrologies (categories, indicators) that held good across disparate locations but rather in terms of frameworks ('infra-language') for communication and discussion and for further reflection upon and development of the research itself. (For an interesting treatment of the largely unaccomplished project of comparative anthropology, see Gingrich and Fox 2002.)

ictPR and EAR, then, were both complex assemblages that mobilized and connected extremely varied components, and each of the component projects was itself a complex assemblage partly constituted in relation to other entities (e.g., stakeholders, institutional forms, other associated projects) that it did not share with the other projects, not to speak of the fact that the projects were located in four countries (which included five entirely different regions of India). Implementation of the EAR approach across these different projects was, as it should have been, very diverse, as will be discussed below. However, it is important to note that the ways in which we all understood and sought to achieve commonalities and coherence were not methodological or epistemological but rather took the form of institutional innovations and arrangements. Firstly, as noted, one full-time researcher was employed at each project and was also expected to be an active project worker in non-research activities. Hence there were grounds for long-term experimentation and reflection on the relations between knowledge and practice. Secondly, the programme began with a week-long training workshop that included both generic training in EAR, and working with researchers to develop research designs for their own individual projects; there were further week-long workshops throughout the life of the programme, each focused on appropriate stages of research and project development, and was designed to support both individual projects and conversations across the programme. Thirdly, the two academic researchers – Jo Tacchi and myself – carried out a rolling programme of visits in which we each had several week-long stays with each project, working closely with the researchers as well as developing our own sense of what was going on, and our involvement was supported by a full-time research officer in the UNESCO Delhi office (Savithri Subramanian), who was particularly important in supporting the writing of research documents, as well as a project officer (Ian Pringle), who was also visiting all the projects regularly and who was both exceptionally knowledgeable and supportive of the research approach. Finally, the researchers were supported remotely by Tacchi and myself through email and chat, but also through a research website. The intention was to provide a space in which not only to support research but also to positively enact the idea of research as conversation and learning process: for example, researchers could see others' material and field notes, as well as reflections, and respond to their innovations, questions and concerns or adapt them to their own milieu. In reality this was both exciting and frustrating. In retrospect it probably worked better than I thought at the time. To sum up all these arrangements, they were clearly extremely 'networky': the aim was not to forge a common knowledge through the application of standardized questions, metrics and methods, but rather to provide structures that would sustain dialogues that could both feed and be fed by our diverse explorations. In a word, the aim was to learn.

On being allowed to learn

EAR, then, was unusually blessed as a social research and development experiment in being fully implemented and supported within a UNESCO programme with very decent levels of staffing and a cogent and institutionally internalized understanding of what it was trying to accomplish. It was a good fit in that everyone was concerned with how to learn and was generally candid about their ignorance. My aim in the discussion is not to evaluate EAR as a methodology (which could only be ironic in this context) or to promote it. Rather, I think that as an experiment the tensions it produced revealed issues about how knowledge functions and circulates within development. Specifically, what tensions arose in trying to develop and legitimate a different modality of knowledge in the context of development institutions and academic ICT for development?

The central tensions between modes of research came through most clearly in what I came to think of as 'Jaya's question', or as the periodic 'rehearsal of the bottom line': at the regular research workshops that assembled the whole research team from across the programme, the visionary UNESCO Director of the Division for Communication Development in the Delhi field office, W. Jayaweera, who was responsible for both the Sri Lanka research and ictPR, had an unnerving habit of concluding our long and fascinating group discussions of the meaning of poverty or social processes around ICTs in particular projects by leaning way back in his chair, staring at the ceiling and asking, 'And so what exactly *is* the impact of ICTs on poverty reduction?'

Aside from filling me with terror, Jaya was clearly enunciating the 'bottom line' of knowledge as it determined the fate of the programme within UNESCO and its status in wider communities. However meaningless we may all have confidently (or smugly) come to feel the question to be when put this way, it was the question all of our claims to knowledge and rational practice would primarily confront, and by which we would be judged. From Jaya's perspective, as someone who had to represent and defend us at precisely these interfaces, the question was literally a rehearsal: how could we or he answer it? A quote from the management consultant's final report on ictPR to UNESCO gives a flavour of what EAR sounded like when translated into evaluation language: 'It is hoped that the action research component will provide disinterested comparative policy advice on matters relating to poverty impacts in time for interim adjustments to be made to project methodology.' Not quite how we'd have put it.

Moreover, 'Jaya's question' not only rehearsed conversations that were inevitably going to happen further up the UNESCO command chain; it also articulated a sequence of necessary translations within Jaya's own practice as communications officer. In that he was responsible for a veritable empire of ICT projects that stretched across all of Asia, a fundamental functional requirement of his job was to generalize findings – as policies, directives on best practice, reasons for funding allocations – across a huge landscape of incommensurable places. He did this through a vocabulary of 'indicators', 'benchmarks', 'best practices', 'impacts' and 'log-frame analyses' whose entire purpose was to get him from here to there, to be able to place unique localities within a singular and legitimating frame. All knowledge in development – or, more accurately, all *official* as opposed to practical, tacit, on-the-ground knowledge – increasingly takes the form of monitoring and evaluation (Mueller-Hirth 2012; Powell 2006; Power, Maury and Maury 2002): that is to say, ways of clearly accounting for investments of resources in terms of the securing of outcomes and impacts that were already predicted in the original project proposal and which can be reliably generalized as causal relationships across a potentially universal domain. There can be nothing more incompatible with learning anything new, let alone making learning a serious basis for managing development interventions. 'Jaya's question' simply rehearsed the forms and aesthetics of knowledge that are required in development, and did so – shockingly for us – in a context where those forms had been temporarily suspended.

The tension enunciated through 'Jaya's question' – roughly, the tension between managerial equivalence and ethnographic singularity – was continuously replicated at the level of everyday research and researchers. As much of the development literature agrees, this tension is part of becoming a development professional and part of building a successful, funded project. For example, a central issue for ictPR was to convince researchers and other people *not* to fit their findings into the concepts, claims and models that they believed to be officially approved and legitimate within the world of development agencies (or the academic worlds they may have come from or wanted to get to): it was hard to get researchers to stop filling their reports, or – far worse – their field notes, with references to the information society, empowerment or the power of media or ICTs, and to stop treating particular observations as illustrations of the entities ('poverty', 'digital divide') they thought they were expected to find in the field.

This was a version of telling us what they thought we or UNESCO wanted to hear (that their world fitted the models we approved), and dealing with this involved recognizing the complex and contradictory conditions under which the researchers' knowledge was being produced and evaluated. These conditions included not just their project's place in UNESCO, but also the place of this research work in their own careers and educational progress: the researchers had generally progressed thus far by profoundly internalizing academic categories, styles of thought and research, and normative narratives of development and social analysis, and by replicating these in exams, interviews, essays, and so on. EAR could be challenging to this (and threatening in terms of what they reckoned their future progress depended upon). Closely related was the problem of encouraging researchers to see field-generated information as valuable and interesting in its own right, and for where it may (unpredictably) lead, rather than to be valued only insofar as it confirmed official discourses or the promises made in initial project proposals. Defined as a learning process, ictPR discussions and documents made a big point of valuing mistakes, failures, disconfirming or even initially unintelligible or inexplicable material, of declaring that the troubling and surprising stuff is the good stuff. However, UNESCO personnel had to go to some lengths to convince researchers that they would not be penalized for openly reporting such 'negatives'; indeed, quite the contrary. Early reports and even fieldwork posted on the research website (both, in some cases, pre-vetted by stakeholders with a very different view of the programme) read more like public relations or like monitoring and evaluation reports: presentations of evidence not of social processes but of the project's success in achieving its initially stated aims, with a few strategic references, for plausibility, to problems that could easily be rectified so that project implementation could be judged successful, and all expressed in accepted and standardized development and ICT languages.

Rather bizarrely, in an age supposedly dominated by 'information', information was actually the least valued object in circulation, and indeed very hard to circulate within development networks. There was a wealth of models, concepts and theories, and there were many forms (literally: paper forms to fill in, forms that *structured* information in abstract and pre-conceptualized ways), but it was very difficult to inject the rich material and experiences of the field, the raw data as it were, into any kind of discussion (see Powell 2006). Development projects and programmes are required to produce ever more information in the sense of monitoring and evaluation, and project documentation. It is unclear what if any of this material is read or how it is read, or how the production of knowledge in these forms structures organizational learning processes. However, it was this kind of dynamic that finally killed off ictPR itself after its first biennium, on the basis of an external evaluation conducted by a consultant who of course had never seen the projects or the information generated by them, but only reports structured into the appropriate UNESCO forms. The issues stated in his report went right to the heart of the present discussion: the evaluation report praised such things as the programme's embeddedness in community and stakeholder networks, and their 'substantial role in providing ideas' and designing and running projects (i.e., we had clearly ticked the box marked 'participatory development'). The 'bottom line', however, concerned models and theories: 'This is an innovative and enterprising project from several viewpoints. However, when assessed in relation to the reduction of poverty, especially extreme poverty, the model it relies on has unproven or untested elements.' End of story. Similarly, the report continued: 'Clearly, the enhancement of voice, empowerment and autonomy of poor populations are important aspects of poverty reduction. It is, however, unclear how the primarily means-based approaches adopted by the project will lead to or be the cause of long-term reductions in poverty and deprivation for its target group in measurable terms.' Of course, the point was to find this out, including the important possibility that the large amount of resources pouring into ICT4D at that time might be having little or no effect on poverty reduction, and that the causal relations blithely assumed by this sentence (e.g., between voice and poverty reduction) are unfounded or not understood.

The very idea of ethnography itself became a relay for all of these kinds of tensions. Ethnography involves a kind of devolution of theory and interpretation to fieldwork and fieldworker, a principle of 'subsidiarity' that allocates the responsibility of analysis to the most immediate possible level of experience. Researchers were asked to treat their work as a process of incrementally making sense rather than filling in blanks through data collection. The idea of being responsible for interpreting, theorizing, analysing, could be experienced as not only complicated but also dangerous. (What if we come to conclusions that are counter-intuitive, opposed to or incomprehensible to stakeholders or officials?) The flipside of this problem was the notion that in an ethnography 'everything is material', at least in principle; we can learn from any mode of engagement with the field, and should not discount any channel for learning. Researchers initially experienced this as a chaotic situation (see Law 2004), to which many responded by trying to observe and record *everything*, worried that UNESCO would penalize them if they missed anything at all, however trivial it might seem. And while ethnography promoted a more 'academic' idea of knowledge (open investigation which challenges underlying concepts and assumptions, with the expectation that the 'relevance' or 'usefulness' of knowledge is likely to be delayed, mediated, indirect, complicated), stakeholders or project colleagues often wanted knowledge to have, or at least signify, a more immediate functionality (see Cottrell and Parpart 2006; Roper 2002)

Under these circumstances, EAR, unsurprisingly, took a considerable range of different forms even within our own few projects, and it changed over time in each individual project. At one extreme, for example, Nabanna (see Box 6.1) was conceived fundamentally as a knowledge project in the first place: its aim was to get women's groups to generate and categorize their own knowledges, and to build up information systems around their categorizations. Although there was a designated researcher, all staff were research-active by virtue of the way the project was defined. In Darjeeling, by contrast, the stakeholders had no interest in the research aspects, and in order to implement what arose from the research process, the researcher effectively had to take over significant elements of the overall project. TANUVAS, the project detailed at the start of Chapter 4, was an interestingly complex story: partly because this was designed by a senior academic with long experience of extension education, EAR sat uncomfortably with already well-established research methodologies. Two of the young researchers were already committed to academic careers in which their future clearly lay with more conventional knowledge production, and they were in the difficult position of having to give UNESCO enough of this weird ethnographic stuff to keep it happy while producing enough 'legitimate' stuff to keep themselves happy. Some of this was accomplished by fudging (interviews were carried out, but tightly structured ones that were then fitted into more rigid analytical frameworks). By contrast the third TANUVAS researcher was not part of this academic structure (yet), and was, moreover, physically located in the villages, and took on board the underlying ethnographic logic of the project: she produced some of the most interesting research material, and very local project innovations, but had very little impact on the project as a whole (this project remaining tightly committed to its original proposal).

The knowledge issues raised around EAR are possibly similar to those encountered by ethnography in almost any institutional context, including academic funding councils: ethnography proposes an open-ended exploration whose findings and conclusions are not contained within or predictable from its starting premises (such as project proposals or hypotheses) and are difficult to fit into a clear and direct functional or instrumental niche within bureaucratic management and accountability. It is more naturally thought of as a learning process than a process of connecting generals and particulars through routine forms of proof. Indeed, we might rather refer to Pickering's notion of 'ontological theatre' (Pickering 2010): ethnography (like the cybernetics he is discussing) provides the kind of space in which is staged the emergence of new objects, and is adept at playing with the different dispositions and configurations of entities in the world. As Green puts it:

> [A]nthropological knowledge resists application to templates and grids. It is this attribute of anthropological knowledge, possible because of anthropological creativity through criticism and analogical analysis, which renders it so importantly 'useless' in terms of its instrumental utility to other disciplines (Strathern, [2006]: 78, 87), although of course insights from this creativity are frequently appropriated by them. (Green 2009: 396)

By the same token, ethnography is unpredictable and destabilizing to any institution (career or organization) that needs to standardize the measurement of its own progress. Moreover, given that the aim of EAR was to explore new ways of integrating research into project development, the solutions involved a fundamental rethink of both research and organization, not a simple fitting of the two together.

Development as an Assemblage

How can we make analytical sense of the tensions we have been describing? In particular, how can we understand the ways in which different forms of knowledge and research practice mediate between the unique particularities of places and the needs of the wider institutional networks for generalization and for standardized forms of knowledge? Our response to these questions can build on some relatively recent and exemplary ethnographies of development institutions and practices that engage development as a complex assemblage (Green 2000, 2003, 2009; Green, Harvey and Knox 2005; Lewis and Mosse 2006; Mosse 2004, 2005, 2011; Mosse and Lewis 2006; Riles 2000). All of these studies emphasize detailed ethnographic attention to the ways in which development practices and projects are assembled and sustained, how networks of participants are enrolled, organized and connected, and how and at what different levels development is made to cohere or is represented as coherent: in a word, as Mosse puts it, 'the question is not whether but *how* development projects work', including the work of translation, alliance building and brokering through which development knowledges, theories and policies are put together, deployed and mobilized by 'interpretive communities' (2004: 646). Policies do not explain practices; rather, assembling development practices includes the generation of development as an apparently rational, or rationalizable, and representable thing. This involves considerable attention to the forms of knowledge and representation not as texts or epistemic structures but rather as material practices. For example, often the ethnographic gaze has to settle on literal forms (reporting templates and rhetorical structures through which knowledge has to be routinely, and normatively, organized, and in enforceable, sanctioned ways) as well as the broader informational forms and aesthetic conventions that form both the map and the path of development organization (as in Riles' [2000] explorations of the 'network form' as the normative informational form of development organizing, and simultaneously her attention to the actual written forms and modes of address and communication through which that network form is enacted). As Mosse puts it, we should be attending to the texts that circulate within development not in a search for 'discursive determinism', not to establish the effectivity of texts as representations or epistemic structures, but, to the contrary, 'a sociology of the document is needed to dispel the discursive hold of the text' (2005: 15). How are actual material inscriptions passed around offices, villages and meetings so as to enrol allies, mobilize participation, legitimate allocations of money and time, integrate particular projects within larger programmes and policies, and so on?

More broadly, this attention to the role of knowledge and representation in the material assemblage of development is a cogent response to the question: what is the relation between policy and practice in development? In Mosse's account, there has been a disabling obsession with the question of whether or not development policy produces or governs development practice, an obsession that Green (2009) also relates to an anthropological focus on texts and their effectivity and discursive structure. One might also trace this obsession through postcolonial and post-structuralist theory, including the Foucauldian focus on discourse: there is a desire to find in policy documents and discussions the underlying logic or rationality that does or should generate development practice.

In this respect, Mosse identifies two previous approaches to the policy/practice relation – instrumental and critical accounts – that have been not only inadequate (particularly in obscuring practice and the ways in which practice produces policy) but also weirdly homologous. Instrumental accounts are concerned with policy as problem solving, with identifying the effective, because technically correct, knowledge that will secure development. The presumption is that practice flows from analytically cogent and evidence-based policy formulations, such that success or failure of development should flow from knowledge and research; conversely, the task of research and policy is to get the theory right so that successful development will follow. We can also link this formulation to McFarlane's notion of a 'rationalist conception of knowledge' in development, in which knowledge is construed in classically modernist terms as 'objective, universal and instrumental' (2006b: 288). The key point for McFarlane (particularly as a geographer) is that these terms entail a specific model of how knowledge moves and circulates: firstly, it is a static entity that travels in a linear way, 'to transfer . . . not to transform' (2006b: 289); and, secondly, knowledge exists at a God's-eye level of objectivity and universality that supports a 'spatial ontology informed by an imagination that information and knowledge circulate globally, and can be "applied to" . . . local places' (2006b: 289). This modality of knowledge, McFarlane notes, underwrites the division of global exchange between northern theory and southern data that has concerned us throughout the book, and here can be glossed as 'knowledge transfer': development is about applying universal truths to particular places. This analysis also echoes Freire's account of oppressive pedagogy (discussed below) as movements of knowledge that are governed by metaphors of 'banking' and 'deposit': knowledge is understood as a form of capital (generally accumulated in the North) that is to be transferred to and deposited in the passive and unthinking heads of subaltern beneficiaries.

Mosse's concern is specifically with the presumption that practices should be or are governed by such knowledges. Such a presumption, perversely, also allows for the alternative, *critical*, model of the policy/practice relationship: the failure of policy to govern development practice, and hence to secure development success, is accounted for by the real aims and logics of policy – the extension of state power and post-colonial dependencies – which are secured behind the backs of the developers. This alternative formulation has largely been enunciated from a Foucauldian position, from the 1990s onwards, paradigmatically represented by the work of Ferguson (1994, 2006) and Escobar (1995, 2000). However, it is significant that this position has spread out (partly through the extension of Foucault more generally) into adjacent fields that collaborate with development, notably postcolonial studies (McEwan 2009), geography (e.g. McFarlane 2006a, 2006b, 2011) and critical management studies (Cooke and Kothari 2001; Dar and Cooke 2008; Dar 2008). This has clearly been a powerful critique, particularly with respect to the issues raised here: the production of epistemic objects and subjects through which state power and governmentality are extended, along with attention to the discursive means by which this is accomplished.

However, critical and Foucauldian accounts are prone to a presumption of discursive effectivity; to assume that the knowledge forms that are unearthed in discursive enunciations actually have significant social currency and effect; that they really give us access to the logic by which social practices are organized and carried out. Moreover, they do so without giving a clear account of the *how* of assemblage (the relays, mechanisms, associations, through which practice is accomplished). They are therefore prone to read into practice the organizing presence of monolithic, coherent and effective discourses.

We identified the instrumental account of the policy/practice relationship with a technicist and 'rationalist' view of knowledge as an entity that can be transferred from place to place, or from universal source to local instance. It is equally important to identify the critical account of knowledge with the project of critical social science, another kind of technical solution to social development in which knowledge experts seek a science that will tell us what is *really* going on, whatever participants may think. Critique implies a relationship between academic knowledges (in this case anthropology) and development knowledges that is equally asymmetrical and unreflexive: on the one hand, in instrumental accounts (and in more technical 'development anthropology'), academic knowledges appear to stand outside development practices, supplying correct and functional expertise to those practices; on the other hand, in critical accounts, academic disciplines appear to stand outside development in the sense of offering a critical truth, unavailable to development practitioners, that reveals its true significance and impacts (power, oppression, underdevelopment, etc.). Hence, as Green puts it, 'If development is a matter of knowledge, anthropology always knows better and is always critical' (2009: 397). But the price of this critical distance is a fundamental, and familiar, asymmetry:

> Understanding why development and anthropology use knowledge differently and recognize different knowledge entails apprehending both in the same terms. We cannot, therefore, explain development practices in terms of an unspecified social, leaving anthropology in a position of analytical unassailability. To assert that development is socially constructed but that anthropology can perceive the truth of this is to reassert the relation of criticism rather than account for how anthropology comes to claim its particular truths. . . . As Callon and others have demonstrated, the asymmetry of 'normal' anthropology and sociology ensures that the practices and assumptions of scientists and others who are not sociologists are interrogated as artefacts of the social relations through which their knowledge comes to be credible yet leaves the social constitution of equivalent practices which permit this perception to be claimed by the social sciences unacknowledged. (Green 2009: 397–8)

Similarly, Riles (2000) addresses the conundrum of social sciences that share the same informational form as the practitioners they study (notably, the concept of 'network' itself), such that the relationship between academic and development knowledges cannot be anything but muddy. At a considerably lower level of abstraction, there has been a healthily growing literature (e.g., Cottrell and Parpart 2006; Heuser 2012; Lloyd, Wright, Suchet-Pearson et al. 2012; Roth 2012) that looks at the problems of collaboration between academic researchers, 'indigenous researchers' and development researchers, problems which can often be traced to the different rules of the game of knowledge as characterized by Green.

Finally, one can hear in Riles and Green echoes of Latour's denunciations of critical sociology, a standpoint that is not only mired in untenable claims that only it knows what is *really* going on in the world, but that in making these claims becomes deaf and blind to the ways in which actors are in fact making up the world in terms of their own sense of what is going on. To the extent that analysts replace the logic by which actors associate (but which the analyst discounts) with their own critical logic, the sociologist actually makes the important stuff disappear from view. But there is an even older and more overtly political echo to be heard here: in his critique of the 'banking' model of pedagogy, discussed further at the end of this chapter, Freire argued that it is not only knowledge that cannot be transferred, like a commodity, into people's heads; critique cannot be given to people, least of all by an educator who considers him- or herself 'the proprietor of revolutionary wisdom' (Freire 2005 [1970]: 60–1).

Policy, theory, research

The argument that development practices cannot be deduced from or explained by policy or discursive structure is entirely convincing, but still leaves us to deal with the fact that throughout development work, practitioners are *expected* to be governed by theory, to render their practices and professionalism rational by appeals to theory, and to act *as if* their practices were theoretically driven and generated. This is in many respects the world described by accounts of 'audit society' (Power 1997; Strathern 2000) or 'virtualism' (Carrier and Miller 1998) in that practitioners are institutionally required to labour under the fiction that practice should be and is driven by policy, and in a clearly linear and line-management sort of way. Hence, in the case of ictPR and EAR, the nerve-jangling properties of 'Jaya's question', and the many other ways in which researchers experienced the imperative to subsume their particular experiences under general categories: one gains legitimacy by being able to represent one's practice as a local instance of a larger model. Thus, in terms of the more specific concern of this chapter – research and the practices of producing knowledge – the idea that 'policy does not produce practice' feels experientially odd as well as an indicator of failure: the rationality of one's practice is generally defined in terms of fitting the particular data into the general model.

As most development ethnographies have clearly acknowledged, theories, models and generalizations are not disposable elements of development, or problems to be critiqued out of the picture. We might relate this back to our characterization of development and development theorists in Chapter 4: theorizing social change in order to formulate strategies and forms of action is a virtually existential condition. To act at any historical moment, under conditions of in principle shaky knowledge, involves producing models or theories or analyses that map out the relevant actors and events in the world, specify relationships and causal connections between them and try to identify likely conditions, variables and risks that impact on what might happen or open up possibilities for better courses of action. The present is a problem that we have to solve, both practically and analytically. The representations that inform strategic action are shared within epistemic or 'interpretive communities', or – more accurately – are institutionalized within different social arrangements (family projects, corporate command structures, social movements) that rely on or enforce some shared assumptions and models as to how the world works. These representations are often treated as if they were real and true, and in the line management structures of development work they can become the governing fictions of practical action, the official reality, the story in terms of which actors have to give reasons for the rationality of what they do.

Conversely, development practitioners generally enact a routinely split consciousness in which they have constantly to negotiate and translate between the official story and the unofficial, tacit, pragmatic and embodied knowledges and theories that make up their lived practice. (Development studies has increasingly drawn on organizational theory, and particularly notions of tacit knowledge, to define learning institutions: an excellent example is McFarlane [2006b]; for organizational theory see Howells 2002; Nicolini, Gherhardi and Yanow 2003; Rooney, Hearn and Ninan 2005.) Development work, like any practice, generally involves multilinguality, the ability to work within multiple interpretive frameworks for different types and registers of action. Some of the tensions produced by EAR, and ethnography in general, could be explained by the attempt to reverse the relation between official models and 'local instances', and to treat tacit knowledge as official knowledge, to structure everyday experiences into formal knowledge.

Against this backdrop we can raise two overarching but interrelated issues about the role of research in development. We will then look briefly at how they play out in the specific field of participatory research and development. Firstly, what is at stake in development theories and models is 'the struggle for interpretive power' (Cornwall, Harrison and Whitehead 2007a, 2007b). This phrase comes from an extended examination of the 'gender myths' that have been 'mainstreamed' into development policy and practice, and that include assumptions of the same logical type as, in our case, 'new media produce a globalized knowledge society': 'sloganized generalities' (Cornwall, Harrison and Whitehead 2007b: 4) such as women are less corrupt than men, poor women always have successful survival strategies, women are 'closer to the earth'. At one level, the problem is straightforward: interpretive power is about control over the development narratives through which realities are formulated but also through which action, including research and further knowledge production, is structured. The problem is not so much truth or falsity but the 'pressures to simplify, sloganize and create narratives with the "power to move" that come to depend on gender myths and give rise to feminist fables' (Cornwall, Harrison and Whitehead 2007a: 13). This pressure is underpinned by the way knowledges have to be structured into reporting forms and policy languages, and to be circulated within very unequal terms of trade between agencies and researchers. The upshot is that problematic findings and ideas, the knowledges that are inventive, unexpected, contrary to the model or simply too difficult for the narrative to digest, are ignored (or deemed 'too academic').

Moreover, the amount of labour and thinking devoted to interpretive and representational work, to fitting experience into the model, can be enormous, and can squeeze out knowledgeable attention to even the most urgent everyday instrumentalities (Mosse 2005: 233). To what extent can a learning process be sustained when experiences have to be translated into policy terms that are remote from practical exigencies, or that devalue features that are important in everyday practice, or that require the kind of split consciousness that is summed up in the distinctions between tacit and formal knowledge, official and unofficial knowledge? In somewhat cruder terms, how much time and effort is wasted, how much that could be done is not done, because of the detour through official structures of knowledge and representation?

Secondly, the analysis of 'gender myths' as organizing knowledge through generalized narratives also points to the different forms of knowledge in development. Cornwall, Harrison and Whitehead (2007a, 2007b) argue that 'gender myths' have to be understood as part of a game of legitimating action rather than a game of truth or evidence: as in Mosse, policy (including the forms of knowledge and narrative that underpin it) is a matter of mobilizing and enrolling support and alliance. But this rather understates the complexity of this process and very much understates the ways in which knowledges take entirely different formal properties in relation to their specific institutionalization. As Green puts it very succinctly:

> Competency in development . . . entails the capacity to work creatively with scalable concepts for the purposes of government. This is not concerned with critique so much as reconstruction, of making concepts work – to have effects, to 'do things' (Austin, 1975) within the distinct representational orders of policy space. Making concepts work is not in actuality a property of concepts or representations as Timothy Mitchell (1988) suggests, or their place within the frame of representational ordering, but of their situation within the social relations of government and development (see also Hart, 2004). There is no clear break between representation and action, between policy and implementation (Green, 2007). (Green 2009: 400)

Policy may not produce practice, but the forms of knowledge that are rendered legitimate and actionable through institutional arrangements and their representation are experienced by practitioners as pressures, constraints and expectations and as the fictions under which they have to labour.

Moreover, this opens up the same kind of analytical gap that we explored in Chapters 2 and 3: while Mosse's Latourian-inflected focus on the assemblage of policy and practice through everyday exigencies and alliances – his 'sociology of the document' – is entirely correct, we require equal attention to informational forms or modalities. This is not to return to the text, discourse or representation in the older Foucauldian sense of a socially effective epistemic structure; rather, it is to find the ways in which the *content* of the document is indeed situated within social relations.

Participating, Theorizing and Learning

I would like briefly to develop this issue – modalities of knowledge in development – by looking at the modality of knowledge that lay beneath EAR. In retrospect, ictPR and EAR are very obviously variants of a wider movement towards participatory development and participatory research that had been gathering steam from the late 1980s (Chambers 2005, 2010). Coming from a non-development background, I was only dimly aware of this at the time, though I and several of those involved drew on a related history of community arts, community media and particularly community radio, all stemming from the 1970s (my own background, as noted in Chapter 1, was in community photography). All of these shared a commitment to elicit and to valorize the knowledges of beneficiaries and stakeholders, and to position them as knowledgeable subjects rather than as objects of knowledge; to recognize 'beneficiaries' as capable of and entitled to represent themselves; and to engage them more generally as agents in their own development. The relation between knowledge and development was reconfigured in terms of a different relationship between developer and developed (though these two roles remained clearly identifiable). Above all, the relationship was ideally grounded in a process of open-ended learning, in which a right to voice and self-representation was connected to a belief that knowledge does not come from outside experts: as in the Freirian metaphor already cited, knowledge is not transferred from authorities but – to be transformative – has to emerge from the people's capacity to make sense of their conditions, which itself requires dialogue and communication.

At the same time, the original aims of participatory research and development took the form of claims about knowledge in development: it was not just a positive claim about the right to learn but also a statement about the reasons for the failures and sins of past development. There were many features to this critique, not always consistently assembled. As Mosse's account would indicate, a central issue was the presumption that policy and knowledge should, normatively, govern development practice; in this case, the problem was that top-down, expert knowledges were too often wrong and misguided, producing disasters particularly in the shape of entirely unanticipated and unintended consequences that arose from local conditions and processes. Local knowledges, in this analysis, were not simply the democratically enunciated voice of the people concerned, their right to participate in social processes; local knowledges were more knowledgeable, correct, informed and reliable, and might in fact produce more intended results. Correlative to this, the mobilization of local knowledges also publicly enacts democratic participation and inclusion which increases the legitimacy and sense of ownership of the project, both of which increase the chance of sustainability and long-term mobilization.

I've put this somewhat cynically in order to point to a fissure or tension within this model of knowledge in development, and one that should resonate with our earlier discussion of network ethics, of tools versus transformation: Is participation a means or an end? An instrumental mobilization of resources to accomplish development more efficiently? Or an ethical expansion of the agency and sociality of beneficiaries, of their ability to articulate and organize individually and collectively around their needs, rights, desires, culture, identity, and so on? Is participation the ground of control or of learning? The issue takes us again back to 'Jaya's question': in the moment of asking 'And so what exactly *is* the impact of ICTs on poverty reduction?', Jaya undermined one modality of knowing with another. Internally, ictPR was genuinely and consistently constituted as an open-ended learning process about as far as anyone could take it, and this was grounded in learning, or participatory research, as an end in itself, as in principle a process of transformation. Jaya's question, for external translation, translated the entire programme and process into an instrumental tool for more effective development – what generalizable models, indicators, best practices, could it generate? In an instant, all the rich ethnographic particulars had value solely in their ability to feed theory, to play their part in 'struggles for interpretive control' at the higher reaches of UNESCO bureaucracy.

Mosse raises this kind of issue in relation to the move, over the past decade, from project-based development like ictPR to wider governance relationships. The desire to produce a more holistic approach to development can result in the whole of social life being transformed into 'development tools': '[A]s social life is instrumentalized as "means" in the new international public policy, donor-driven ideas such as social capital, civil society or good governance theorize relationships between society, democracy and poverty reduction so as to extend the scope of rational design and social engineering from the technical and economic realm to the social and cultural' (Mosse 2004: 642).

Critiques of participatory research and development are now legion and almost ritualistic, almost too easy; and many of them round on issues close to the instrumentalization critique I've deployed: participatory approaches are easily co-opted and subsumed into the machinations of the wider institutions, which also generally define the conceptual universe (the models and policies) and the 'ends', the goals and objectives of the programme as a whole. Again, development ethnographies properly demand that we are extremely careful about the grounds on which we launch such critiques (the relation between policy and practice is too complicated to warrant claims, for example, that participatory development is *merely*, reductively, in reality an exercise of power – or, bizarrely, 'the new tyranny' [Cooke and Kothari 2001]). But we do need to attend to – and be reflexive in our practical lives about – the different informational modalities through which the same practices and knowledges could be apprehended. Jaya's question itself provided a salutary learning experience because it made viscerally obvious the different forms of knowledge at play in our world.

The fudging of the distinction between the normative and the instrumental or technical value of 'participation', then, runs through participatory approaches to knowledge and research, and comes out in a number of tensions around this modality of knowledge. Out of all this, I'll briefly take up three issues that most sharply focus on the lost ethics of agency and sociality, and of transformative learning.

Firstly, there is the danger of a kind of ventriloquism lurking in participatory research, a danger that is recognizable in ethnography itself: the opportunity or temptation to speak through others, to find a suitable indigenous voice or assemble the stereotypically correct stakeholders for participation. Riles (2000: Chapter 6) gives a deep account of this in terms of the network's need to appeal to a real world and to people outside itself, its 'desire for the real'. The instrumentalization of participatory research and development as methodologies (indeed they are often a requirement for project funding) complexifies this danger to a meta-level: participants are already well versed in how to act as 'participants' as defined by the rules of this particular game. It is not hard to find the right people and voices. An additional problem is that these assertions of participation and community involve assumptions about authenticity, an expectation that participatory methodologies should elicit the true voice of a beneficiary community. (We could instead regard these methodologies as simply a new playing field, in which case the issue is not whether truth will out, but what 'participants' do with these 'hybrid forums' [Callon 1998a; Callon, Lascoumes and Barthe 2009], what opportunities present themselves, what kinds of conversations ensue, how these forms format action, dialogue and politics.)

The way in which 'participation', as a form of knowledge, might be used to instrumentalize participants and communities comes out clearly in fieldwork generously donated by Daiana Beitler (2013) concerning the One Laptop per Child (OLPC) programme. Uruguay remains the only country to have fully implemented an OLPC programme, in which an MIT XO computer was handed out to every student and teacher, accompanied by the technical, organizational and educational infrastructure for this roll-out. One dimension of this programme concerns the normative forms of knowledge and knowledge practice that frame the XO and are in various ways scripted into the object and its software, as well as the ways in which these modalities are translated up and down the development chain, from Boston through to the hinterlands of Uruguayan schools. Briefly, the whole programme has been driven by a pedagogic model ('constructivism') associated with Seymour Pappert (himself massively – and for this discussion somewhat ironically – influenced by Paulo Freire) which provided a very particular view of empowerment: the aim was to give people tools that are entirely about learning how to learn, about their own self-discovery and about non-prescriptive learning (knowledge should be the result of their learning, not MIT teaching or knowledge transfer). In the self-understanding of those running the OLPC programme, they were providing an entirely bottom-up learning capacity that should allow for the expression or discovery of 'Uruguayan' knowledges and informational skills.

Uruguayans, on the whole, did not see it this way: the OLPC clearly came wrapped in a visionary ethos associated with MIT, Negroponte and Pappert, which was materially inscribed in the technology itself as well as the surrounding discourses, presentations and training. The OLPC ethos was not a neutral space of enabling empowerment; it was a very particular northern vision which had to be negotiated and mediated in a specific Latin American history, including decisions as to what to accept or reject or to reinterpret out of all recognition. This mediation could be inscribed in very specific contestations (the education system through which the machine was implemented had to square this 'liberating technology' with existing curricula, with the training and ethos of already overworked teachers, with vocational needs, etc.). The imposition of liberation is in so many ways constraining. (The situation is homologous to Rose's [1991, 1992, 1998] Foucauldian account of the neoliberal imposition of an enterprising self, the requirement to remake oneself as self-governing, 'responsibilized' and free [cf. Nederveen Pieterse 2005).

This could be construed as a deeper kind of ventriloquism: Uruguayans were being asked – as a conditionality of participation – to voice not only specific propositions about knowledge, technology and learning, but also meta-claims or ethics concerning the nature of spaces of freedom and the very shape of the political. The point here, however, is not to debunk OLPC as a northern plot to impose western liberalism by stealth, but rather to see that Uruguayans did indeed recognize the knowledge model as located, enunciated, indeed northern, and clearly recognized – in various and variously successful or sophisticated ways – that that was simply one of many things they had to deal with. For example, at a major launch conference there was considerable local laughter in response to the visionary speech of a Negroponte clone visiting from MIT and spouting the latest nonsense about genomes and memes, but there was also a hall filled with innovative software, including games programmed by local school kids. Uruguayans, as Beitler develops this analysis, had actually embarked on the OLPC route specifically *because* of historical Uruguayan concerns with core values such as social inclusion, particularly as effected through education: that is to say, issues of knowledge and participation were Uruguayan starting points, not an import from Boston, and what was interesting was not the struggle between a Pappertian liberation philosophy and Uruguayan indigenous knowledges, but rather a complex engagement between many different views of the relation between knowledge and development and of the modelling of each.

Of course, we could analyse ictPR in the same way: EAR *required* that its researchers question all fundamental premises (What is poverty? What is an ICT?) and adopt a stance of radical openness which we derived from a combination of ethnographic training and radical community politics. I'm sure I frequently presented this stance not as (just) my view of knowledge but as the ground upon which democratic knowledge could be erected; then again I was after all just another participant operating from within my own frame of reference. The point here is not to seek a purified process with no presumptions or power, nor reductively to realize – guiltily – that my ostensibly democratic research was *really* just a deeper form of 'knowledge transfer' (a transfer and imposition of the forms, models and protocols of knowledge production). As in the Uruguayan case and as in development ethnographies, what is more productive is to look at how, over the course of the programme (as discussed above), this engagement was used in very various ways, and it was adopted, contested, debated and changed, and partly through discussion about the nature of knowledge and research itself: from outright conversion to rejection to a complex tactical game with stakeholders.

A second and related issue concerns how we understand politics and contestation within participatory approaches to new media and development. Participation in research and development is often understood in what might be called liberal or pre-Foucauldian terms. On the one hand, if communication is rendered two-way, then 'voices' should, indeed must, emerge, and express themselves, and development must be held accountable to them. On the other hand, this is usually construed as a relatively non-conflictual emergence: once free to speak, a voice is heard, and if voices conflict, they can be brought to consensus within the same participatory procedures. This pressure to achieve consensus has already been critiqued along numerous lines, some of which are related to the danger of ventriloquism: perhaps participation is a way of managing voice into the support of projects that are in fact still designed and implemented from donor capitals and the head offices of INGOs and ODAs, ways of mobilizing and functionalizing communities through new technical means that make them subjects of development only in a Foucauldian sense of ethically adapted subjectivities? There has in particular been considerable comment on the will to consensus in development, the extent to which participatory research is intended to forge a consensual mobilization rather than a space of debate, conflict, clash of interests and identities. Indeed, participatory research sometimes sounds like an even more banal version of multiculturalism (we could all get together if we just respected each other's essentialized differences).

The mechanisms for this drive to consensus can partly be traced to a particular view of politics in which politics is understood as the formation of consensus and collective will, or (in more contemporary, communitarian formulations) shared cultures or imaginaries. In this view, politics is not about contestation, and indeed participatory research can be regarded as part of a machinery for generating 'anti-politics' (as the term is used by Barry [2001, 2002] rather than Ferguson [1994]): these definitions of politics are designed to close down contest, conflict and disagreement rather than to open them up. Politics is identified with the formation of a common will and community rather than with the ability to produce, articulate and challenge difference. Similar communitarian, Taylorian definitions of the political infuse media studies (Couldry, Livingstone and Markham 2010), in which, again, communication aims at commonality rather than at the consequential enactment of conflictual difference. Otherwise put, in knowledge and communication, the expression of consequential difference is regarded as failure when it might actually be the only real indication of success: it is only to the extent that I can passionately challenge the other's deepest discursive assumptions that I can be said to be political at all.

Thirdly and finally, participatory research and development can be formalist in the sense of a knowledge based on ticking the right boxes: we have consulted the right numbers of the right categories of person; we have done so through procedures such as PRAs (participatory rural appraisals), focus groups, expert interviews; we have related the local information upwards through models and policy considerations that are shared across institutions, and expressed them in terms of mainstreamed values such as empowerment and gender equality. This formalism clearly returns us to the issues of 'interpretive power' and the implementation of knowledge forms throughout development chains, but there is one feature I'd like to emphasize: formalist box-ticking depends on the presumption of a fairly reified world in which specific categories of persons, communications and value are pre-given and the role of participatory research is to give them voice and effectivity. They may be 'empowered' but they are not meant to be transformed. We have already visited this in relation to Castells' distinction between Net and Self in Chapter 4, where the issue was a 'tool user' view of development which is premised on ethical fixity: people need resources in order more effectively to be who they really are rather than – through the emergence of new material, technical and social mediations – to become something else entirely. Again, the form of knowledge instrumentalises participatory development and closes down its potential ethics of open-ended learning: the job of research is simply to find the best fit between new means and naturalised ends and end users. This is another way of asking if the process of participation is itself consequential rather than merely technical.

The limits of consequential transformation can be glimpsed in the constant invocation of Sen (e.g., Hatakka and Lagsten 2912; Kleine, Light and Montero 2012; Wresch and Fraser 2012) and the capabilities agenda within participatory research and development. The use of Sen (e.g., 1985, 1987, 1999) to legitimate voice has been extremely important, useful and productive but also somewhat formulaic (Mansell 2002, 2006). What it is clearly good for is detaching development from a narrow and empty association with economic growth, indexed by GDP, and connecting it rather to the substantive qualities of life that are to be sustained (including their equitable distribution). However, while Sen's language of functionings and capabilities seems to open up a space in which people are self-defined, or defined within their own communicative arenas, nonetheless people and objects look rather conventional within the capabilities approach: after deliberation on desired forms of life, people have culturally specific needs, and they need objects and skills with determinate properties to meet those needs. The problem with this view is very material cultural: in Sen we still have a kind of tool-using person who imagines a form of life and then should be provided with the means to realize it. It obviously requires both material means and skills in order to be able to talk about real capability or functionings. And yet both skills and material means look rather alike in this view as properties that can be added onto the unchanging person. This is even more mechanistic in Nussbaum (2006, 2011), where we are given an actual list of capabilities that can be bolted on to persons. This hardly does justice to the transformative powers of engagement, what happens in the process of articulating and pursuing interests, not least when the resources in question (such as new media and ICTs) are themselves the means of knowledge production and circulation.

The Symmetries of 'Learning'

The desire to implement ICTs as tools of development can easily lead to instrumentalizing or technicizing not only these new means of communication but also knowledge, information and communication themselves. The two quotations at the beginning of the chapter point to alternative ways of framing knowledge in development: the World Bank identifies knowledge as the latest 'magic bullet' in the global war on poverty; by contrast, for Freire – whom we have cited several times already – the greatest barrier to development is precisely this attitude to knowledge, too often held by both technocrats and supposed revolutionaries who equally regard knowledge (and critique) as something that they possess and need to transfer or 'deposit' – like a transfer of capital – to those who need it. This version of the relation of knowledge prevents the forms of 'dialogue, reflection and communication' (Freire, 2005 [1970]: 66) on which any real development depends. Freire's complex understanding of communication feeds a view of knowledge as learning that depends on a series of symmetries – student/teacher; oppressor/ oppressed – whose very acknowledgement is transformative and ruptural as well as capable of promoting action based on critical reflection. Moreover, Freire's view of knowledge depends on a further symmetry – between subject and object, thought and world – that is even more radical and prescient (amongst other things, Freire's formulation sometimes sounds like a direct precursor of the subject–object relations delineated in both ANT and material culture studies). And it is a model of learning that can lead us directly back from these questions of knowledge and research to the questions from which the book started: the ways in which overarching terms like new media, development and globalization organize our worlds and structure our dialogues. For Freire, such imposed categorial frameworks preclude 'conscientization' (conscientização), Freire's term for 'attention to naming the world', giving voice and developing critical consciousness by knowledgeably constituting the world through full use of one's learning capacity. To the extent that the North does the theory and the South provides the data, their relationship exemplifies the very opposite of conscientization, as captured in Freire's 'banking concept of education'

> in which the scope of action allowed to the students extends only as far as receiving, filing, and storing the deposits. They do, it is true, have the opportunity to become collectors or cataloguers of the things they store. But in the last analysis, it is the people themselves who are filed away through the lack of creativity, transformation, and knowledge in this (at best) misguided system. (2005 [1970]: 72)

This is not a critique of instrumentally ineffective development theory or practice but an ethical critique of dehumanization, of the reduction of the agent to object on the very grounds that should constitute it as an agent: the world-making capabilities of everyday human praxis. To be 'filed away' under media, development, globalization or the next buzzword to be transported down the (information) highway from up North, to file oneself away, is to cede the very ground on which one can make sense and act. 'Authentic liberation' means 'adopting instead a concept of women and men as conscious beings, and consciousness as consciousness intent upon the world' (2005 [1970]: 79). Indeed, ' "Problem-posing education", responding to the essence of consciousness – *intentionality* – rejects communiqués and embodies communication' (2005 [1970]: 79).

The language of essences and authenticity might sound like an intellectual *faux pas* to the contemporary academic ear, as might the phenomenological idiom, but Freire takes this argument in a direction that is uncompromisingly radical in a contemporary sense. Freire understands social cognition in terms of 'generative themes' that characterize a historical moment – 'a complex of ideas, concepts, hopes, doubts, values, and challenges in dialectical interaction with their opposites' (2005 [1970]: 101). Themes – such as the three terms of our title, and their conjuncture – are to be understood not as abstract knowledge or truth claims, or simply as representations, but also as the problems, tasks and strategies that mark out the ground of action, the 'thematic universe' people inhabit and within or through which people formulate and carry out their projects. We could refer this kind of notion back to Williams' structures of feeling, Riles' aesthetic forms, Latour's panoptica or the notion of modalities proposed in Chapter 3. In any of these cases, Freire's conclusion would be entirely appropriate:

> [T]he generative theme cannot be found in people, divorced from reality; nor yet in reality, divorced from people; much less in 'no man's land.' It can only be apprehended in the human–world relationship. To investigate the generative theme is to investigate people's thinking

about reality and people's action upon reality, which is their praxis. For precisely this reason, the methodology proposed requires that the investigators and the people (who would normally be considered objects of that investigation) should act as co-investigators. The more active an attitude men and women take in regard to the exploration of their thematics, the more they deepen their critical awareness of reality and, in spelling out those thematics, take possession of that reality. (2005 [1970]: 106)

To abrogate the right to define these 'thematics' to the privileged, to the managers, to the career development bureaucrats, to the academics and to the teachers, to act as if a 'thematic universe' was a good that could be deposited or 'banked' in people's heads, to 'name the world' and constitute it for others, to make our thematics of new media, development and globalization into the grounds of everyone's praxis – this is for Freire the ultimate form of symbolic violence. And it is to preclude even the possibility of reflective action, of change through learning, because the elaboration of thematics is the very foundation of 'pedagogy': 'The more active an attitude men and women take in regard to the exploration of their thematics, the more they deepen their critical awareness of reality and, in spelling out those thematics, take possession of that reality' (2005 [1970]: 107). And, finally, Freire explicitly ties this pedagogy to dialogue and communication: 'If it is in speaking their word that people, by naming the world, transform it, dialogue imposes itself as the way by which they achieve significance as human beings. Dialogue is thus an existential necessity' (2005 [1970]: 88).

This conclusion to the chapter, as to the book, is necessarily but appropriately utopian. Freire's re-modelling of the teacher–student relationship provides the best paradigm I've yet found for re-modelling the relations of knowledge and theory between North and South: teachers learn and students teach as they 'become jointly responsible for a process in which all grow. . . . Here, no one teaches another, nor is anyone self-taught. People teach each other, mediated by the world, by the cognizable objects' (2005 [1970]: 80). This is a radical and open-ended vision, and Freire's language is full of challenges to take risks, to court chaos, to discover, while at the same time he constantly reminds us that the safe and manageable categorical frameworks through which we formalize and standardize knowledges are disastrous for social learning. Moreover, his texts and life were full of institutional and practical inventiveness, finding new ways of constructing situations that make for radical and democratic discovery. And this utopic vision in which the naming and the making of the world is carried out under symmetrical relations, relations of mutual respect between equally struggling (re)searchers, strikes me as a powerful formulation of the 'network ethics' that, I argued, were expressed in many of the discourses that have been projected onto the material culture of new media, new economy and network society, new possibilities of agency and sociality that should be extended without restriction along the new medial routes of social change and social connection.

Notes

Chapter 1   Introduction: Frames and Dialogues

1 I heard this phrase from the Indian sociologist André Béteille, himself a formidable southern producer of theory, at a conference at the Delhi School of
Economics in December 2006. I have not been able to trace a published reference, but the phrase neatly sums up a growing move towards 'southern
theory' that is intrinsic to (if not always accomplished by) postcolonial
studies, and is increasingly promised by sociology and anthropology (notably
Comaroff and Comaroff 2011; Connell 2007, 2008).
2 There are complicated terminological issues, especially if one is centrally
concerned with how actors, including oneself, classify the entities we are
trying to understand. 'New media' was chosen for the title because it is widely
understood but relatively neutral; it also connected to the concerns of Chapters 2–3: how has the idea of 'media' organized so many themes in modern
western thought? In later chapters, I tend to use terms like ICTs more because
this is in most common use in development thinking, not least because of the
influence of information systems research. Digital culture is another useful
label, but so too are social media, mobile media, and so on. As ever, the terms
need to be deployed tactically.

Chapter 3   Media Forms and Practices

1 This section is based on arguments developed with Joanne Entwistle, and
jointly published as Entwistle and Slater (2012, 2013).

Chapter 4   Making Up the Future: New Media as the Material Culture of Development

1   Choice of terminology is strategic. I've largely talked about media and new media in the previous chapters, whereas the final three chapters are organized more around the idea of IT or ICTs. This is at least partly because the development industry has increasingly defined policy and practice in this area around 'ICTs' – as in 'ICT4D' – not least to assert a strategic distinction from older 'media' and development traditions (e.g., 'community media'). The term is as vague as any other: in common parlance, ICTs are generally synonymous with new media and digital media, mapping out a world with the computer at its centre, then internet-enabled computers plus phones; and including peripherals such as printers, cameras, CDs, DVDs and VCDs and other machines that can directly network with computers. The label 'ICT' can of course be used more inclusively (any technology old or new that processes or circulates information or communication, such as radio), and sometimes is, but it has generally been used to draw an exclusionary line in the sand between older communicative technologies (the 'media') and those newer ones that involved some element of computing.

2   Alternatively:

> New information technologies are integrating the world in global networks of instrumentality. Computer-mediated communication begets a vast array of virtual communities. Yet the distinctive social and political trend of the 1990s is the construction of social action and politics around primary identities, either ascribed, rooted in history and geography, or newly built in an anxious search for meaning and spirituality. The first historical steps of informational societies seem to characterize them by the pre-eminence of identity as their organizing principle. (Castells, 1996b: 22)

3   'By "modernity" I mean the ephemeral, the fugitive, the contingent, the half of art whose other half is the eternal and immutable. . . . This transitory, fugitive element, whose metamorphoses are so rapid, must on no account be despised or dispensed with' (Baudelaire 1986: 37).

Chapter 5   Scaling Practices and Devices: Globalizing Globalization

1   This section draws heavily on collaborative fieldwork and analysis conducted with Tomas Ariztia-Larraine, and published as a report to our funders (Slater and Ariztia-Larrain 2007), as well as a meta-commentary that used the fieldwork to explore the idea of scaling research (Slater and Ariztia-Larrain 2009).

References

Abu-Lughod, L. (1997) 'The interpretation of culture(s) after television', *Representations* 59: 109–33.

Anderson, B. (1986) *Imagined Communities*. London: Verso.

Angell, I. O. and F. M. Ilharco (2004) 'Solution is the problem: a story of transitions and opportunities', in C. Avgerou, C. Ciborra and F. Land (eds), *The Social Study of Information and Communication Technology: Innovation, Actors, and Contexts*. Oxford: Oxford University Press.

Appiah, K. A. (2006) *Cosmopolitanism: Ethics in a World of Strangers*. London: Allen Lane.

Askew, K. and R. Wilk (eds) (2002) *The Anthropology of the Media: A Reader*. Oxford: Blackwell.

Aune, J. B. (2000) 'Logical Framework Approach and PRA – mutually exclusive or complementary tools for project planning?', *Development in Practice* 10 (5): 687–90.

Austin, J. L. (1975) *How to Do Things with Words*. Cambridge, MA: Harvard University Press.

Avgerou, C., C. Ciborra and F. Land (eds) (2004) *The Social Study of Information and Communication Technology: Innovation, Actors, and Contexts*. Oxford: Oxford University Press.

Bakardjieva, M. (2005) *Internet Society: The Internet in Everyday Life*. London: Sage.

Barlow, J. P. (1996) 'A declaration of independence of cyberspace'. Available at: https://projects.eff.org/~barlow/Declaration-Final.html (accessed 31 May 2013).

Barry, A. (2001) *Political Machines*. London: Athlone Press.

Barry, A. (2002) 'The anti-political economy', *Economy and Society* 31 (2): 268–84.

Barry, A. (2006) 'Technological zones', *European Journal of Social Theory* 9 (2): 239–53.

Barry, A., T. Osborne and N. Rose (eds) (1996) *Foucault and Political Reason*. London: UCL Press.

Bassett, C. (1997) 'Virtually gendered: life in an on-line world', in K. Gelder and S. Thornton (eds), *The Subcultures Reader*. London: Routledge.

Bateson, G. (2000 [1972]) *Steps to an ecology of mind*. Chicago: University of Chicago Press.

Baudelaire, C. (1986) 'The painter of modern life', in *My Heart Laid Bare and Other Prose Writings*. London: Soho Book Company.

Bausinger, H. (1984) 'Media, technology and everyday life', *Media, Culture and Society* 6 (4): 343–51.

Beitler, D. (2013) National programmes, technical projects: translations of XO laptops in Uruguay's CEIBAL programme. Ph.D. thesis, London School of Economics, Department of Sociology.

Boellstorff, T. (2010) *Coming of Age in Second Life: An Anthropologist Explores the Virtually Human*. Princeton: Princeton University Press.

Bourdieu, P. (1984) *Distinction: A Social Critique of the Judgement of Taste*. Cambridge, MA: Harvard University Press.

Bourdieu, P. (1990) 'The Kabyle house, or the world reversed', in P. Bourdieu (ed.), *The Logic of Practice*. Stanford: Stanford University Press.

Bowker, G. C. and S. Leigh Star (2000) *Sorting Things Out: Classification and Its Consequences*. Cambridge, MA: MIT Press.

Boyd-Barrett, O. (1977) 'Media imperialism: towards an international framework for analysis', in J. Curran, M. Gurevitch and J. Woollacott (eds), *Mass Communication and Society*. London: Methuen.

Boyd-Barrett, O. (1982) 'Cultural dependency and the mass media', in M. Gurevitch, T. Bennett, J. Curran and J. Woollacott (eds), *Culture, Society and the Media*. London: Methuen.

Boyer, D. (2006) 'Turner's anthropology of media and its legacies', *Critique of Anthropology* 26 (1): 47–60.

Bräuchler, B. and J. Postill (eds) (2010) *Theorising Media and Practice*. New York: Berghahn Books.

Brow, J. (1996) *Demons and Development: The Struggle for Community in a Sri Lankan Village*. Tucson: University of Arizona Press.

Burrell, J. (2012) *Invisible Users: Youth in the Internet Cafés of Urban Ghana*. Cambridge, MA: MIT Press.

Callon, M. (1998a) 'An essay on framing and overflowing: economic externalities revisited by sociology', in M. Callon (ed.), *The Laws of the Market*. Oxford: Blackwell Publishers/The Sociological Review.

Callon, M. (1998b) 'Introduction: the embeddedness of economic markets in economics', in M. Callon (ed.), *The Laws of the Market*. Oxford: Blackwell Publishers/The Sociological Review.

Callon, M., P. Lascoumes and Y. Barthe (2009) *Acting in an Uncertain World: An Essay on Technical Democracy*. Cambridge, MA: MIT Press.

Cameron, A. and R. Palan (2004a) 'Empiricism and objectivity: post-structural empiricism and the imagined economies of globalization'. Lancaster: Institute of Advanced Studies and Department of Politics and International Relations, Lancaster University. Cultural Political Economy Working Paper Series 4.

Cameron, A. and R. Palan (2004b) *The Imagined Economies of Globalization*. London: Sage.

Campbell, C. (1989) *The Romantic Ethic and the Spirit of Modern Consumerism*. Oxford: Basil Blackwell.

Carrier, J. and D. Miller (eds) (1998) *Virtualism: A New Political Economy*. Oxford: Berg.

Castells, M. (1996a) 'The Net and the self: working notes for a critical theory of the informational society', *Critique of Anthropology* 16 (1): 9–38.

Castells, M. (1996b) *The Power of Identity*. Oxford: Blackwell.

Castells, M. (1996c) *The Rise of the Network Society*. Oxford: Blackwell.

Castells, M. (1999) *Information Technology, Globalization and Social Development*. UNRISD Discussion Paper No. 114 (September). Geneva: United Nations Research Institute for Social Development.

Castells, M. (2000) 'Materials for an exploratory theory of the network society', *British Journal of Sociology* 51 (1): 5–24.

Castells, M. (2001) *The Internet Galaxy: Reflections on the Internet, Business and Society*. Oxford: Oxford University Press.

Chambers, R. (2005) *Ideas for Development*. London: Earthscan.

Chambers, R. (2010) 'Paradigms, Poverty and Adaptive Pluralism'. Institute of Development Studies, University of Sussex, IDS Working Paper No. 344. Available at: http://onlinelibrary.wiley.com/doi/10.1111/j.2040-0209.2010.00344_2.x/pdf (accessed 24 May 2013).

Ciborra, C. (2004) 'Encountering information systems as a phenomenon', in C. Avgerou, C. Ciborra and F. Land (eds), *The Social Study of Information and Communication Technology: Innovation, Actors, and Contexts*. Oxford: Oxford University Press.

Colle, R. D. and R. Roman (2003) 'Challenges in the telecenter movement', in S. Marshall, W. Taylor and X. Yu (eds), *Closing the Digital Divide: Transforming Regional Economies and Communities with Information Technology*. London: Praeger.

Comaroff, J. and J. L. Comaroff (2011) *Theory from the South: Or, How Euro-America Is Evolving Toward Africa*. Boulder, CO: Paradigm Publishers.

Connell, R. (2007) 'The northern theory of globalization', *Sociological Theory* 25 (4): 368–85.

Connell, R. (2008) *Southern Theory: The Global Dynamics of Knowledge in Social Science*. London: Allen & Unwin.

Cooke, B. and U. Kothari (2001) *Participation: The New Tyranny?* London: Zed Books.

Cornwall, A., E. Harrison and A. Whitehead (2007a) 'Gender myths and feminist fables: the struggle for interpretive power in gender and development', *Development and Change* 38 (1): 1–20.

Cornwall, A., E. Harrison and A. Whitehead (2007b) 'Introduction: feminisms in development: contradictions, contestations and challenges', in A. Cornwall, E. Harrison and A. Whitehead (eds), *Feminisms in Development: Contradictions, Contestations and Challenges*. London: Zed Books.

Cottrell, B. and J. Parpart (2006) 'Academic–community collaboration, gender research, and development: pitfalls and possibilities', *Development in Practice* 16 (1): 15–26.

Couldry, N. (2004a) 'Theorizing media as practice', *Social Semiotics* 14 (2): 115–32.

Couldry, N. (2004b) 'Transvaluing media studies or, beyond the myth of the mediated centre', in J. Curran and D. Morley (eds), *Media and Cultural Theory: Interdisciplinary Perspectives*. London: Routledge.

Couldry, N. (2008) 'Mediatization or mediation? Alternative understandings of the emergent space of digital storytelling', *New Media & Society* 10 (3): 373–91.

Couldry, N. (2012) *Media, Society, World: Social Theory and Digital Media Practice*. Cambridge: Polity Press.

Couldry, N., S. Livingstone and T. Markham (2010) *Media Consumption and Public Engagement: Beyond the Presumption of Attention*. Basingstoke: Palgrave Macmillan.

Couldry, N. and A. McCarthy (2004) *MediaSpace: Place, Scale and Culture in a Media Age*. London: Routledge.

Dale, R. (2003) 'The logical framework: an easy escape, a straitjacket, or a useful planning tool?', *Development in Practice* 13 (1): 57–70.

Dar, A. and B. Cooke (eds) (2008) *The New Development Management: Critiquing the Dual Modernization*. London: Zed Books.

Dar, S. (2008) 'Real-*izing* Development: Reports, Realities and the Self in Development NGOs', in A. Dar and B. Cooke (eds), *The New Development Management: Critiquing the Dual Modernization*. London: Zed Books.

Dibbell, J. (1994) 'A rape in cyberspace: or, how an evil clown, a Haitian trickster spirit, two wizards, and a cast of dozens turned a database into a society', in M. Dery (ed.), *Flame Wars: The Discourse of Cyberculture*. London: Duke University Press.

Dzidonu, C. (2003) *An Integrated ICT-Led Socio-economic Development Policy and Plan Development Framework for Ghana*. June. Accra: United Nations Economic Commission for Africa.

Elmer-Dewitt, P. (1993) First nation in cyberspace. *Time International*, 6 December.

Entwistle, J. and D. R. Slater (2012) 'Models as brands: critical thinking about bodies and images', in J. Entwistle and E. Wissinger (eds), *Fashioning Models: Image, Text and Industry*. Oxford: Berg.

Entwistle, J. and D. R. Slater (2013) 'Reassembling the cultural: fashion models, brands and the meaning of 'culture' after ANT', *Journal of Cultural Economy*.

Escobar, A. (1995) *Encountering Development: The Making and Unmaking of the Third World*. Princeton, NJ: Princeton University Press.

Escobar, A. (2000) 'Beyond the search for a paradigm? Post-development and beyond', *Development* 43 (4): 11–14.

Featherstone, M. and R. Burrows (eds) (1995) *Cyberspace, Cyberbodies, Cyberpunk: Cultures of Technological Embodiment*. London: Routledge.

Ferguson, J. (1994) *The Anti-Politics Machine*. Minneapolis: University of Minnesota Press.

Ferguson, J. (2006) *Global Shadows: Africa in the Neoliberal World Order*. London: Duke University Press.

Floridi, L. (1999) *Philosophy and Computing: An Introduction*. London: Routledge.

Floridi, L. (2010) *Information: A Very Short Introduction*. Oxford: Oxford University Press.

Floridi, L. (2011) *The Philosophy of Information*. Oxford: Oxford University Press.

Foth, M. and G. Hearn (2007) 'Networked individualism of urban residents: discovering the communicative ecology in inner-city apartment buildings', *Information, Communication & Society* 10 (5): 749–72.

Freire, P. (2005 [1970]) *Pedagogy of the Oppressed: 30th Anniversary Edition*. New York: Continuum.

Frisby, D. (1988) *Fragments of Modernity*. Cambridge: Polity Press.

Gadamer, H.-G. (1994) *Truth and Method*. London: Continuum International Publishing.

Giddens, A. (1981) *A Contemporary Critique of Historical Materialism*. London: Macmillan.

Giddens, A. (1984) *New Rules of Sociological Method*. London: Hutchinson.

Giddens, A. (1999) *Runaway World: How Globalisation Is Reshaping Our Lives*. London: Profile.

Giddens, A. (2001) *The Global Third Way Debate*. Cambridge, MA: Polity Press.

Gingrich, A. and R. G. Fox (2002) *Anthropology, By Comparison*. London: Routledge.

Gonzalez, S. (2006) 'Scalar narratives in Bilbao: a cultural politics of scales approach to the study of urban policy', *International Journal of Urban and Regional Research* 30 (4): 836–57.

Goody, J. (1986) *The Logic of Writing and the Organization of Society*. Cambridge: Cambridge University Press.

Green, M. (2000) 'Participatory development and the appropriation of agency in Southern Tanzania', *Critique of Anthropology* 20 (1): 67–89.

Green, M. (2003) 'Globalizing development in Tanzania: policy franchising through participatory project management', *Critique of Anthropology* 23 (3): 123–43.

Green, M. (2007) 'Delivering discourse: some ethnographic reflections on the practice of policy making in international development', *Critical Policy Analysis* 1 (2): 139–53.

Green, M. (2009) 'Doing development and writing culture: exploring knowledge practices in international development and anthropology', *Anthropological Theory* 9 (4): 395–417.

Green, N. and L. Haddon (2009) *Mobile Communications: An Introduction to New Media*. Oxford: Berg.

Green, S., P. Harvey and H. Knox (2005) 'Scales of place and networks: an ethnography of the imperative to connect through information and communications technologies', *Cultural Anthropology* 46 (5): 805–25.

Guillory, J. (2010) 'Genesis of the media concept', *Critical Inquiry* 36 (2): 321–62.

Habermas, J., C. Cronin and P. De Greiff (1998) *The Inclusion of the Other: Studies in Political Theory*. Cambridge, MA: MIT Press.

Haddon, L. (2004) *Information and Communication Technologies in Everyday Life: A Concise Introduction and Research Guide*. Oxford: Berg.

Haddon, L. (2011) 'Domestication analysis, objects of study, and the centrality of technologies in everyday life', *Canadian Journal of Communication* 36 (2): 311–24.

Hart, G. (2004) 'Geography and development: critical ethnographies', *Progress in Human Geography* 28: 91–100.

Hatakka, M. and J. Lagsten (2012) 'The capability approach as a tool for development evaluation – analyzing students' use of internet resources', *Information Technology for Development* 18 (1): 23–41.

Hearn, G. and M. Foth (2007) 'Editorial preface: communicative ecologies', *Electronic Journal of Communication* 17 (1–1). Available at: http://www.cios.org/www/ejc/v17n12.htm#introduction (accessed 28 May 2013).

Held, D., A. McGrew, D. Goldblatt and J. Perraton (1999) *Global Transformations*. Cambridge: Polity Press.

Hepp, A. (2009) 'Transculturality as a perspective: research media cultures comparatively', *Forum Qualitative Sozialforschung/Forum: Qualitative Social Research* 10 (1): Art. 26. Available at: http://nbn-resolving.de/urn:nbn:de:0114-fqs0901267 (accessed 24 May 2013).

Heuser, E. A. (2012) 'Befriending the field: culture and friendships in development worlds', *Third World Quarterly* 33 (8): 1423–37.

Hine, C. (2000) *Virtual Ethnography*. London: Sage.

Hine, C. (ed.) (2005) *Virtual Methods: Issues in Social Research on the Internet*. Oxford: Berg.

Horst, H. and D. Miller (2005) 'From kinship to link-up: cell phones and social networking in Jamaica', *Current Anthropology* 46 (5): 755–78.

Horst, H. and D. Miller (2006) *The Cell Phone: An Anthropology of Communication*. Oxford: Berg.

Howells, J., R. L., (2002) 'Tacit knowledge, innovation and economic geography', *Urban Studies* 39 (5–6): 871–84.

Innis, H. A. (2008) *The Bias of Communication*. Toronto: University of Toronto Press.

Innis, H. A. and A. J. Watson (2007) *Empire and Communications*. Toronto: Dundurn Press.

Jazeel, T. and C. McFarlane (2010) 'The limits of responsibility: a postcolonial politics of academic knowledge production', *Transactions of the Institute of British Geographers* 35 (1): 109–24.

Kelly, K. (1999) *New Rules for the New Economy: 10 Radical Strategies for a Connected World*. London: Penguin.

Kleine, D., A. Light and M.-J. Montero (2012) 'Signifiers of the life we value? Considering human development, technologies and Fair Trade from the perspective of the capabilities approach', *Information Technology for Development* 18 (1): 42–60.

Knorr Cetina, K. D., E. von Savigny and T. R. Schatzki (2000) *The Practice Turn in Contemporary Theory*. London: Routledge.

Kumar, K. (1978) *Prophecy and Progress*. London: Penguin.

Laidlaw, J. (2002) 'For an anthropology of ethics and freedom', *Journal of the Royal Anthropological Institute* 8: 311–32.

Lakoff, A. and S. J. Collier (2004) 'Ethics and the anthropology of modern reason', *Anthropological Theory* 4 (4): 419–34.

Latour, B. (1986) 'Visualisation and cognition: drawing things together'. Available at: http://www.bruno-latour.fr/sites/default/files/21-DRAWING-THINGS-TOGETHER-GB.pdf (accessed 24 May 2013).

Latour, B. (1988a) 'On actor-network theory: a few clarifications plus more than a few complications'. Available at: http://www.bruno-latour.fr/sites/default/files/P-67%20ACTOR-NETWORK.pdf (accessed 24 May 2013).

Latour, B. (1988b) *The Pasteurization of France*. Cambridge, MA: Harvard University Press.

Latour, B. (1991) *We Have Never Been Modern*. Hemel Hempstead: Harvester Wheatsheaf.

Latour, B. (2005) *Reassembling the Social: An Introduction to Actor-Network Theory*. Oxford: Oxford University Press.

Latour, B. (2009) 'Spheres and networks: two ways to reinterpret globalization', *Harvard Design Magazine* 30: 138–44.

Latour, B. (2010) 'Networks, societies, spheres: reflections of an actor-network theorist'. International Seminar on Network Theory, Annenberg School for Communication and Journalism.

Law, J. (2004) *After Method: Mess in Social Science Research*. Abingdon: Routledge.

Lewis, D. and D. Mosse (2006) 'Encountering order and disjuncture: contemporary anthropological perspectives on the organization of development', *Oxford Development Studies* 34 (1): 1–13.

Lister, M., J. Dovey, S. Giddings, I. Grant and K. Kelly (2009) *New Media: A Critical Introduction*. Milton Park, Abingdon: Routledge.

Livingstone, S. (2009a) 'Foreword: coming to terms with "mediatization"', in K. Lundby (ed.), *Mediatization: Concept, Changes, Consequences*. New York: Peter Lang.

Livingstone, S. (2009b) 'On the mediation of everything: ICA Presidential Address 2008', *Journal of Communication* 59: 1–18.

Lloyd, K., S. Wright, S. Suchet-Pearson, L. Burarrwanga and B. Country (2012) 'Reframing development through collaboration: towards a relational ontology of connection in Bawaka, North East Arnhem Land', *Third World Quarterly* 33 (6): 1075–94.

Lundby, K. (ed.) (2009) *Mediatization: Concept, Changes, Consequences*. New York: Peter Lang.

McEwan, C. (2009) *Postcolonialism and Development*. London: Routledge.

McFall, L. (2009) 'The *agencement* of industrial branch life assurance', *Journal of Cultural Economy* 2 (1): 49–65.

McFarlane, C. (2006a) 'Crossing borders: development, learning and the North–South divide', *Third World Quarterly* 27 (8): 1413–37.

McFarlane, C. (2006b) 'Knowledge, learning and development: a post-rationalist approach', *Progress in Development Studies* 6 (4): 287–305.

McFarlane, C. (2011) 'The city as assemblage: dwelling and urban space', *Environment and Planning D: Society and Space* 29: 649–71.

McKemmish, S., F. Burstein, S. Faulkhead, J. Fisher, A. J. Gilliland, I. McLoughlin and R. Wilson (2012) 'Working with communities', *Information, Communication & Society* 15 (7): 985–90.

McKemmish, S., F. Burstein, R. Manaszewicz, J. Fisher and J. Evans (2012) 'Inclusive research design', *Information, Communication & Society* 15 (7): 1106–35.

McLuhan, M. (1974) *Understanding Media*. London: Abacus.

McLuhan, M. and Q. Fiore (1967) *The Medium Is the Message: An Inventory of Effects*. Harmondsworth: Penguin Press.

McRobbie, A. (1998) *British Fashion Design: Rag Trade or Image Industry?* London: Routledge.

Madianou, M. and D. Miller (2012) *Migration and New Media*. London: Routledge.

Manovich, L. (2001) 'Data beautiful'. Available at: http://www.virtualart.at/database/general/work/data-beautiful.html (accessed 24 May 2013).

Manovich, L. (2002) *The Language of New Media*. Cambridge, MA: MIT Press.

Manovich, L. (2003) 'New media from Borges to HTML', in N. Wardrip-Fruin and N. Montfort (eds), *The New Media Reader*. Cambridge, MA: MIT Press.

Mansell, R. (2002) 'From digital divides to digital entitlements in knowledge societies', *Current Sociology* 80 (3): 407–26.

Mansell, R. (2006) 'Ambiguous connections: entitlements and responsibilities of global networking', *Journal of International Development* 18 (6): 901–13.

Marres, N. (2012) *Material Participation: Technology, the Environment and Everyday Publics*. London: Palgrave Macmillan.

Marx, K. (1966) *The Poverty of Philosophy*. Peking: Foreign Languages Press.

Massey, D. (1992) 'A place called home?', *New Formations* 17 (Summer): 3–15.

Massey, D. (1995) 'The conceptualization of place', in D. Massey and P. Jess (eds), *A Place in the World? Places, Cultures and Globalization*. Oxford: Oxford University Press/Open University.

Massey, D. (1996) *Space, Place and Gender*. Cambridge: Polity Press.

Meyrowitz, J. (1986) *No Sense of Place: The Impact of Electronic Media on Social Behaviour*. New York: Oxford University Press.

Miller, D. (1987) *Material Culture and Mass Consumption*. Oxford: Basil Blackwell.

Miller, D. (1992) 'The young and the restless in Trinidad: a case of the local and the global in mass consumption', in R. Silverstone and E. Hirsch (eds),

Consuming Technologies: Media and Information in Domestic Spaces. London: Routledge.

Miller, D. (1994) *Modernity – An Ethnographic Approach: Dualism and Mass Consumption in Trinidad*. Oxford: Berg.

Miller, D. (1997) *Capitalism: An Ethnographic Approach*. Oxford: Berg.

Miller, D. (1998) *A Theory of Shopping*. Cambridge: Polity Press.

Miller, D. (2001) 'The poverty of morality', *Journal of Consumer Culture* 1 (2): 225–44.

Miller, D. (2011) *Tales from Facebook*. Cambridge: Polity Press.

Miller, D. (2012) *Consumption and Its Consequences*. Cambridge: Polity Press.

Miller, D. and D. R. Slater (2000) *The Internet: An Ethnographic Approach*. London: Berg.

Miller, D. and D. R. Slater (2003) 'Ethnography and the extreme internet', in T. Eriksen (ed.), *Globalization: Studies in Anthropology*. London: Pluto Press.

Miller, D. and D. R. Slater (2005) 'Comparative ethnography of new media', in J. Curran and M. Gurevitch (eds), *Mass Media and Society*. London: Hodder Arnold.

Miller, D., D. R. Slater and L. Suchman (2004) 'Anthropology', in M. Price and L. Nussenbaum (eds), *The Academy and Internet*. New York: Peter Lang.

Mitchell, T. (1988) *Colonizing Egypt*. Berkeley: University of California Press.

Miller, P. and N. Rose (2008) *Governing the Present*. Cambridge: Polity Press.

Moores, S. (2003) 'Media flows and places', Media@LSE Electronic Working Papers 6.

Moores, S. (2005) *Media/Theory: Thinking about Media and Communications*. London: Routledge.

Moores, S. (2012) 'Loose ends: lines, media and social change'. Working Paper for the EASA Media Anthropology Network's 40th e-Seminar, 19 June–3 July.

Morley, D. (1986) *Family Television: Cultural Power and Domestic Leisure*. London: Comedia.

Morley, D. (1992) *Television, Audiences and Cultural Studies*. London: Routledge.

Morley, D. (2007) *Media, Modernity and Technology: The Geography of the New*. London: Routledge.

Morley, D. (2008) 'For a materialist, non-media-centric media studies', *Television & New Media* 10 (1): 114–16.

Mosse, D. (2004) 'Is good policy unimplementable? Reflections on the ethnography of aid policy and practice', *Development and Change* 35 (4): 639–67.

Mosse, D. (2005) *Cultivating Development: An Ethnography of Aid Policy and Practice*. London: Pluto Press.

Mosse, D. (ed.) (2011) *Adventures in Aidland: The Anthropology of Professionals in International Development*. Oxford: Berghahn.

Mosse, D. and D. Lewis (eds) (2006) *Development Brokers and Translators: The Ethnography of Aid and Agencies*. Bloomfield, CT: Kumarian Press.

Mueller-Hirth, N. (2012) 'If you don't count, you don't count: monitoring and evaluation in South African NGOs', *Development and Change* 43 (3): 649–70.

Nederveen Pieterse, J. (2005) 'The Human Development Report and cultural liberty: tough liberalism', *Development and Change* 36 (6): 1267–73.

Negroponte, N. (1996) *Being Digital*. New York: Coronet.

Nicolini, D., S. Gherhardi and D. Yanow (2003) *Knowing in Organizations: A Practice-Based Approach*. New York: M. E. Sharpe.

Nussbaum, M. C. (2006) 'Reply: in defence of global political liberalism', *Development and Change* 37 (6): 1313–28.

Nussbaum, M. C. (2011) *Creating Capabilities: The Human Development Approach*. Cambridge, MA: Harvard University Press.

Ong, W. (2002) *Orality and Literacy*. London: Routledge.

Pickering, A. (2010) *The Cybernetic Brain: Sketches of Another Future*. Chicago: University of Chicago Press.

Pieterse, J. N. (2006) 'Emancipatory cosmopolitanism: towards an agenda', *Development and Change* 37 (6): 1247–57.

Piore, S. and C. Sabel (1984) *The Second Industrial Divide*. New York: Basic Books.

Polanyi, K. (1957) 'The economy as instituted process', in K. Polanyi, C. Arensberg and H. Pearson (eds), *Trade and Markets in Archaic Societies*. Glencoe, IL: Free Press.

Poster, M. (1995a) 'Cyberdemocracy: Internet and the public sphere'. Available at: http://www.hnet.uci.edu/mposter/writings/democ.html (accessed 24 May 2013).

Poster, M. (1995b) 'The Net as a public sphere'. Available at: http://www.wired.com/wired/archive/3.11/poster.if.html (accessed 24 May 2013).

Poster, M. (1995c) 'Postmodern virtualities', in M. Featherstone and R. Burrows (eds), *Cyberspace, Cyberbodies, Cyberpunk: Cultures of Technological Embodiment*. London: Routledge.

Poster, M. (1995d) *The Second Media Age*. Cambridge: Polity Press.

Poster, M. (2001) *What's the Matter with the Internet?* Minneapolis: University of Minnesota Press.

Postman, N. (1987) *Amusing Ourselves to Death: Public Discourse in the Age of Show Business*. Harmondsworth: Penguin.

Powell, M. (2006) 'Which knowledge? Whose reality? An overview of knowledge used in the development sector', *Development in Practice* 16 (6): 518–32.

Power, G., M. Maury and S. Maury (2002) 'Operationalising bottom-up learning in international NGOs: barriers and alternatives', *Development in Practice* 12 (3–4): 272–84.

Power, M. (1997) *The Audit Society*. Oxford: Oxford University Press.

Rahnema, M. and V. Bawtree (1997) *The Post-Development Reader*. London: Zed Books.

Rantanen, T. (2005) *The Media and Globalization*. London: Sage.

Rheingold, H. (1993) *The Virtual Community: Homesteading on the Electronic Frontier*. Reading, MA: Addison-Wesley Publishing.

Ricoeur, P. (1984) *Time and Narrative*. Chicago: University of Chicago Press.

Riles, A. (2000) *The Network Inside Out*. Ann Arbor: University of Michigan Press.

Rival, L., D. R. Slater and D. Miller (1998) 'Sex and sociality: comparative ethnography of sexual objectification', *Theory, Culture and Society* 15 (3–4): 295–322.

Robbins, L. (1935) *An Essay on the Nature and Significance of Economic Science*. London: Macmillan.

Robins, K. (1995) 'Cyberspace and the world we live in', in M. Featherstone and R. Burrows (eds), *Cyberspace, Cyberbodies, Cyberpunk: Cultures of Technological Embodiment*. London: Routledge.

Robins, K. (1997) 'What in the world's going on?', in P. du Gay (ed.), *Production of Culture, Cultures of Production*. London: Sage.

Robins, K. and F. Webster (1986) *Information Technology: A Luddite Analysis*. London: Ablex.

Robins, K. and F. Webster (1999) *Times of the Technoculture: From the Information Society to the Virtual Life*. London: Routledge.

Rooney, D., G. Hearn and A. Ninan (2005) *Handbook on the Knowledge Economy*. Cheltenham: Edward Elgar.

Roper, L. (2002) 'Achieving successful academic–practitioner research collaborations', *Development in Practice* 12 (3–4): 338–45.

Rose, N. (1991) *Governing the Soul: The Shaping of the Private Self*. London: Routledge.

Rose, N. (1992) 'Governing the enterprising self', in P. Heelas and P. Morris (eds), *The Values of the Enterprise Culture: The Moral Debate*. London: Routledge.

Rose, N. (1998) *Inventing Our Selves: Psychology, Power, and Personhood*. Cambridge: Cambridge University Press.

Rose, N. (1999) *Powers of Freedom: Reframing Political Thought*. Cambridge: Cambridge University Press.

Rostow, W. (1952) *Stages of Economic Growth: A Non-Communist Manifesto*. Cambridge: Cambridge University Press.

Roth, S. (2012) 'Professionalisation trends and inequality: experiences and practices in aid relationships', *Third World Quarterly* 33 (8): 1459–74.

Savage, M., G. Bagnall and B. Longhurst (2005) *Globalization and Belonging*. London: Sage.

Schatzki, T., K. Knorr Cetina and E. von Savigny (eds) (2001) *The Practice Turn in Contemporary Theory*. London: Routledge.

Schoonmaker, S. (2007) 'Globalization from below: free software and alternatives to neoliberalism', *Development and Change* 38 (6): 999–1020.

Schulz, W. (2004) 'Reconstructing mediatization as an analytical concept', *European Journal of Communication* 19 (1): 87–101.

Sen, A. (1985) *Commodities and Capabilities*. Amsterdam: Elsevier.

Sen, A. (1987) *On Ethics and Economics*. Oxford: Basil Blackwell.

Sen, A. (1999) *Development as Freedom*. New York: Anchor Books.

Sennett, R. (2000) *The Corrosion of Character: The Personal Consequences of Work in the New Capitalism*. New York: W. W. Norton and Co.

Shields, R. (ed.) (1996) *Cultures of Internet: Virtual Spaces, Real Histories, Living Bodies*. London: Sage.

Shove, E. (2005) 'Consumers, producers and practices: understanding the invention and reinvention of Nordic walking', *Journal of Consumer Culture* 5 (1): 43–64.

Shove, E., M. Hand, J. Ingram and M. Watson (eds) (2007) *The Design of Everyday Life*. Oxford: Berg.

Shove, E. and M. Pantzar (2005) *Manufacturing Leisure: Innovations in Happiness, Well-Being and Fun*. Helsinki: National Consumer Research Centre, Finland.

Silverstone, R. and E. Hirsch (eds) (1992) *Consuming Technologies: Media and Information in Domestic Spaces*. London: Routledge.

Silverstone, R., E. Hirsch and D. Morley (1992) 'Information and communication technologies and the moral economy of the household', in R. Silverstone and E. Hirsch (eds), *Consuming Technologies: Media and Information in Domestic Spaces*. London: Routledge.

Slater, D. R. (1995) 'Domestic photography and digital culture', in M. Lister (ed.), *The Photographic Image in Digital Culture*. London: Routledge.

Slater, D. R. (1997a) *Consumer Culture and Modernity*. Cambridge: Polity Press.

Slater, D. R. (1997b) 'The object of photography', in J. Evans (ed.), *The Camerawork Essays: Context and Meaning in Photography*. London: Rivers Oram Press.

Slater, D. R. (1999) 'Marketing mass photography', in J. Evans and S. Hall (eds), *Visual Culture: The Reader*. London: Sage/Open University.

Slater, D. R. (2000a) 'Consumption without scarcity: exchange and normativity in an internet setting', in P. Jackson, M. Lowe, D. Miller and F. Mort (eds), *Commercial Cultures: Economies, Practices, Spaces*. London: Berg.

Slater, D. R. (2000b) 'Political discourse and the politics of need: discourses on the good life in cyberspace', in L. Bennett and R. Entman (eds), *Mediated Politics*. Cambridge: Cambridge University Press.

Slater, D. R. (2002) 'Making things real: ethics and order on the Internet', *Theory, Culture and Society* 19 (5–6: Special issue: Sociality/Materiality): 227–45.

Slater, D. R. (2003) 'Modernity under construction: building the Internet in Trinidad', in P. Brey, T. Misa and A. Rip (eds), *Modernity and Technology: The Empirical Turn*. Boston: MIT Press.

Slater, D. R. (2004) 'Social relationships and identity online and offline', in R. C. Allen and A. Hill (eds), *The Television Studies Reader*. London: Routledge.

Slater, D. R. (2008) 'Glimpsing God in the Internet', in D. Held and H. Moore (eds), *Cultural Politics*. Cambridge: Polity Press.

Slater, D. R. and T. Ariztia-Larrain (2007) *Cultural Maps and Cultural Development: A Study of Youth Culture, Technology and Cultural Policy*. London/ Aviles, LSE/Enterprise LSE/CCON.

Slater, D. R. and T. Ariztia-Larrain (2009) 'Assembling Asturias: scaling devices and cultural leverage', in I. Farias and T. Bender (eds), *Urban Assemblages: How Actor-Network Theory Changes Urban Studies*. London: Routledge.

Slater, D. R. and J. Kwami (2005) 'Embeddedness and escape: Internet and mobile use as poverty reduction strategies in Ghana'. Information Society Research Group Working Paper 4, University of Adelaide.

Slater, D. R. and J. Tacchi (2003) 'Modernity under construction: comparative ethnographies of internet (Moderniteit in opbouw: een vergelijkende etnografie van het internet)', *Amsterdams Sociologisch Tijdschrift* (Special Issue: Digitaal Contact): 205–22.

Slater, D. R. and J. Tacchi (2004) *Research: ICT Innovations for Poverty Reduction*. New Delhi: UNESCO.

Slater, D. R., J. Tacchi and G. Hearn (2003) *Ethnographic Action Research Manual*. London: UNESCO.

Slater, D. R., J. Tacchi and P. Lewis (2002) *Ethnographic Monitoring and Evaluation of Community Multimedia Centres: A Study of Kothmale Community Radio Internet Project, Sri Lanka*. London, DfID/UNESCO.

Springer, C. (1996) *Electronic Eros: Bodies and Desire in the Postindustrial Age*. Austin: University of Texas Press.

Strate, L. (2004) 'A media ecology review', *Communication Research Trends* 23 (2): 3–48.

Strathern, M. (1990) *The Gender of the Gift*. Berkeley: University of California Press.

Strathern, M. (1995a) *The Relation: Issues in Complexity and Scale*. Cambridge: Prickly Pear Press.

Strathern, M. (1995b) *Shifting Contexts: Transformations in Anthropological Knowledge*. London: Routledge.

Strathern, M. (1996) 'Cutting the network', *Journal of the Royal Anthropological Institute* 2 (3): 517–35.

Strathern, M. (2000) *Audit Cultures: Anthropological Studies in Accountability, Ethics and the Academy*. London: Routledge.

Strathern, M. (2004 [1991]) *Partial Connections*, updated edition. Lanham, MD: Rowman and Littlefield.

Strathern, M. (2006) 'Useful knowledge', *Proceedings of the British Academy* 139: 73–109.

Suchman, L. (2007) *Human–Machine Reconfigurations: Plans and Situated Actions*. Cambridge: Cambridge University Press.

Taussig, M. (1980) *The Devil and Commodity Fetishism in South America*. Chapel Hill: University of North Carolina Press.

Taussig, M. (1993) *Mimesis and Alterity: A Particular History of the Senses*. London: Routledge.

Taussig, M. (1997) *The Magic of the State*. New York: Routledge.

Terranova, T. (2004) *Network Culture: Politics for the Information Age*. London: Pluto.

Thompson, G. (1986) 'The firm as a "dispersed" social agency', in G. Thompson (ed.), *Economic Calculation and Policy Formation*. London: Routledge and Kegan Paul.

Thompson, J. B. (1995) *The Media and Modernity: A Social Theory of the Media*. Cambridge: Polity.

Thrift, N. (1997) 'The rise of soft capitalism', *Cultural Values* 1 (1): 29–57.

Thrift, N. (1998) 'Virtual capitalism: the globalization of reflexive business knowledge', in J. Carrier and D. Miller (eds), *Virtualism: A New Political Economy*. Oxford: Berg.

Thrift, N. (2000) 'Performing cultures in the new economy', *Annals of the Association of American Geographers* 90 (4): 674–92.

Thrift, N. (2005) *Knowing Capitalism*. London: Sage.

Toft, A. (2011) 'Contextualizing technology use: communication practices in a local homelessness movement', *Information, Communication & Society* 14 (5): 704–25.

Turkle, S. (1995) *Life on the Screen: Identity in the Age of the Internet*. New York: Simon and Schuster.

Turner, T. (1992) 'Defiant images: the Kayapo appropriation of video', *Anthropology Today* 8 (6): 5–16.

Varnelis, K. (2008) 'Conclusion: the meaning of network culture', in K. Varnelis (ed.), *Network Publics*. Cambridge, MA: MIT Press.

Warde, A. (2005) 'Consumption and theories of practice', *Journal of Consumer Culture* 5 (2): 131–53.

Wastell, S. (2001) 'Presuming scale, making diversity: on the mischiefs of measurement and the global: local metonym in theories of law and culture', *Critique of Anthropology* 21 (2): 185–210.

Waters, M. (1995) *Globalization*. London: Routledge.

Wellman, B. and C. Haythornthwaite (eds) (2002) *The Internet in Everyday Life*. Oxford: Blackwell.

Wilk, R. (1994a) 'Colonial time and TV time: television and temporality in Belize', *Visual Anthropology Review* 10 (1): 94–102.

Wilk, R. (1994b) 'Consumer goods as dialogue about development: colonial time and television time in Belize', in J. Friedman (ed.), *Consumption and Identity*. Chur, Swizerland: Harwood Academic Publishers.

Wilk, R. (1995) 'Learning to be local in Belize: global systems of common difference', in D. Miller (ed.), *Worlds Apart: Modernity through the Prism of the Local*. London: Routledge.

Wilk, R. (2006) *Home Cooking in the Global Village: Caribbean Food from Buccaneers to Ecotourists*. London: Berg.

Williams, R. (1977) *Marxism and Literature*. New York: Oxford University Press.

Williams, R. (1978) *Television: Technology and Cultural Form*. London: Fontana.

Williams, R. (1980 [1961]) *The Long Revolution*. Harmondsworth: Penguin.

Wittfogel, K. (1956) *The Hydraulic Civilizations*. Chicago: University of Chicago Press.

World Bank (1998) *WDR: 1998/99: Knowledge for Development*. Oxford: Oxford University Press.

Worsely, P. (1957) *The Trumpet Shall Sound*. London: MacGibbon and Kee.

Wresch, W. and S. Fraser (2012) 'ICT – enabled market freedoms and their impacts in developing countries: opportunities, frustrations, and surprises', *Information Technology for Development* 18 (1): 76–86.

WSIS (2005) 'Tunis Commitment'. 18 November. Available at: http://www.itu.int/wsis/docs2/tunis/off/7.html (accessed 31 May 2013).

Yankah, K. (1995) *Speaking for the Chief: Okyeame and the Politics of Akan Royal Oratory*. Bloomington: Indiana University Press.

Index